VATICAN II

THE CRISIS AND THE PROMISE

ALAN SCHRECK

SERVANT
BOOKS

PUBLISHED BY ST. ANTHONY MESSENGER PRESS
CINCINNATI, OHIO

Nihil Obstat: Father James Dunfee
Imprimatur: Bishop Daniel Conlon,
                Diocese of Steubenville, Ohio
                May 16, 2005

Excerpts from Vatican II documents are taken from Walter M. Abbott, ed. *The Documents of Vatican II* (New York: Guild Press, 1966).

Unless otherwise noted, Scripture passages have been taken from the *Revised Standard Version*, Catholic edition. Copyright 1946, 1952, 1971 by the Division of Christian Education of the National Council of Churches of Christ in the USA. Used by permission. All rights reserved.

Cover design by Steve Eames
Cover photo: Larry Chiger / SuperStock
Book design by Phillips Robinette, O.F.M.

Library of Congress Cataloging-in-Publication Data

Schreck, Alan.
  Vatican II : the crisis and the promise / Alan Schreck.
      p. cm.
  Includes bibliographical references (p.   ) and index.
  ISBN 0-86716-609-6 (pbk. : alk. paper)
  1. Vatican Council (2nd : 1962-1965) 2.   Catholic Church—Doctrines—History—20th century. I. Title: Vatican 2. II. Title.
  BX8301962 .S34 2005
  262'.52—dc22

                        2005006978

ISBN 0-86716-609-6

Published by Servant Books, an imprint of St. Anthony Messenger Press
28 W. Liberty St.
Cincinnati, OH 45202
www.AmericanCatholic.org

Printed in the United States of America

Printed on acid-free paper

05 06 07 08 09 8 7 6 5 4 3 2 1

Table of Contents

Acknowledgments

I would like to thank Mrs. Patty Virtue for her invaluable assistance in producing this book, and Cindy Cavnar for her encouragement and editorial assistance.

I am also grateful to my family and especially to my wife, Nancy, whose prayers and support make this, and all my work, possible.

PART ONE

THE CRISIS OF VATICAN II

CHAPTER ONE

Vatican II: The Crisis and the Critics

At this writing we are approaching the fortieth anniversary of the close of the Second Vatican Council. Even after forty years, the mere mention of "Vatican II" evokes strong opinions and even fiery emotions among many Catholics. Perhaps this is because the Second Vatican Council has become a symbol for nearly everything that Catholics like or dislike in the church today, or at least it symbolizes the direction that the Catholic Church has taken in the past forty years. In fact, much of the life of the Catholic Church today has been shaped and directed by the Second Vatican Council, especially when we consider the comprehensive scope of its teaching and its ambitious agenda of renewal.

So what does Vatican II symbolize? What does it stand for?

Does it stand for the renewal of the sacred liturgy or its destruction? Does it stand for bringing the church into "the world," or allowing "the world" to infiltrate and desecrate the church? Does the Council sacrifice fundamental Catholic principles in its effort to update church teaching? Is it the harbinger of a new evangelistic effort or of a decline in evangelization, with its focus on ecumenism, dialogue and understanding others' beliefs?

Does the Council stand for revitalization of priesthood and religious life, or is it responsible for creating the confusion and unrest that led to a decline in priestly and religious vocations? And if the Council called for lay holiness, why did so many lay Catholics stop going to confession and regularly attending Mass? Did the concept of "collegiality" and a more "pastoral" approach by bishops and clergy undermine discipline and the exercise of legitimate pastoral authority?

Questions such as these have led many Catholics to ask, "What went wrong with Vatican II?"[1] And if people become convinced that there *was* something wrong with the Council itself or its teaching, it certainly becomes difficult to rally the faithful to study, believe in and live what the Second Vatican Council taught. This, I believe, is the "crisis of Vatican II."

Critics of the Council

Those who criticize the Second Vatican Council, of course, have different concerns and perspectives. Some reject outright the authority of the Council or particular points of its teaching, seeing these as distortions of or breaks from authentic Catholic teaching and tradition. Some see themselves as the "loyal opposition," still deeply committed to the Catholic Church but genuinely convinced that some of the teaching or direction given by the Council was erroneous or misguided.

On the other hand, there are those who criticize Vatican II for not going far enough in *aggiornamento,* that is, in updating the church. Some in this group appeal to the "spirit" of the Council to justify going beyond its actual teachings and directives. Some say whatever they think and attribute it to Vatican II or to the "spirit of Vatican II." No wonder the Council is misunderstood!

Let us look at some of the actual statements of these critics of the Council. Michael Davies, an English Catholic, published in the mid-1970s a biting three-volume critique of the Council. In Volume II, entitled *Pope John's Council,* he observes:

> The Church is at present undergoing what must certainly be her worst crisis since the Arian heresy. There is hardly an aspect of traditional

Catholic dogma, morality, or practice which has not been questioned, ridiculed, or contradicted "within the bosom of the Church." The Liturgy above all has been reduced to a condition which varies from banality to outright profanity and sacrilege. The question to be answered is whether these are the fruits of the Council itself, not the fruits which the majority of the Fathers intended or even expected but, nevertheless, the direct result of the Council.[2]

His answer is that the "worst crisis" of the church now underway is a direct result or "fruit" of Vatican II, which opened the way to "neo-modernism" in the Catholic Church. Davies observes:

There are a good many sincere and exemplary Catholics who, like the Pope, believe that the paradox of the actual as opposed to the intended fruits of the Council can be solved by making a distinction between the so-called "Spirit of Vatican II" and the conciliar documents themselves. Adherence to these documents, they claim, would have brought about an unprecedented renewal. Once again it must be stressed that a good tree *cannot* bring forth bad fruit. There was no "spirit" of Trent or Vatican I working in a contradictory sense to the expressed intentions of these councils because their documents are *not* open to such an interpretation.[3]

Davies' conclusion is clear: if the "fruit" of Vatican II is bad, then the "tree," the Council itself, must be bad. He insists: "No rational person can deny that up to the present Vatican II has produced no good fruits."[4]

Davies suggests that Pope John XXIII's decision to call the Council, which the pope saw as a heavenly inspiration, was actually a subtle temptation of Satan.[5] He claims that Pope John had "lost most of his illusions" about the Council before his death.[6] Likewise, he cites Pope Paul VI's complaints that the church was in a process of "self-destruction"[7] and that the devil had come "to suffocate the fruits of the Vatican Council."[8] Instead of recognizing that the popes were concerned about abuses or false implementations of the

Council, Davies claims that even they came to view the whole council as a terrible mistake, even an instrument that Satan was using to destroy the church.

Michael Davies frequently quotes the late schismatic Archbishop Marcel Lefebvre in support of his views.[9] (Davies authored a three-volume *Apologio Pro Marcel Lefebvre* in defense of Lefebvre's position.) Both Davies and Lefebvre focus their criticism on two themes addressed by Vatican II: liturgical renewal and religious liberty. Regarding the liturgy, Davies writes:

> In his book, *The Devastated Vineyard*, published in 1973, Dietrich von Hildebrand rightly observed that: "Truly, if one of the devils in C.S. Lewis's *The Screwtape Letters* had been entrusted with the ruin of the liturgy he could not have done it better."
>
> This is a statement based on an objective assessment of the reform itself. It is beyond dispute that whether or not the Roman Rite has been destroyed deliberately, it has been destroyed. If this result is simply the consequence of ill-judged decisions by well-meaning men, the objective fact remains unchanged, they could not have destroyed the Roman Rite more effectively had they done so deliberately.[10]

The "villain" whom Davies holds principally responsible for the destruction of the Roman Rite liturgy is one of the principal architects of Vatican II's *Constitution on the Sacred Liturgy (Sacrosanctam Concilium)*, Archbishop Annibale Bugnini. "That Archbishop Bugnini has destroyed the Roman Rite is an easily demonstrable historic fact."[11] He also argues that the *Novus Ordo Missae*, the *New Order of the Mass,* approved and promulgated by Pope Paul VI, "bears no relationship to what the Fathers of Vatican II intended when they gave almost unanimous approval to the *Constitution on the Sacred Liturgy.*"[12] Here we find a shift away from blaming liturgical abuses on the council and toward blaming the pope and others in the church, including the bishops. These allegedly have diverged from the true meaning of the *Constitution on the Liturgy* and the intention of the Council fathers who approved it.

Michael Davies also wrote *The Second Vatican Council and Religious Liberty*, in which he attacks an aspect of Vatican II's *Declaration on Religious Liberty (Dignitatis Humanae)*. He claims that the Council's teaching that a person or group cannot be prevented from expressing or practicing religious beliefs in public is "a contradiction of traditional [Catholic] teaching."[13] This position Davies calls "the Liberal position," but he notes that it "could be more accurately called the anti-Catholic position."[14]

The "villain" who is ultimately responsible for this alleged corruption of Catholic teaching is Father John Courtney Murray, an American Jesuit who wrote an influential book, *We Hold These Truths: Catholic Reflections on the American Proposition*, in 1960. Cardinal Spellman of New York brought Father Murray to the Council as a *peritus* (a theological advisor). There, according to Davies, "Father Murray was determined to ensure that Church teaching was brought into line with the American Constitution," even if "the teaching of Pope Pius IX and his successors is fundamentally incompatible with the principles of Liberalism, exemplified by the American Constitution. If the Council Fathers were to accept the principles of the American Constitution [concerning religious liberty] they would either have to contradict or at the very least abandon the traditional Catholic teaching."[15]

Davies is convinced that "the triumph of the Murray brand of Liberalism was assured when Pope John XXIII decided to convoke an Ecumenical Council."[16] Even though the pope himself was no liberal, Davies is convinced that Vatican II was not led or controlled by the Holy Spirit but by the *Zeitgeist*, the spirit of the age, which is (according to Michael Davies), "liberalism" or elsewhere "modernism." Davies sees this as another example of Vatican II's break from authentic and established Catholic tradition. "Not a sentence can be found in any papal pronouncement agreeing with Vatican II on the question of religious freedom in the external forum."[17] His argument leads to only one conclusion: here, as elsewhere, we must question and at length reject what Vatican II teaches on this issue.

7

Opening the Floodgate of Dissent

Michael Davies is only one of many who have vocally dissented from the teaching of Vatican II. For some this may involve only one, two or a few issues. For others like Davies, it is dissent *against* the Council itself.

Those who come from Davies's perspective, however, usually object to the term *dissenter*. They see themselves as defenders of authentic Catholic doctrine and tradition. It is the Council itself, they say, that was corrupted by the influence of possible Freemasons like Archbishop Bugnini or "liberals" like John Courtney Murray. These critics point to the results of the Council as nearly a *prima facie* demonstration of the correctness of their evaluation.

These commentators have convinced or influenced many concerned Catholics. I will not analyze here the tragic schism from the Catholic Church of the late Archbishop Marcel Lefebvre and his Priestly Society of Pope St. Pius X, as I would like to focus in this book on the true understanding of Catholic doctrine as found in the documents of Vatican II and on its proper implementation. It is enough to observe that after every ecumenical council of the Catholic Church there have been strong reactions against conciliar teaching and even schisms. Note the schism after Vatican I of the "Old Catholics" led by Ignatius Döllinger, who could not accept the definition of papal infallibility and primacy.

A number of books and authors in recent years have rejected Vatican II for reasons similar to those of Michael Davies and Marcel Lefebvre. In 1997 Atila Sinke Guimarães published *In The Murky Waters of Vatican II*, volume 1 of a collection *Eli, Eli, Lamma, Sabacthani?* The author claims to have an attitude of "love, obedience and fidelity to the Holy Catholic Church, the Successor of Peter."[18] To expound authentic Catholic doctrine, this author looked to the documents of Vatican II but discovered an inherent problem in the "ambiguities" he claims to have found in them. Guimarães explains:

> For the most part, conciliar language appeared to us to have been written so that it could be interpreted either from the standpoint of sound and traditional Catholic doctrine or, surprisingly enough, from that of the doctrines of the neo-Modernist current, which has billeted itself into so many key positions of the contemporary Church.... An immediate consequence of such ambiguities is to make an analysis of the conciliar texts sterile and fruitless.[19]

What is the cause of this "ambiguity"? As usual, there were "villains" behind it. As Guimarães explains: "Since the letter of the conciliar documents is ambiguous because of the clash between the thinking of two currents, the documents as a whole cannot be understood as having a unity of thought.... Everyone knows that the perennial thinking of the Church, as well as her spirit, is habitually crystalline, most holy and upright.[20]

However, at Vatican II this perennially "crystalline" thinking of the church was undermined by the "progessivists" (or "progressives") who introduced ambiguity. "Crisis of unity, crisis of authority, crisis of vocations, crisis of Faith: These are the outlines of the present crisis in the Church, born of the ambiguity in [the] conciliar documents."[21] This echoes Michael Davies's statement that "there was no 'spirit' of Trent or Vatican I working in a contradictory sense to the expressed intentions of these councils because their documents are *not* open to such an interpretation."[22]

In short, these authors claim that many current problems in the church are the result of deficiencies and ambiguities in the teaching of the Second Vatican Council. Though it is not my purpose to answer the objections of the Council's critics at this point, I cannot resist observing that many people have interpreted the sacred Scriptures in a variety of conflicting ways. Does this mean that the sacred Scriptures are ambiguous and that we should abandon our trust in them as inspired by God? Guimarães seems to think that the documents of Vatican II should be so "unambiguous" that they would not require authoritative (that is, magisterial) interpretation and proper implementation by the appropriate church authorities. If this were the case, this would be the first council in the history of the church that did not require official interpretation and implementation by proper church authorities!

Out of his "objective and severe analysis" Guimarães concludes his book with three questions or propositions:

First, "given the fundamental ambiguity of Vatican II, its variance on certain points with the earlier Magisterium of the Church, and the crisis it has generated, could one not advocate that it is null?" Since Guimarães finds the Council "ambiguous" and cannot discern how the Council's teaching can be reconciled, in his own mind, with past magisterial teaching on certain points, he seriously proposes that the Twenty-First Ecumenical Council of the Catholic Church be considered simply "null"—that is, invalid, a mistake, meaningless (even though a pope validly convened Vatican II and over two thousand bishops attended during its three years!).

His second proposition is that since the Council's texts are inherently ambiguous and subject to varying interpretations, the only way to interpret them is "to study the spirit of the Council, the thinking of the men who designed, wrote and applied it, as well as the fruits it has generated."

Finally, he invites the reader in his coming volumes to accompany him in *his* "analysis of the spirit of Vatican II," "taking a stance of resolute vigilance before the enemies of the Church" and confident of the victory of Christ and Mary in the church (see Matthew 16:18).[23] In other words, the only way to understand the Council's true meaning is not to listen to the bishops but to follow Atila Sinke Guimarães in his analysis and interpretation of a Council that he deeply mistrusts and finds "ambiguous."

The Liberal Plot

Another commentator on Vatican II, Robert Sungenis, proposes that while "easily 90% of Vatican II's teachings are traditional and ortho-dox, it is that extra 10% that has caused such controversy in the last 40 years." Some of that ten percent, Sungenis contends, (mainly teachings concerning religious liberty and ecumenism) have "little, if any precedent in Catholic tradition," and the remainder are (as Guimarães claims) "ambiguous."

How did these questionable statements get into the Vatican II documents? Sungenis says a carefully orchestrated plot of liberal or "modernist" prelates took control of (or "hijacked") Vatican II. He comments:

> Vatican II, at least the 10% with which we have problems, was written in such a way as to escape blatant heresy yet with enough cleverness and ambiguity to allow future progressivists to interpret it the way they want, and get away with it, at least for now. They are very smart. The devil never shows his pitched fork and red suit. He comes look-ing just like Christ (2 Corinthians 11:13-15).
> …But this means the Holy Spirit allowed Vatican II's documents to contain these ambiguities.

Here is some more fascinating reasoning by the Council's critics! Sungenis claims that even though Satan was behind the "cleverness and ambiguity" of the "progressivists," the Holy Spirit allowed Vatican II's documents to contain these ambiguities." Why? He holds that God allowed it to eventually bring judgment upon the "hijack-ers" of Vatican II and upon all "progressivists" who would interpret the Council's teaching "contrary to nineteen centuries of established Catholic dogmas."

"Unfortunately," Sungenis concludes, "the sheep suffer for what the shepherds do wrong, and as a result we have been wandering in a spiritual desert of liberal theology for the past 40 years."[24]

Sungenis proceeds to cite statistics of the declining number of priests and religious over this period, as well as polls documenting the steady erosion of belief in basic doctrines among Catholics. While stopping short of calling the teaching of Vatican II "heresy," he concludes that a good portion of the teaching is either misleading or ambiguous. His response to those (apparently including Pope John Paul II) who claim that we are entering into a "new springtime" of faith as a result of Vatican II is simply: "Some 'springtime'!"

Two Men and a Book

Surprisingly, the approaches of Sungenis, Guimarães and even Davies appear relatively mild and civil when compared with the frontal assault on the Second Vatican Council launched by Christopher A. Ferrara and Thomas E. Woods, Jr., in their 2002 book *The Great Façade: Vatican II and the Regime of the Novelty in the Roman Catholic Church.* In their analysis there are two clearly defined and opposing "camps": "traditionalists," who are the authentic Catholics, and "neo-Catholics," who believe "that with the advent of the Second Vatican Council a new sort of orthodoxy arose in the Church—an orthodoxy stripped of any link to ecclesiastical traditions once considered an untouchable sacred trust."[25] What particularly irks these two authors is that "the distinctive legacy of Vatican II that the neo-Catholic celebrates and demands that we all embrace does not consist in doctrine, but in *a defense of ecclesial novelties,* many of which were explicitly reproved before the Council."[26]

While Guimarães criticizes Vatican II primarily on the basis of the *ambiguity* of its teaching, Ferrara and Woods denounce the "novelty" of the practices fostered by the Council.

In sum, neo-Catholics gladly defend and practice a form of Catholicism that would have horrified any Pope before 1960. To appreciate this, one need only imagine Pope St. Pius X attending what today's neo-Catholic would consider a "reverent Novus Ordo Mass," with women, their heads uncovered, serving as "lectors," altar girls assisting the priest and holding the sacred vessels, the priest facing the people over a table, horrendous and doctrinally suspect vernacular translations proclaimed entirely in a loud voice, ecumenically oriented "Eucharistic prayers" that omit every reference to the Mass as propitiatory sacrifice, banal hymns and even pop music, the handshake (or hug) of peace, Communion in the hand, and lay men and women distributing the Sacred Host and Precious Blood to standing communicants. How would St. Pius X react to this spectacle? Obviously, he would react as traditionalists do; and, as Pope, he would order it to cease immediately. But for the neo-Catholic, the same spectacle poses no problem whatever, and in his view of the situation calls only for "obedience" to the ruinous innovations that produced it.

Whether he knows it or not, therefore, the neo-Catholic has broken with Tradition.[27]

According to Ferrara and Woods, the "neo-Catholic" follower of Vatican II is not only "anti-traditional" but also prone to join "one of the more overtly pathological, anti-traditional 'ecclesiastical movements,'" such as the "Catholic charismatic renewal" or the "neo-Catechumenal Way." The two authors' descriptions of these movements make no effort to mask their utter disdain for them and make no pretense of presenting them with either justice or charity. The authors are forced to grudgingly acknowledge of the "neo-Catechemunal Way" that "the sect is armed with a letter of commendation from the Pope himself—which, sad to say, is quite authentic." They totally disregard the many statements of Paul VI and John Paul II encouraging and commending the Catholic charismatic renewal, which finds its doctrinal basis in Scripture and Catholic tradition, as well as in the teaching of Vatican II.[28]

After commenting that "one could multiply the examples of neo-Catholic movements that have sprouted like weeds in the devastated vineyard of the postconciliar Church," Ferrara and Woods complete their tirade against neo-Catholics with a litany of traditional

Catholic doctrines they have abandoned as a result of Vatican II.[29]

Ferrara and Woods even caricature the submission of "neo-Catholics" to the direction and teaching of the present pope: "The neo-Catholic 'follows' the Pope, no matter what. 'I would rather be wrong with the Pope than right with him' is one of the more visible neo-Catholic bromides." Since I have never heard a "neo-Catholic" say this, perhaps it is a backhanded way of justifying what is apparently the authors' own position on Vatican II: "I would rather be right without the Pope than wrong with him." (We'll discuss what Pope John Paul II says about Vatican II in the next chapter.)

In summary, Ferrara and Woods have drawn these "battlelines" and have launched a frontal assault against the Second Vatican Council and those who seek to adhere to its "novelties." The conclusion to their first chapter sets forth the basic hypothesis of the book:

> In sum, traditionalists are convinced that the correct answer to the current ecclesial crisis is a total restoration of the ecclesiastical and apostolic traditions that were abandoned or suppressed an historical moment ago for the sake of the unprecedented postconciliar experiment in reform, and a return as well to the uncompromising Scholastic clarity and vigor of the preconciliar Magisterium. The neo-Catholics, on the other hand, see no fundamental problem with the approved postconciliar novelties (all of which they defend as consistent with Catholic Tradition), and tend to question the Catholicity of traditionalists for believing otherwise.
>
> These, then, are the parties—traditionalist and neo-Catholic—and this is the controversy between them. The final outcome of the controversy may well determine the direction of the Roman Catholic Church in the Third Millennium.[30]

Moderate Critics of the Council

The authors just discussed consider the documents of Vatican II, in whole or in part, to be seriously flawed. They still consider themselves loyal Catholics because they claim that Vatican II was a "pastoral" council whose teachings were not infallible and hence not requiring good Catholics to accept them, at least where they contradict or diverge from past papal or Catholic magisterial teaching. To support the contention that Vatican II's teaching is not infallible, Michael Davies quotes a statement of Pope Paul VI from a general audience of January 12, 1966:

> In view of the pastoral nature of the Council, it avoided any extraordinary statements of dogmas endowed with the note of infallibility, but it still provided its teaching with the authority of the Ordinary Magisterium which must be accepted with docility according to the mind of the Council concerning the nature and aims of each document.[31]

Davies and other extreme critics of Vatican II overlook Paul VI's directive that these documents, even if they express only the authority of the Ordinary Magisterium, "must be accepted with docility." Davies's remark on this quotation is simply: "What could be more clear? Pope Paul states unequivocally that the documents of Vatican II do not pertain to the Extraordinary Magisterium, and that they are not endowed with the note of infallibility."[32]

Would one be correct in inferring that these traditionalists believe that the only church teaching that Catholics are bound to follow are infallibly defined dogmas? Do they hold to this standard when they cite the teachings of past popes and councils to justify their dissent against current Catholic teaching, such as the teaching of Vatican II?

There are others whose criticisms of Vatican II are more moderate and limited. One example is eminent Catholic historian James Hitchcock. In his 1979 book *Catholicism and Modernity,* Hitchcock called for a critical evaluation of many of the changes in the church:

> Crucial to such a review should be *a priori* agreement on the criteria which would govern it: the authentic teachings of the Church, especially as they culminate in the decrees of the Second Vatican Council.

These decrees remain among the great unread documents of modern times. Although practically everyone, Catholic and non-Catholic, has an impression of what the Council said and did, relatively few demonstrate an intimate familiarity with its actual statements. Even theologians have been known to censor some of its blunter passages, preferring to rely on the vaguer formulations which lend themselves to free interpretation.[33]

While in 1979 Hitchcock praised Vatican II and warned against those who would focus on "vaguer formulations which lend themselves to free interpretation," more recently Dr. Hitchcock has become more critical of the Council and has adapted his own "free interpretation" of the Vatican II texts to justify his criticism. In his 2003 article "The End of *Gaudium et Spes*?" Hitchcock characterizes Vatican II as a "pastoral" council that was highly influenced in its teaching by "the worldwide cultural phenomenon now popularly known as 'the Sixties.'"

The result of this, according to Hitchcock, was that Vatican II, and particularly the *Pastoral Constitution on the Church in the Modern World (Gaudium et Spes)*, adopted a stance of unrealistic and "dreamy" optimism with regard to the modern world, an optimism that is not suitable nor historically justifiable. He claims that this naïvete of the Council fathers, as expressed in *Gaudium et Spes*, "unintentionally helped to erode the crucial distinction between hope and optimism." Hitchcock claims that what Vatican II promotes is not true Christian faith or hope but a "compulsory optimism" that requires "that Catholics ignore what history has taught them."[34]

In the next chapter we will examine what *Gaudium et Spes* actually taught about these issues based on the actual statements of the document and without "censoring its blunter passages." The point here is that even former defenders of the Second Vatican Council have now become critics, enhancing the "crisis of Vatican II."

Pope John Paul II's Response

At the vortex of this maelstrom during his long pontificate was Pope John Paul II. As a staunch defender of the Second Vatican Council, he also was an object of attack. For example, John Paul II supported the principle of religious liberty as enunciated by Vatican II's *Declaration on Religious Liberty (Dignitatis Humanae)*. One of the most controversial points of this document is that the rights of individuals and groups to proclaim and practice their religion must be respected, even in predominantly Catholic countries, as long as this practice does not violate basic human rights nor disrupt the "just requirements of the public order" of the country. Opponents of Vatican II believe that only the true religion (Catholicism) has an unrestricted right to religious freedom. Michael Davies comments:

> In his visit to Brazil in October 1991 Pope John Paul II urged Catholics to crusade against sects offering what he termed "false mirages" to an impoverished people. But he did not suggest legal action to restrict such sects. As a disciple of Vatican II, how could he? In a visit to Malta in December 1989 he assured the President that the Church did not seek a privileged status at the expense of the State but that, rather, the Church "desires to balance her activity within the areas of competence proper to her with the activities of the State in the realm of its own competence." Malta is now saturated with every variety of sects, and no action is taken by the government to restrict their activities. How could such action be taken? It is for the government to decide what constitutes unworthy proselytism according to *Dignitatis humanae*, but it cannot do so because, according to *Dignitatis humanae*, it is incompetent to pronounce on religious questions! The disastrous effects of modifying the constitutions of countries such as Malta where Church and State were united, in order to implement *Dignitatis humanae*, make clear the wisdom of Pope St. Pius X [who condemned the concepts of the absolute separation of Church and State in his 1906 encyclical letter *Vehementer nos*].[35]

○ for continuing to support the United Nations;

○ for failing to see Islam as a threat to the church and approaching it "in conventionally 'ecumenical' ways";

○ for repudiating war as a viable approach for resolution of conflicts among nations.

While carefully avoiding a direct denunciation of Pope John Paul, Hitchcock observes how "ironic" it is that his pontificate was marked by systematic attacks on sexual morality and the priest sexual abuse scandals. Hitchcock claims that the pope has "not been deeply shocked" by these scandals and sees no need for "an agonizing reappraisal of clerical discipline."[38]

While Hitchcock says that the pope would never have made the mistake of trivializing religious faith and making it into a sort of "dreamy optimism," he goes on to say, "But recently a Catholic writer lauded the Pope's 'faith' in the possibility of a peaceful solution for international quarrels—a sentimental reduction of 'faith' to wishful thinking, a reduction which is characteristic of modern religious liberalism."[39]

The conclusion that the reader invariably draws from Hitchcock's analysis is that Pope John Paul II was not realistic in his historical appraisal of the threats to the church, and hence his responses were inadequate. Hitchcock attributes this unfounded "optimism" of the pope largely to his being a disciple of Vatican II, a council that Hitchcock thinks did not realistically evaluate or address the threats to the church, perhaps due to the "euphoria" and optimism of the 1960s.

The main difference, it appears, between the more radical critics of Pope John Paul II and Vatican II and the moderate critics is that the latter do not counsel a return to the policies of the church before Vatican II but urge a more realistic analysis of and response to today's

A critic of John Paul II's application of Vatican II from another perspective is Gregory Baum, an influential *peritus* (theological consultant) at the Council, who stated in a recent interview:

> Some Catholics claim that the Council has been poorly applied in the life of the Church. Hans Küng has said repeatedly that Pope John Paul II betrayed the Council by reversing the conciliar orientation toward collegiality and decentralization....
>
> The Vatican Council envisaged a participatory Church. In my opinion, it is not unjust to say that Pope John Paul II has reversed the orientation toward participation and restored the monarchial regime in the Catholic Church.... The pope's bold teaching on social democracy and religious pluralism prompts Catholics to expect participation and pluralism within the Church. The malaise of many Catholics today is that the official Church is in contradiction with itself, affirming one ideal for humanity and another for the Catholic community.[36]

James Hitchcock also criticized John Paul II for the way he interpreted and applied the teaching of Vatican II. "John Paul II obviously regards himself as a man of the Council to the very core of his being, someone who truly understands the message of that Council. He is perhaps described as an orthodox optimist, one who boldly affirms all Catholic teaching but seems almost to consider the spirit of *Gaudium et Spes* to be obligatory on believers."[37]

Here again Hitchcock implies that even Pope John Paul II failed to distinguish between hope and optimism. He criticizes the pope on a number of counts:

○ for failing to discipline erring bishops and clergy;

○ for "minimizing the post-conciliar disasters" by "indicating that the Church's loss of members [which Hitchcock calls 'mass apostasy'] is not as significant as the genuine spiritual renewal which has taken place";

situation. Both the radical and moderate critics agree that the Second Vatican Council and its doctrine are either erroneous or flawed and hence are at least partially responsible for the problems and even crises that have plagued the Catholic Church since the Council's close.

CHAPTER TWO

The Deeper Crisis in the Church Since the Council

Most of the dissenters to whom I alluded in the previous chapter would be angered by the suggestion that they are disloyal Catholics or that they are a "problem" in the church. They would claim that they are simply responding to the *real* crisis in the Catholic Church over the past forty years: a loss of true Catholic identity and a betrayal of authentic Catholic teaching.

It is logical that these critics would conclude that Vatican II is the primary cause of the real crisis in the church. Those responsible for the crisis often claim to be following the teaching of the Second Vatican Council. Some of these claim that their understanding of Vatican II, though not exactly what the Council taught, is a legitimate extension or development of the Council. Some have even taken as a motto "Beyond the Council."[1]

Signs of Crisis

What would support the conclusion that the church is in a serious crisis of identity and betrayal of doctrine? Here is a sample of the situation of the church as the critics of Vatican II see it:

○ There has been widespread confusion over the meaning and nature of the priesthood, open debate about the requirement of priestly celibacy in the Latin Rite and a dramatic decline in vocations to the priesthood. More recently the Catholic Church in America has been rocked by a series of clerical sexual abuse scandals.

○ Similarly, Vatican II's call for renewal of religious life brought about radical changes and sometimes divisions in religious communities. In the West there has been a drastic decline in vocations to religious life. The feminist movement raised many hotly debated questions that, in the wake of Vatican II, deeply affected many women's religious communities.

○ Liturgical changes have created "mass confusion" (pun intended) regarding the language of the liturgy, liturgical music, art and architecture, fast and abstinence, proper participation of laypeople and their involvement in liturgical ministries and adaptations of the rubrics of the Mass, the sacraments and other liturgies. Particularly in the West, there has been an unprecedented drop in regular Sunday Mass attendance, while Sunday increasingly has become just another day of work or worldly activity.

○ Overall there has been a tremendous erosion of traditional Catholic moral practice, especially with regard to the sacredness of sexuality and human life. Catholic divorce, use of artificial contraception, abortion and other prohibited practices have steadily increased and are increasingly *defended* among Catholics. The question of Catholic identity has become critical here.

○ Related to the moral crisis has been the growing influence of modern means of social communication, which often promote anti-Christian positions and values and attack the Catholic faith.

○ There has been a growing debate over the purpose and even the necessity of missionary activity. Many missionary orders have placed more emphasis on human development and social programs and less on bringing people to believe in Jesus (basic evangelization) and instructing them in the truths of the Catholic faith (catechesis). Contributing to the controversy has been the question of the meaning and legitimacy of "liberation theology."

○ Related to the above, there has been confusion about how Catholics are to view and approach non-Christians as well as Protestants, Orthodox and other separated churches or ecclesial bodies. Some Catholics have understood the purpose of dialogue with these groups to be simply building cordial relationships with them. These discussions sometimes deny, distort or compromise Catholic doctrines.

○ In countries of the West hundreds of Catholic schools have been closed over the past forty years, and many that have remained open have become more like secular private schools. The purpose, goals and values of Catholic education have become unclear to many Catholics.

○ In the name of openness to new theologies, dissent from Catholic doctrines and the teaching office (the magisterium) of the Catholic Church have become common, leaving the faithful confused about Catholic beliefs and about whom to believe and follow.

Not only critics of Vatican II would agree with these observations. Many Catholics, including prominent Catholic leaders, have expressed grave concern about the church's situation since the Second Vatican Council. Pope Paul VI stated at a general audience on the ninth anniversary of his pontificate, June 29, 1972:

> Satan's smoke has made its way into the temple of God through some crack.... One no longer trusts the Church; one trusts the first profane prophet that comes along.... Doubt has entered our consciences and it entered through windows which should have been open to the Light. It was believed that after the Second Vatican Council there would be a day of sunshine in the history of the Church. There came instead a day of clouds, storm and darkness, of search and uncertainty. This came about through an adverse power; his name is the Devil.... We believe that some preternatural thing has come into the world precisely to disturb, to suffocate the fruits of the Ecumenical Council and to stop the Church from breaking out into a hymn of joy by sowing doubt, uncertainty, problems, unrest, and discontent.[2]

Critics of Vatican II often refer to this quotation inaccurately, saying that Paul VI blamed the Council for the entrance of the "smoke of Satan" into the church.[3] Clearly Paul VI was troubled about the condition of the church but blamed Satan, the "father of lies," not the Second Vatican Council. He spoke even more explicitly about the existence of the devil and his responsibility for the crisis in the church in an address on November 15, 1972.[4]

Likewise, Cardinal Joseph Ratzinger, now Pope Benedict XVI, as prefect of the Vatican congregation overseeing doctrine, spoke on numerous occasions of the crisis he saw in the church. Ten years after the Council's close he commented, "It is incontestable that the last ten years have been decidedly unfavorable for the Catholic Church."[5] He noted specifically that Christians are a greater minority in the world today than they have been "since the end of antiquity." In *The Ratzinger Report,* published twenty years after the close of the Council, he reiterated his judgment:

What the Popes and the Council Fathers were expecting was a new Catholic unity, and instead one has encountered a dissension which—to use the words of Paul VI—seems to have passed over from self-criticism to self-destruction. There had been the expectation of a new enthusiasm, and instead too often it has ended in boredom and discouragement. There had been the expectation of a step forward, and instead one found oneself facing a progressive process of decadence that to a large measure has been unfolding under the sign of a summons to a presumed "spirit of the Council" and by so doing has actually and increasingly discredited it.[6]

In short, Pope Benedict XVI expressed the belief that, to be honest, "we must speak…of a crisis of faith and of the Church. We can overcome it only if we face up to it forthrightly."[7]

To recognize the crisis in the church is not to be a "prophet of gloom" (such as Pope John XXIII warned against in his opening speech to the Council in 1962), but a realist. We cannot afford to be like the emperor who prided himself on his beautiful new clothes when he actually had none on.

This leads us to the critical question of our analysis: What happened? What went wrong? Vatican II was to adorn the church with a beautiful set of "new clothes" to show forth her splendor and beauty, and instead we find the church "exposed"—dragged through the mud and mire of confusion.

If we return to the catalogue of crises, it appears that much trouble has arisen not from the teaching of the Second Vatican Council but from distortions, partial presentations and misunderstandings of the Council's teaching. It is a common observation that in the Council's aftermath much was done in the "name" of Vatican II or according to the "spirit" of Vatican II. But this "spirit" is nowhere to be found (or not accurately found) in the Council documents.

Whether these things were done intentionally (as a conscious plan or strategy to undermine or distort the Council in order to promote other views or agendas) or through ignorance is another fascinating and important question. I have no doubt that some people appealed to the authority of Vatican II to support certain views that they knew were not taught nor clearly advocated by the Council documents. Some of these people undoubtedly did so in good conscience because they believed that there was a "spirit" of Vatican II in support of whatever they were advocating. This "spirit" of Vatican II was usually vaguely associated with "openness" to the world or to new ideas and approaches, such as a democratization of the church.[8] However, the real problem is that the "spirit of Vatican II" can mean "anything anyone wants it to mean."[9]

Undoubtedly, many Catholics have advocated unjustified positions in the "name" of Vatican II or in its "spirit" simply out of ignorance of what the Council taught. Ignorance, however, can be culpable or inculpable—one can and should be blamed for making little or no effort to discover what the Council taught. Usually one doesn't know whether a person is consciously distorting the council's teaching or is just "clueless" about what the council taught. For example, Catholic presidential candidate John Kerry publicly stated during his 2004 campaign that he didn't have to oppose abortion because Vatican II taught that Catholics needed to follow their consciences in moral decision making.[10]

I mention this example because it represents one of the most egregious distortions of both Catholic tradition and of the Second Vatican Council. The Catholic tradition dating from the early second century clearly and consistently condemns abortion. Vatican II's *Pastoral Constitution of the Church in the Modern World* (*Gaudium et Spes*) has a beautiful description of conscience, which explains the necessity of its being "guided by objective norms of morality" (no. 16). The constitution later goes on to condemn some crimes against life itself "such as...murder, genocide, abortion, euthanasia, or willful self-destruction" (no. 27). Article 51 of *Gaudium et Spes* could not be clearer or more forceful: "Life must be protected with the utmost care from the moment of conception: abortion and infanticide are abominable crimes."

Now, it is conceivable that some Catholics may not be liable to God's judgment when "conscience...errs from invincible ignorance" (*Gaudium et Spes,* 16). Perhaps there are some nuanced Catholic teachings that are more difficult to understand and require explanation, such as some issues in the emerging field of bioethics. However, is it *possible* that the Catholic teaching on such issues as abortion and euthanasia (repeated again in Vatican II) is unknown to any mature Catholic? Has the pro-life movement, which exists to educate and speak out on these issues, been totally invisible or ineffective?

This is one of the more obvious examples of the crisis imperiling the Catholic Church since the Second Vatican Council. An increasing number of Catholics appear either to be ignorant of Catholic teaching and practice or to have knowingly rejected it. What do we say of Catholics who

❍ do not attend Sunday Mass or frequent the sacraments?

❍ either advocate or see nothing wrong with abortion, euthanasia, artificial means of birth regulation, cheating on tax reporting or breaking other civil laws?

❍ accept as "normal" Catholic marriages that end in divorce (with or without an annulment) and priests and religious who see their ordination and vows as something they can choose to reject?

❍ see little value in reading and studying the sacred Scripture, in praying or seeking to achieve holiness in their lives?

○ have little interest in sharing their Catholic faith with others or in supporting the church's efforts in missionary activity or in seeking unity with other Christians?

○ disagree with the idea that Catholics must submit to and follow the teachings of the pope, their own bishop or ecumenical councils such as Vatican II, while believing instead that theologians, media personalities or other religions may articulate religious truth just as fully as the Catholic hierarchy?

○ see truth, including religious truth, as something purely subjective, not as something that is objective and binding and capable of being expressed with fullness and clarity by an institution such as the church?

○ think that all religions are equally valid ways to approach God or to find meaning in life, reflecting the great diversity of cultures and world civilizations?

○ think that traditional Catholic teaching on a celibate, all-male priesthood, on same-sex monogamous marriage for life, on homosexuality and on other teaching regarding gender and sex roles are all outmoded, reflecting social mores of a particular time and culture?

All of these positions represent what some would term "modern" or "progressive" Catholicism. And yet *none* of them is taught or supported by any of the sixteen documents of the Second Vatican Council. As one writer noted, ever since a conference was held in Brussels in 1970 and adopted as a slogan and mission statement "Beyond the Council," this tendency to go beyond what the Council taught has been growing.[11]

What can be done, then, to correct or respond to these widespread but erroneous beliefs about the council and its teaching? One place to start is to educate Catholics in the authentic teaching of the Second Vatican Council. Many Catholic thinkers and leaders have advocated this. James Hitchcock, who in his *Catholicism and Modernity* pointed out the error of many of the false "renewals" in the church after Vatican II, states that "the beginnings of authentic renewal would require a massive and comprehensive program of education in the true meaning of the Second Vatican Council."[12]

Six years later Hitchcock's recommendation was confirmed by the then Cardinal Joseph Ratzinger and by the 1985 Extraordinary Synod of Bishops, called by Pope John Paul II to assess the effects and implementation of Vatican II twenty years after the Council's close. The Synod, after noting many of the problems and errors that had arisen in the church after the Council, stated that "these and other deficiencies show the need for a deeper reception of the Council." This would come in four phases: "a deeper and more extensive knowledge of the Council, its interior assimilation, its loving reaffirmation and its implementation." The Synod went on to suggest some practical steps to accomplish this:

It is suggested that a pastoral program be implemented in the particular churches for the years to come, having as its objective a new, more extensive and deeper knowledge and reception of the Council. This can be attained above all through a new diffusion of the documents themselves, through the publication of studies that explain the documents and bring them closer to the understanding of the faithful. The conciliar doctrine must be proposed in a suitable and continued way by means of conferences and courses in the permanent formation of priests and seminarians, in the formation of men and women religious, and also in the catechesis of adults. Diocesan Synods and other ecclesial conferences can be very useful for the application of the Council. The opportune use of the means of social communication (mass media) is recommended. For a correct understanding and implementation of the Council's doctrine, great help will be had from the readings and the practical implementation of what is found in the various Apostolic Exhortations, which are, as it were, the fruit of the Ordinary Synods held beginning in 1969.[13]

When Cardinal Joseph Ratzinger was interviewed in 1985, he also stated clearly that the problems besetting the church were not the result of the Council. Rather the study of the authentic teaching of Vatican II is the essential *remedy* to those problems.

> He says: "I am convinced that the damage that we have incurred in these twenty years is due, not to the 'true' Council, but to the unleashing *within* the Church of latent polemical and centrifugal forces; and *outside* the Church it is due to the confrontation with a cultural revolution in the West: the success of the upper middle class, the new 'tertiary bourgeoisie,' with its liberal-radical ideology of individualistic, rationalistic and hedonistic stamp."
>
> Hence his message, his exhortation to all Catholics who wish to remain such, is certainly not to "*turn back*" but, rather, "to *return to the authentic texts of the original Vatican II.*"
>
> For him, he repeats to me, "to defend the true tradition of the Church today means to defend the Council."[14]

In this interview the former Cardinal, now pope, referred to the church after Vatican II as a massive construction site in which there was chaos because the blueprints had been lost. The documents of Vatican II are those blueprints. Cardinal Ratzinger also stated that Vatican II's teachings were actually "prophetic" in that they address problems and issues that were just beginning to emerge at the time. As he put it:

> Today, in fact, we are discovering its "prophetic" function: some texts of Vatican II at the moment of their proclamation seemed really to be ahead of the times. Then came the cultural revolutions and the social convulsions that the Fathers in no way could have foreseen but which have shown how their answers—at that time anticipatory—were those that were needed in the future. Hence it is obvious that return

to the documents is of special importance at the present time: they give us the right instrument with which to face the problems of our day. We are summoned to reconstruct the Church, not *despite,* but *thanks* to the true Council.[15]

Finally, the strongest advocate for following the teachings of Vatican II as the key to confronting erroneous beliefs was Pope John Paul II. In 1972, while still a cardinal, Karol Wojtyla wrote *Sources of Renewal: The Implementation of Vatican II,* which he called "a vade mecum introducing the reader to the relevant documents of Vatican II, but always from the point of view of translating them into the life and faith of the Church." He explained that he wrote the book "to acquit himself of a debt"—a debt to the Holy Spirit who spoke through the Council in a way "particularly expressive and decisive for the Church." Cardinal Wojtyla stated further:

> Our sense of the debt we owe to the Council is linked with the need for a further response, called for by faith, which itself is essentially a reply to the word of God, to the Spirit as it speaks to the Church.... It would be a mistake to not consider the implementation of Vatican II as the response of faith to the word of God as it proceeded from the Council. It is to be hoped that this implementation will be guided by the idea that the renewal which it set on foot is an historical stage in the self-realization of the Church. Through the Council, the Church has not only shown clearly what it thinks of itself, but also in what way it wishes to be realized. The teaching of Vatican II stands revealed as the image, proper to our time, of the Church's self-realization, an image which in various ways should pervade the minds of the whole people of God.[16]

After his election to the papacy in 1978, Pope John Paul II made the proper implementation of the Council his main objective. Anyone who has read his encyclicals and apostolic letters, weekly catechetical lectures or homilies knows that John Paul II's teaching is pervaded with the thought of Vatican II (both in references and quotations), just as they are replete with references to sacred Scripture and to the fathers and doctors of the church. It is clear that, next to the sacred Scripture itself, the teaching of the Second Vatican Council holds an unmistakable "pride of place" in John Paul II's pastoral and theological teaching. He himself declared in the Apostolic Constitution *Fidei Depositum* of 1992:

> After its conclusion, the Council did not cease to inspire the Church's life. In 1985 I was able to assert: "For me, then—who had the special grace of participating in it and actively collaborating in its development—Vatican II has always been, and especially during these years of my Pontificate, the constant reference point of my every pastoral action, in the conscious commitment to implement its directives concretely and faithfully at the level of each Church and the whole Church."[17]

The *Catechism of the Catholic Church,* which this Apostolic Constitution introduces, may rightly be called "The Catechism of Vatican II," just as the catechism that expressed the doctrine of the church formulated at Trent was commonly known as the "Catechism of the Council of Trent." Lengthy and numerous sections of the recent *Catechism of the Catholic Church* are direct quotations of, paraphrases of or close references to Vatican II documents.[18]

In his apostolic letter of January 6, 2001, *Novo Millennio Ineunte (At the Dawn of the New Millennium),* Pope John Paul II gave one of his most powerful affirmations of the importance of the Second Vatican Council, particularly for us today as we enter the third millennium of Christianity:

> What a treasure there is, dear brothers and sisters, in the guidelines offered to us by the Second Vatican Council! For this reason I asked the Church, as a way of preparing for the Great Jubilee, to *examine herself on the reception given to the Council.* Has this been done? The Congress held here in the Vatican was such a moment of reflection, and I hope that similar efforts have been made in various ways in all

the particular churches. With the passing of years, *the Council documents have lost nothing of their value or brilliance.* They need to be read correctly, to be widely known and taken to heart as important and normative texts of the Magisterium, within the Church's Tradition. Now that the Jubilee has ended, I feel more than ever in duty bound to point to the Council as *the great grace bestowed on the Church in the twentieth century:* there we find a sure compass by which to take our bearings in the century now beginning.[19]

In conclusion, if this education in the Council's teaching were to be accomplished, perhaps not every Catholic would *accept* the Council's teaching, but at least everyone would be clearer on what the Catholic Church actually teaches and where he or she really stands on the critical issues confronting the church today. And it might at least end efforts to defend various bogus beliefs as being based on the teaching or the "spirit" of Vatican II. In the next chapter we will review some of the key points that such a study would reveal about what the Catholic Church truly teaches.

CHAPTER THREE

Setting the Record Straight

In 1870 Cardinal John Henry Newman remarked in a letter that "it is rare for a council not to be followed by great confusion."[1] The greatest danger I see in the confusion arising after Vatican II is that it has been used as an excuse to discount the significance of the Council and to question or even reject its authority. Now it is time to set the record straight.

The first and essential question about Vatican II concerns its authority. This usually leads to a discussion of whether Vatican II was "pastoral" or "doctrinal" and then to consideration of its mode of teaching: Infallible or non-infallible? With extraordinary or ordinary magisterium? Then the discussion moves to the interpretation of the Council: who interprets the Council, and how is it to be interpreted at each point?

These questions certainly ought to be considered, but the primary question about the Second Vatican Council is the one Jesus asked about John's baptism after his own authority was questioned: Is it from heaven or from men? Divinely guided or merely human? (See Matthew 21:23-27; Luke 20:1-8.) Either the Holy Spirit of God spoke through the Council, or it doesn't really matter what we think of it or how we interpret it.

Continuity with the Faith

If we are Catholics, we believe that God speaks to the church through an ecumenical council in a way that is, as Cardinal Wojtyla put it in

1972, "particularly expressive and decisive for the Church" and that "the implementation of Vatican II is the response of faith to the word of God as it proceeded from that Council."[2] Cardinal Ratzinger made it exceedingly clear that "Vatican II is upheld by the same authority as Vatican I and the Council of Trent, namely, the Pope and the College of Bishops in communion with him." He goes on to explain that it is impossible to be "for" Vatican I and the Council of Trent and "against" Vatican II, or vice versa, because all ecumenical councils are based on the same authority—God's, particularly through the guidance of the Holy Spirit.[3] Likewise, Pope Benedict XVI, Pope John Paul II, the Extraordinary Synod of 1985 and others have stressed the continuity of the teaching of Vatican II with previous ecumenical councils (and other magisterial teachings), rather than a discontinuity or "break" with past tradition.[4]

Of course, Vatican II's teaching is not simply a repetition of past conciliar or magisterial teaching. As Pope John XXIII said in his opening speech to the Council, for this a council would not have been necessary. Instead he speaks of a deeper "doctrinal penetration" and an expression of doctrine "expounded through the methods of research and through the literary forms of modern thought." He also emphasizes the pastoral thrust of the Council.[5]

From this we can conclude that through the Second Vatican Council the Holy Spirit is speaking a new word to strengthen the church and to promote her renewal. It is a new word, but one that is in continuity with past church teaching, since God cannot contradict himself but sends the Holy Spirit as Jesus promised to guide his followers into the truth (see John 16:13). As Cardinal Ratzinger succinctly put it, "Vatican II surely did not want 'to change' the faith, but to represent it in a more effective way."[6] In a speech given in the Vatican on February 27, 2000, Pope John Paul II said, "To interpret the [Second Vatican] Council on the supposition that it marks a break with the past, when in reality *it stands in continuity with the faith of all times,* is a definite mistake."[7]

Part of "setting the record straight," therefore, is to clarify that Vatican II is in harmony with past Catholic teaching while not simply repeating previous formulations of our faith. As we discussed in chapter one, some critics of Vatican II claim that it contradicts prior papal teaching on some points, such as religious liberty. There is no question that previous popes condemned "freedom of conscience" (as well as freedom of speech and of the press), yet they did this because in their historical contexts these liberties were being promoted with total disregard to the obligations they entail, especially the obligation to seek and submit to the truth.

The teaching of the Second Vatican Council is a true advance or development of Catholic tradition in that it discusses the meaning of religious liberty in a broader context, taking into account the intrinsic nature of religious belief, the dignity of the human person, proper and improper understandings of religious freedom and the limits of this freedom—all of this based on both right reason and the example and teaching of Jesus Christ.

This deeper understanding of the teaching of Christ illustrates what the *Dogmatic Constitution on Divine Revelation* (*Dei Verbum*) says about Tradition: "This tradition which comes from the apostles develops in the Church with the help of the Holy Spirit. For there is a growth in the understanding of the realities and the words which have been handed down.... For, as the centuries succeed one another, the Church constantly moves forward toward the fullness of divine truth until the words of God reach their complete fulfillment in her" (no. 8).

So there is a difference between the "plentitude of divine truth" and our comprehension of it, which "makes progress" or "grows" in the church through the work of the Holy Spirit. The teachings of Vatican II are another step in this advance toward the fullness of divine truth under the guidance of the Holy Spirit.

Does this mean, as some have said, that we should not take the teaching of Vatican II too seriously because it is not the "final" word of the church, or that it is even only the first step in the emergence of a truly "updated" church that is continually developing? Some have said, following this logic, that we have already surpassed Vatican II and are ready for Vatican III, a new council for a new time.[8]

The response of most church leaders to this viewpoint is that we are not ready for Vatican III because Vatican II is still perfectly relevant to the situation in the church today. In fact, we have not even begun to implement this Council fully and effectively. Cardinal Ratzinger commented, "I believe…that the true time of Vatican II has not yet come, that its authentic reception has not yet begun…. The reading of the *letter* of the documents will enable us to discover their true *spirit*. If thus rediscovered in their truth, those great texts will make it possible for us to understand just what happened and to react with a new vigor."[9]

The 1985 Extraordinary Synod of Bishops echoed this belief. The bishops stated in their final report that the Second Vatican Council "remains the *Magna Carta* for the future [of the church]" (Synod, 68). Pope John Paul II confirmed this when he called the Council "a sure compass by which to take our bearings in the century now beginning."[10] He also said, in addressing a conference at the Vatican on the implementation of Vatican II on February 27, 2000, "The Second Vatican Ecumenical Council was truly a prophetic message for the Church's life; it will continue to be so for many years in the third millennium which has just begun."[11]

Guiding Principles

If the Vatican II documents are a "sure compass" for the church, how do we answer the objection that they are ambiguous and therefore cannot produce unity in the church? As was mentioned earlier, it would even be possible to call the sacred Scriptures ambiguous if ambiguity means "susceptible to different interpretations." The greater issue, I propose, is to find principles of interpreting the texts of Vatican II that are valid and usable, just as scholars must recognize and agree on valid principles of biblical interpretation.

Pope John Paul II noted in his February 27, 2000, address that "the Church has always known the rules for a correct hermeneutic of the content of dogma. These rules are set *within the fabric of faith* and not outside it."[12] Equally important is the question of authority: does anyone have particular *authority* to interpret the texts, or is one person's interpretation as authoritative as anyone else's? (We will return to this question of the authority to interpret Vatican II later in this chapter.)

Cardinal Avery Dulles summarized the principles for the interpretation of Vatican II presented in the final report of the 1985 Extraordinary Synod of Bishops:

○ Each passage and document of the Council must be interpreted in the context of all the others, so that the integral teaching of the Council may be rightly grasped.

○ The four constitutions of the Council (on liturgy, church, revelation and the church in the modern world) are the hermeneutical key to the other documents— namely, the Council's nine decrees and three declarations.

○ The pastoral import of the documents ought not to be separated from, or set in opposition to, their doctrinal content.

○ No opposition may be made between the spirit and the letter of Vatican II.

○ The Council must be interpreted in continuity with the great tradition of the church, including earlier councils.

○ Vatican II should be accepted as illuminating the problems of our own day.[13]

Dulles concludes, "These principles seem to me to be sound." When he first presented this same summary in 1987, he remarked:

> If the Synod's principles are followed, the Council need no longer be brought into discredit by one-sided interpretations, as has sometimes happened in the past. The Synod's hermeneutical principles will make it clear that...Vatican II is fundamentally self-consistent, stands in substantial continuity with earlier church teaching, and remains valid in its essentials for our own day.[14]

Nonetheless, in a 2003 *America* article Cardinal Dulles noted that many of the "quarrels" over Vatican II have had to do with conflicting interpretations of the documents. Some of these conflicts, he says, come from the fact that the Council documents "reflect some compromises." The Council fathers sought to formulate the documents in such a way as to "express the consensus of the whole episcopate, not the ideas of one school." This is important to understand, and it belies the oft-stated claim that Vatican II represents the "victory" of one school of thought (the "progressive" bishops or the so-called "European alliance") over another (the "conservative" bishops and those of the Roman Curia).

Two things should be noted about these compromises. First, the Second Vatican Council, guided by the Holy Spirit, did not achieve simply a compromise among various opinions but a remarkable *integration* of the Catholic theology and insights of the various Council fathers, representing both the tradition of the church and important new perspectives. Yves Congar describes the impact of this remarkable integration:

> A very serious attempt at integration was made at Vatican II. There was, for instance, no Scripture without Tradition and no Tradition without Scripture. There was no sacrament without the Word. There

was no Christology without pneumatology and no pneumatology without Christology. There was no hierarchy without the people and no people without the hierarchy. There was no episcopate without the Pope and no Pope without the episcopate.

There was no local Church that was not missionary and no mission that was not ecclesial. There was no Church which was not mindful of the whole Church and which did not provide universality within itself and so on.[15]

Second, ecclesial "politics" certainly were part of the Council, but the bishops who attended often reflect on how the Holy Spirit acted in a powerful way to enable them to experience and to express in their teaching the "collegiality" that they speak of in the Council documents, thus transcending and overcoming partisan ecclesiastical politics. Pope John Paul II said that the bishops of Vatican II experienced the council as the *"seminary of the Holy Spirit."*[16] Cardinal John Krol concluded in his closing address to the 1985 Extraordinary Synod of Bishops, "*In primis*, we have celebrated and relived the experience of communion that characterized the period of the Council."[17]

The Question of Authority

Even if the pope and the bishops who attended the Second Vatican Council had not experienced this deep sense of communion (and certainly some of them did not), the important and salient fact for the church (then and now) is the *authority* of the Council's teaching and the authority of the bishops, in communion with the pope, to interpret and implement that teaching. Here again we must "set the record straight."

An ecumenical council—a universal council of Catholic bishops—is the church's most authoritative collegiate teaching body. There have been only twenty-one of these councils in the church's two thousand-year history. As Vatican II's *Dogmatic Constitution on the Church (Lumen Gentium)* states, "The supreme authority with which this college [of bishops] is empowered over the whole Church is exercised in a solemn way through an ecumenical council" (no. 22), and later, "Bishops, teaching in communion with the Roman Pontiff, are to be respected by all as witnesses to divine and Catholic truth. In matters of faith and morals, the bishops speak in the name of Christ and the faithful are to accept their teaching and to adhere to it with a religious assent of soul" (no. 25). This same article goes on to explain that the bishops in union with the pope also have the authority to define a doctrine as infallibly true.[18]

Some have claimed that Catholics are not obliged to obey or follow the teaching of the Second Vatican Council either because the Council made no infallible definitions or because the Council's teaching is "pastoral," not doctrinal. Yes, there is an important distinction between infallible church teaching (that is, formally defined dogmas) and other teaching. Vatican II states that infallibly defined doctrines, being revealed by God and part of the "deposit of faith"[19] require the "loyal and obedient assent of faith" (*Lumen Gentium,* 25) or the "obedience of faith" (*Dei Verbum,* 5).

However, even when an ecumenical council of the Catholic Church does not define any doctrines, it still has great authority. It is the most solemn and universal vehicle of teaching of all the bishops in union with their visible head, the pope. Anyone who has studied the history of the Council knows how lengthy and painstaking was the formulation of the wording of each line of the documents and how many drafts (*schemata*) were produced and discussed before the final vote on each document was taken.

In itself this does not demonstrate nor guarantee the truth or the authority of the documents. This authority rests on the Holy Spirit, the "Spirit of Truth" (John 14:17), who promised to guide the church into the fullness of truth. The Holy Spirit does this, above all, by guiding in a special way the teaching of the apostles and their successors, the bishops. Thus, even the "non-infallible" teaching of the bishops is to be accepted by Catholics with "a religious assent of soul" (*Lumen Gentium*, 25).

This is a response of faith in the Lord who established the church and continues to guide and teach us through his true pastors. As Vatican II's documents on the church *(Lumen Gentium)* and the bishops *(Christus Dominus)* explain, it is the bishops, acting in communion with each other and with the head of the college of bishops, the pope, who carry on the prophetic (teaching) ministry of Jesus with the same authority that he gave to his apostles. This is one way in which Jesus fulfills his promise to remain with the church until the end of time (see Matthew 28:20) and to guide her, by His Spirit, into the fullness of truth (see John 16:13).

This, then, is why Catholics believe that the teaching of the bishops, especially when they are gathered together in a universal council (as we first see in the Acts of the Apostles, chapter 15), has unique authority and cannot be overlooked, even when the bishops are not formally defining doctrine (which was also the case in Acts 15). It is in this context that we can understand why the Extraordinary Synod of Bishops in 1985 said, "Unanimously and joyfully we also verify that the [Second Vatican] Council is a legitimate and valid expression and interpretation of the deposit of faith as it is found in Sacred Scripture and in the living tradition of the Church" (Synod, 38), and why Pope John Paul II referred to the Second Vatican Council documents as "important and normative texts of the Magisterium, within the Church's tradition."[20]

Pastorally Speaking

What about the claim that we do not have to heed the formal teaching of Vatican II because it was a "pastoral" council? First we might ask where this concept came from and what was intended by it. The idea that the Council was "pastoral" came from the one who called it: Pope John XXIII. What did he mean by this?

I think it is adequately explained in his opening speech to the Council of October 11, 1962. To put his idea of "pastoral" in context, we must note that toward the beginning of the speech he said: "The greatest concern of the Ecumenical Council is this: that the sacred deposit of Christian doctrine should be guarded and taught more efficaciously."[21]

As his speech went on, Pope John XXIII explained that teaching Christian doctrine more efficaciously did not mean a discussion or repetition of fundamental doctrines of the church that are "well known and familiar to all." Rather he called for "a step forward" in expounding and penetrating this doctrine, through "the methods of research and through the literary forms of modern thought. The substance of the ancient doctrine of the faith is one thing, and the way in which it is presented is another. And it is the latter that must be taken into great consideration…everything being measured in the forms and proportions of a magisterium which is predominantly pastoral in character."[22]

John XXIII made it clear that what was *pastoral* about the Council was the *way* in which doctrine was explored or studied and the way that this doctrine was presented. He recognized that the way Catholic doctrine is explored and presented today must utilize methods and forms of modern thought if it is to be understood in our time. This is the particular "pastoral" approach of Vatican II.

The essential core of the teachings of Vatican II are doctrine: biblical doctrines, doctrines that have unfolded in sacred Tradition, doctrines about human beings, individually and in society, and doctrines about God and his works, particularly in the church. This is why the Extraordinary Synod of 1985 stated, "It is not licit to separate the pastoral character from the doctrinal vigor of the documents" (Synod, 41). Yves Congar explained:

> A pastoral approach is not without doctrine. It is doctrinal, but in a way that is not satisfied with conceptualizations, definitions, deductions and anathemas. It intends to present the truth of salvation in a

way which is close to men and women of today and which accepts their difficulties and tries to answer their questions. It even does that in a doctrinal form of expression. Vatican II was undoubtedly doctrinal. The fact that it "defined" no new dogmas does not in any way minimize its doctrinal value.[23]

"To present the truth of salvation in a way which is close to men and women of today." This is what Vatican II was all about! Consider the language of the documents. For the most part it is very direct and easy to understand. The sacred Scripture is frequently quoted or referenced. Some documents are addressed to all people, seeking to establish a dialogue:

> …a dialogue described by Pope Paul VI as a "dialogue of salvation." This dialogue was not intended to be limited to Christians alone. It was meant to be open to non-Christian religions, and to reach the whole modern world, including those who do not believe. *Truth, in fact, cannot be confined.* Truth is for one and for all. And if this truth comes about through love (cf. Eph. 4:15) then it becomes even more universal. This was the style of the Second Vatican Council and the spirit in which it took place.[24]

These words of Pope John Paul II call to mind another aspect of Vatican II that needs clarification. What do we mean by the "spirit of Vatican II"?

As we saw earlier, the "crisis of Vatican II" has much to do with an abuse and misrepresentation of the Council and its teaching, often justified by an appeal to the Council's "spirit." However, Pope John Paul II indicates here that there is a true spirit of Vatican II. It is a spirit of openness and boldness in sharing the truth of Jesus Christ and his gospel with others. It is the spirit of the "new evangelization, which originated precisely at the Second Vatican Council."[25] One of the principles of interpretation of the Council taken from the

Extraordinary Synod is that "it is not legitimate to separate the spirit and the letter of the Council" (Synod, 4).

To put it another way, the spirit of the Council can only be inferred from what the Council documents actually teach. Since the Council's close, the popes and various Vatican congregations have issued many documents seeking to clarify its true meaning. Their goal has been that Catholics not be misled by false interpretations or appeals to the "spirit of Vatican II" that are opposed to its actual teaching. Unfortunately, the church has sometimes been criticized for these efforts or even accused of trying to undermine the Council or go back to pre-conciliar positions. Cardinal Avery Dulles summarizes some of these criticisms:

> The Congregation for the Doctrine of the Faith was denounced for its declaration on infallibility, *Mysterium Ecclesiae* (1973), for the new profession of faith issued in 1989, for its ecclesiology of communion in *Communionis Notio* (1991) and for its document on Christ and the Church, *Dominus Iesus* (2000). The Roman document on the collaboration of the laity in the sacred ministry (1997) was angrily dismissed, as was, in some quarters, John Paul II's apostolic constitution *Apostolos Suos*, on the status and authority of episcopal conferences (1998). In each of these cases there was a clamor of protest, but the critics did not convincingly show that the official teaching had departed from the teaching of Vatican II, interpreted according to the principles set forth in the Extraordinary Synod of 1985.[26]

A Question of Authority

The obvious irony here is that all of these popes and Vatican congregations that are part of the teaching office of the Catholic Church are being accused of undermining one of the sources of Catholic doctrine that they exist to defend and proclaim! But this leads us to the final area regarding Vatican II where we must "set the record straight." Who has the *authority* to properly interpret and implement Vatican II, that is, the sixteen documents of the Council?

The answer, of course, is that the final decisions and judgments regarding the interpretation and implementation of the Council belong to the magisterium of the Catholic Church. Responsibility for the general implementation of the Council's teaching in each diocese normally rests with the local diocesan (or archdiocesan) bishop. He acts in communion with the universal college of bishops by following any special directives for the interpretation or implementation of the Council's teaching that come either from the pope or from the Vatican congregation having doctrinal or pastoral oversight in a particular area of the church's life. Thus Catholics can achieve clarity and unity of direction in the various aspects of the Council's teaching, even those that require explanation, interpretation or steps to implement.

Catholics believe that the same Holy Spirit who guided the bishops in writing the Council documents also will guide the bishops in interpreting and implementing them correctly. This isn't just true for the bishops who were there, had participated in the discussions and had voted on the documents. The Holy Spirit guides the pastors of the church in *every* generation in interpreting church doctrine and in properly applying it.

Note that this doesn't mean that every individual bishop is infallible in his own interpretation or implementation of every particular teaching of the church or the Council. Rather, when acting as a member of the college of bishops—listening to the voices of the pope, Vatican congregations and other bishops, as well as to theologians and the priests and people under his care—an individual bishop can have confidence that the Holy Spirit will direct his interpretations and decisions that follow from the Vatican II documents (and other church teaching based on or belonging to sacred Scripture and sacred Tradition). The Catholic faithful can have confidence in their bishops' decisions, trusting that God will help and guide them in "pastoring" the church.

This is part of the church's faith, which is attested to both by the New Testament (see Titus 1:7-9; Hebrews 13:17) and by many writings from the earliest days of the church.[27] To "set the record straight," the source of pastoral guidance and certain teaching that the Lord has provided for his church is not a "magisterium" of theologians (though their insights often may be of value), nor a "magisterium" of a "faithful remnant" of Catholics who adhere only to the past as normative (though their piety and passion for truth is often admirable), but the teaching and pastoral office of the pope and the bishops, to whom Christ has entrusted the care of his church in each age and generation.

We have discussed the fact that the Council's teachings have been called "ambiguous." We see reflected in the *Constitution on Sacred Liturgy (Sacrosanctum Concilium)* two concerns that were vying in the minds of many bishops. These provide an example of the proper understanding of church authority.

On the one hand the bishops wished to affirm continuity with (and the validity of) long-standing traditions such as the use of Latin, Gregorian chant and the pipe organ in the church's liturgical services (see nos. 36, 116, 120). On the other hand, the bishops chose the "full and active participation by all the people as the aim to be considered before all else" in renewal of the liturgy (see no. 14).

Hence, when they wrote approvingly about the traditional forms of liturgical language and music, they also specified that other languages (the vernacular) and forms of music could be adopted, with the intention of extending their use if the bishops decided that this would foster the "full, conscious and active participation" of the faithful. The constitution explains, immediately after speaking of Latin being preserved in the Latin Rite, "But since the use of the mother tongue, whether in the Mass, the administration of the sacraments, or other parts of the liturgy, may frequently be of great advantage to the people, the limits of its employment may be extended" (no. 36, par. 2). The document goes on to state that it is up to the bishops or duly established body of bishops in a region (episcopal conference) "to decide whether, and to what extent, the vernacular language is to be used" (no. 36, par. 3).

Likewise, immediately after speaking of the special place of the traditional music of Gregorian chant and the pipe organ in the liturgy, the constitution says that "other kinds of sacred music" may be used in the liturgy as long as "they accord with the spirit of the liturgical action" (no. 116) and the instruments "are suitable for sacred use, or can be made so" according to the judgment of "competent territorial authority"—once again, the bishops (no. 120). The section on liturgical music refers to article 30 of the constitution, which states: "By way of promoting active participation, the people should be encouraged to take part by means of acclamations, responses, psalmody, antiphons, and songs, as well as by actions, gestures, and bodily attitudes. And at the proper times all should observe a reverent silence."[28]

Although the bishops at the Council did have two concerns that were in "tension" regarding the liturgy—continuity with past tradition and adaptation that would promote fuller participation—the Council documents are not ambiguous. They clearly give authority to the bishops to determine to what extent vernacular language and new forms of music and instrumentation are to be used in the liturgy. The bishops did not violate the "letter" of the Council, nor did they "go beyond" Vatican II, when the vast majority of them discerned that it would be pastorally advantageous to move to a largely (even entirely) vernacular liturgy, often with vernacular hymns and newer forms of instrumental accompaniment, to promote the "full, conscious and active participation" of the faithful.

Perhaps the pendulum swung too far, in that Latin and traditional musical forms totally disappeared in some dioceses. Many bishops are reexamining this situation today and discerning whether or in what ways these traditional forms would promote full participation in their dioceses, according to the norms of Vatican II and subsequent liturgical documents of the church.

Back to Basics

To summarize this chapter is to summarize some of the basic Catholics beliefs about the church that Christ founded. Sometimes those outside the church think of Catholicism as a very confusing system of belief. Or they are scandalized because, although Catholics have a "hierarchy"—a "chain of command"—and a fairly clear set of teachings, many Catholics act as if they can believe whatever they wish. (They often do this under the rubric of "following one's conscience," which they say Vatican II authorized.) We Catholics need to be clear about what we believe and then act according to the faith we have received. Here are some of the key points of Catholic belief that can guide us:

○ Jesus established a body or "college" of apostles to teach, govern and carry on his ministry in the church he founded. Peter had a special leadership role within that "college" of apostles.

○ Since that church is to endure until the end of time, there is a body or college of leaders, called bishops, who are successors of the apostles and carry on their role and mission. The pope carries on the leadership role of Peter in the college of bishops.

○ The college of bishops exercises its leadership role "in a solemn manner" when the bishops gather, with the pope or at least with his approval, in a universal or "ecumenical" council.[29]

○ When an ecumenical council's decrees are agreed upon by the "fathers" of the Council (the bishops) and are confirmed and promulgated by the pope, they have "obligatory force."[30] The precedent for this is in

Acts 15:1-29, when the apostles and elders first met as a group to settle a matter that affected the whole church. They concluded with the statement that "it has seemed good to the Holy Spirit and to us" (Acts 15:28). The bishops of the church, in union with the pope, have the primary responsibility and the authority to interpret the true meaning of the Council and to implement it.

○ Through the guidance of the Holy Spirit, the teaching of the ecumenical councils in the church's history are consistent and, when properly understood, do not contradict each other or other essential church teaching, although there can be a development or growth in understanding the truth of the gospel over the course of time.

The "crisis" of Vatican II has come about largely because these basic, traditional Catholic beliefs have been overlooked or called into question. It should therefore not surprise us that the pope, the Extraordinary Synod of Bishops and the former prefect of the Sacred Congregation of Doctrine of the Faith agree that the solution to the crisis is to study, wholeheartedly embrace and carry out the teaching of the Second Vatican Council. In doing this we will "all attain to the unity of the faith and of the knowledge of the Son of God, to maturity, to the measure of the stature of the fullness of Christ" (Ephesians 4:13).

George Sims Johnston rightly observed:

The council ought to have been followed by a thorough catechesis. This happened in the diocese of Krakow under the future Pope John Paul II, but not much elsewhere. It is to be hoped that a genuine implementation lies in our future. John Paul has told us that the teachings of Vatican II are what his pontificate is all about. They are also the key to a new evangelization of the West. They present a program for Catholic apologetics that avoid both the frozen integralism of the past and the loopy therapeutics of the present. But the texts need to be thoughtfully unpacked.[31]

The remainder of this book is devoted to this important task of properly understanding the teaching of Vatican II.

PART TWO

UNDERSTANDING
VATICAN II

CHAPTER FOUR

Background to Vatican II

In Part I we saw that the "crisis of Vatican II" is the harm that has been done through ignorance, misunderstanding and partial or false implementation of the teaching of the Second Vatican Council. The recent popes and leaders of the Catholic hierarchy concur that the single most important solution for this crisis is a return to the Council documents in order to understand them accurately and implement them fully and correctly. These documents remain, in the words of Pope John Paul II, "a sure compass to guide us on the path of the century that is now beginning."[1]

The purpose of the second part of this book is to present the key teachings of the Second Vatican Council. I have employed a question-and-answer format. At the end of each chapter I have noted references from the *Catechism of the Catholic Church* that quote or refer to the teachings of the Vatican II documents. I have chosen to begin with reflection on the four constitutions of the Council. The Extraordinary Synod of Bishops of 1985 stated, "Special attention must be paid to the four major constitutions of the Council, which contain the interpretive key for the other decrees and declarations" (Synod, 41).

Many readers may not be familiar with the documents of Vatican II nor the history of the Council. In this chapter I will list the documents of Vatican II, beginning with the constitutions, with brief descriptions of their content. I will then present a time line of Council events and other happenings during the Council. Finally, I include a list of figures who were most significant in shaping the

Council's teaching and some suggestions for further reading on the Council.

The Documents of Vatican II

Along with the document titles I give the abbreviations, taken from the Latin titles, that are commonly used to refer to them.

There are four constitutions of Vatican II. Like constitutions of nations or organizations, these documents are solemn, authoritative presentations of basic principles governing the foundational areas of the institution—in this case, the Catholic Church.

Dei Verbum (DV), the *Dogmatic Constitution on Divine Revelation,* explains the Catholic understanding of divine revelation: its origin, transmission, various forms and importance in the church today.

Lumen Gentium (LG), the *Dogmatic Constitution on the Church,* is the central doctrine of Vatican II. It states and explains the Catholic understanding of the nature of the church, which was the focus of the Council. This document answers the question "What is the church?" or "How do we understand the nature of the church today?"

Sacrosanctum Concilium (SC), the *Constitution on the Sacred Liturgy,* states the general principles regarding (or related to) the official communal worship of the Catholic Church, known as the liturgy, and presents norms for its renewal.

Gaudium et Spes (GS), the *Pastoral Constitution on the Church in the Modern World,* complements *Lumen Gentium.* While *Lumen Gentium* speaks of the nature of the church, *Gaudium et Spes* explains the mission of the church, both in its principles (part I) and in particular areas of public life in the modern world (part II).

Then there are the decrees of the Council. These documents, often expanding on the constitutions, provide God's guidance for specific areas of the church's life and mission.

Orientalium Ecclesiarium (OE), the *Decree on Eastern Catholic Churches*, complementing *Lumen Gentium*, extols the dignity and unique place of the various Eastern rite churches within the Catholic Church. These churches and the people they embrace are fully Catholic and in full communion with the pope. Their "rite" is the ancient traditions of worship and Catholic practice that they observe.

Apostolicam Actuositatem (AA), the *Decree on the Apostolate of the Laity*, is the first document of any ecumenical council devoted exclusively to the identity and mission of laypeople in the church and in the world.

Christus Dominus (CD), the *Decree on the Pastoral Office of Bishops in the Church*, *Presbyterorum Ordinis (PO)*, the *Decree on the Ministry and Life of Priests*, and *Perfectae Caritatis (PC)*, the *Decree on the Appropriate Renewal of Religious Life*, develop the teaching of *Lumen Gentium* chapters three and six on the way that bishops, priests and religious, all in their own way, carry out the threefold ministry of Jesus Christ as priest, prophet and king or pastor.

Optatum Totius (OT), the *Decree on Priestly Formation*, gives new direction for the effective formation of priests, especially through major seminaries, stressing the importance of spiritual and pastoral preparation.

Ad Gentes Divinitus (AG), the *Decree on the Missionary Activity of the Church*, underscores the ongoing mission of the church to proclaim the gospel of Jesus Christ to those who have not yet heard or responded to it and to build local church communities among those brought to Christ.

Unitatis Redintegratio (UR), the *Decree on Ecumenism*, a ground-breaking decree, is a mandate for all Catholics to participate actively in restoring unity among Christians. It gives directions and guidelines for participation in the ecumenical movement.

Inter Mirifica (IM), the *Decree on the Means of Social Communication*, presents the Catholic understanding of the proper use of modern forms of social communication. It urges Catholics to use the media to proclaim and teach our faith.

Finally we have declarations of the Council.

Dignitatis Humanae (DH), the *Declaration on Religious Liberty*, explains, using both reason and divine revelation, the rights of individuals and groups to express their religious beliefs and to worship, as well as the limits of these rights.

Nostra Aetate (NA), the *Declaration on the Relationship of the Church to Non-Christian Religions*, expresses the Catholic understanding of non-Christian religions, with special attention to Judaism, with which Christians share a common spiritual heritage. Emphasis is placed on the respect Catholics are to have for these religions because of the truths they possess. The document condemns discrimination against or persecution of adherents to these religions.

Gravissimum Educationis (GE), the *Declaration on Christian Education*, proclaims the right of each person to an education, and of each Christian to a Christian education. The document explains the basic Catholic understanding of the goals and purposes of education and the roles and responsibilities of parents, the church, schools, teachers and civil authorities with regard to education.

I often make note of other documents relating to the Council:

Apostolos Suos (AS), On the Theological and Juridical Nature of Episcopal Conferences, Pope John Paul II, May 21, 1998.

Christifideles Laici (CL), The Lay Members of Christ's Faithful People, Pope John Paul II, December 30, 1988.

Dominicae Cenae (DC), On the Mystery and Worship of the Eucharist, Pope John Paul II, February 24, 1980.

Final Report of the Extraordinary Synod of Bishops of 1985, denoted as "Synod" in citations.

Laborem Exercens (LE), On Human Work, Pope John Paul II, September 14, 1981.

Ordinatio Sacerdotalis (OS), Apostolic Letter on Ordination and Women, Pope John Paul II, May 22, 1994.

Redemptoris Missio (RM), On the Permanent Validity of the Church's Missionary Mandate, Pope John Paul II, December 7, 1990.

Ut Unum Sint (UUS), That They May Be One: On Commitment to Ecumenism, Pope John Paul II, May 25, 1995.

Vicesimus Quintus (VQ), On the Twenty-Fifth Anniversary of the Constitution on the Sacred Liturgy, Pope John Paul II, December 4, 1988.

Time Line of Events Related to the Second Vatican Council

January 25, 1959	Pope John XXIII announces Council.
Pentecost 1959	Ante-Preparatory Commission established. The Central Preparatory Commission consists of 108 members and 27 consultants. During the next two years they prepare 75 schemas for the Council, which are eventually reduced to 20.
December 25, 1961	Pope John XXIII formally convokes the Second Vatican Council with the apostolic constitution *Humanae Salutis.*
July 13, 1962	First seven schemas sent to all the bishops.
July 20, 1962	Letters sent to separated Christian churches and communities inviting them to send delegates or observers to the Council.
October 11, 1962	The Council opens. The first official prayer is *Veni, Creator Spiritus.*
October 11 to December 8, 1962	First Session. Discussion focuses on the schema on the liturgy.
October 20, 1962	Council issues "A Message to Humanity."

June 3, 1963	Pope John XXIII dies.
June 21, 1963	Pope Paul VI (Giovanni Battista Montini) is elected.
September 29 to December 4, 1963	Second Session
October 30, 1963	Orientation vote is taken, favoring sacramentality and collegiality of bishops, the divine right of the episcopal college and restoration of the diaconate as a distinct and permanent order.
December 4, 1963	The second session of the Council closes, with promulgation of the *Constitution on the Sacred Liturgy* and the *Decree on the Means of Social Communication.*
January 4-6, 1964	Pope Paul makes an ecumenical journey to the Holy Land and meets with Patriarch Athenagoras.
May 17, 1964	The Secretariat for Non-Christians Religions is created.
September 14 to November 21, 1964	Third Session

November 21, 1964	The third session closes with promulgation of the *Dogmatic Constitution on the Church,* the *Decree on Ecumenism* and the *Decree on the Eastern Catholic Churches.* Pope Paul proclaims the title of Mary the Mother of the Church.
September 14 to December 8, 1965	Fourth Session
September 15, 1965	Pope Paul, in the apostolic constitution *Apostolica Sollicitudo,* sets the norms governing the new Synod of Bishops, established to help him lead the church.
October 4-5, 1965	Pope Paul goes to New York to address the United Nations General Assembly and reports to the Council on his visit.
October 28, 1965	The following documents are promulgated: the *Decree on the Pastoral Office of Bishops in the Church,* the *Decree on the Appropriate Renewal of the Religious Life,* the *Decree on Priestly Formation,* the *Declaration on Christian Education* and the *Declaration on the Relationship of the Church to Non-Christian Religions.*
November 18, 1965	The Council promulgates the *Dogmatic Constitution on Divine Revelation* and the *Decree on the Apostolate of the Laity.* Pope Paul also

announces the beginning of the reform of the Roman Curia, the introduction of the process for the beatification of Pope Pius XII and Pope John XXIII, a Jubilee period and convocation of the Synod of Bishops not later than 1967.

December 4, 1965

A Prayer Service (Sacra Celebratio) for Promoting Christian Unity takes place at St. Paul's Outside the Walls, where Pope John first announced the Council. Pope Paul VI assists, along with the Council fathers as well as observers and guests delegated to attend the Council.

December 7, 1965

The Council promulgates the *Declaration on Religious Freedom,* the *Decree on the Ministry and Life of Priests,* the *Decree on the Church's Missionary Activity* and the *Pastoral Constitution on the Church in the Modern World.* At Istanbul and Vatican City, a joint declaration affecting the See of Rome and the See of Constantinople is publicly proclaimed.

December 8, 1965

The Council solemnly closes in St. Peter's Square.

Key Figures at the Council

The names of many bishops, cardinals, theologians and others became well known as the Council unfolded. Following is a very partial "honor roll" of leaders, participants, episcopal advisors and observers. As this book is not a history of Vatican II, I will not attempt to detail the contributions of these men nor the positions they took. The bibliography after the list is for readers who wish to explore the nature of their contributions.

Popes of the Council
Angelo Roncalli (Pope John XXIII)
Giovanni Battista Montini (first Cardinal, then Pope Paul VI)

Cardinals, Patriarchs and Bishops (in Alphabetical Order)
Cardinal Gregorio Agagianian (Council moderator)
Cardinal Bernard Alfrink
Cardinal Augustine Bea (President of the Secretariat for Christian Unity)
Cardinal Michael Browne
Cardinal Jose Bueno y Monreal
Archbishop Helder Camara
Bishop Luigi Carli
Cardinal Fernando Cento (Roman Curia)
Cardinal Amleto Cicognani (Vatican Secretary of State)
Cardinal Richard Cushing (Boston)
Cardinal John Dearden (Detroit)
Cardinal Julius Dopfner (Council moderator)
Archbishop Eugene D'Souza
Bishop Arthur Elchinger
Archbishop Pericle Felici (Secretary General of the Council)
Archbishop Ermenegildo Florit
Cardinal Joseph Frings
Archbishop Emile Guerry

Bishop George Hakim
Archbishop Paul Hallinan (Atlanta)
Archbishop John Heenan
Archbishop Denis Hurley
Archbishop Lorenz Jaeger
Cardinal Charles Journet
Cardinal Franziskus Konig
Archbishop John Krol (Philadelphia)
Bishop Donal Lamont
Archbishop Marcel Lefebvre
Cardinal Paul-Emile Leger (Canada)
Cardinal Giacomo Lercaro (Council moderator)
Cardinal Achille Lienart
Archbishop Marcus McGrath
Cardinal Albert Meyer (Chicago)
Cardinal Alfredo Ottaviani (Prefect of the Holy Office)
Archbishop Pietro Parente (Roman Curia)
Cardinal Joseph Ritter (St. Louis)
Cardinal Ernesto Ruffini
Patriarch Maximos IV Saigh
Bishop Fulton Sheen (United States)
Archbishop Geraldo Sigaud
Cardinal Guiseppe Siri
Bishop Emile deSmedt
Cardinal Francis Spellman (New York)
Cardinal Domenico Tardini (Vatican Secretary of State)
Cardinal Eugene Tisserant
Archbishop Egidio Vagnozzi (Papal Delegate to the United States)
Bishop Jan Willebrands
Archbishop Karol Wojtyla
Bishop John Wright (Pittsburgh)
Cardinal Stefan Wyszynski
Archbishop Elias Zoghby

Notable Theologian Advisors (*Periti*)

Father Gregory Baum

Father Anniballe Bugnini

Father Marie-Dominique Chenu, O.P.

Father Yves Congar, O.P.

Father Jean Danielou, S.J.

Father Bernard Haring, C.SS.R.

Father Josef Jungmann, S.J.

Father Hans Küng

Father Henri de Lubac, S.J.

Father John Courtney Murray, S.J.

Father Karl Rahner, S.J.

Father Joseph Ratzinger

Father Edward Schillebeeckx, O.P.

Father Sebastian Tromp, S.J.

Some Notable Ecumenical Observers

Archpriest Vilaly Borovoy

Dr. Oscar Cullmann

Archbishop Geoffrey Fisher (Canterbury)

Dr. George Lindbeck

Bishop John Moorman

Dr. Albert Outler

Dr. Harold Roberts

Dr. Edmund Schlink

Dr. Archpriest Alexander Schmemann

Dr. Kristen Skydsgaard

Pastor Max Thurian

Pastor Lukas Vischer

Dr. Wilhelm Visser 't Hooft

For Further Reading

Fesquet, Henri. *The Drama of Vatican II.* New York: Random House, 1967.

Kaiser, Robert Blair. *Pope, Council and World.* New York: Macmillan, 1963.

Rynne, Xavier. *Vatican Council II.* New York: Farrar, Straus, and Giroux, Inc., 1962-1968.

Wiltgen, Ralph. *The Rhine Flows into the Tiber.* New York: Hawthorne, 1967.

These books, published during or shortly after the Council, reflect popular journalistic views of the proceedings. All focus on the dynamic tensions between the more conservative prelates and the "progressive" bishops and theologians. Fesquet, Kaiser and Rynne (a pseudonym for Father Francis X. Murphy, whose book synthesizes a series of "insider" reports published in the *New Yorker* magazine during the Council) are all sympathetic to the "progressive" side. This is especially true of Rynne, who paints a black picture of the "obstructionist" conservatives. Wiltgen strives for objectivity and is fairly successful, while showing more sympathy for the "conservative" side.

A more recent scholarly study of the unfolding of the council is the three-volume *History of Vatican II,* edited by Giuseppe Alberigo, English version edited by Joseph A. Komonchak (Maryknoll, N.Y.: Orbis, 1995, 1997, 2000).

With this background we will now proceed to study the council documents. There we may "mine" a wealth of theological and pastoral wisdom and discover how the Holy Spirit led the Catholic Church into the third millennium.

CHAPTER FIVE

Knowing and Living God's Word

How do you respond when you notice a clean-cut representative of another religious body, like the Jehovah's Witnesses, approaching your front door? Are you confident that you will be able to explain your faith and its biblical basis in a simple and convincing way? Sadly, many Catholics are unable to do so because they don't understand how their Catholic faith is rooted in God's word as it comes to us in sacred Scripture and Tradition and through the teaching office of the church.

A colleague of mine who became a Catholic after years as a convinced Presbyterian pastor said that he was stunned to discover, when he began to investigate the Catholic faith, that Catholics actually revere the Bible as the Word of God. Further, he was surprised to discover that Catholics draw their basic beliefs, including beliefs about Tradition and the church's magisterium, from the Bible.

To me it is ironic that while informed Catholics are ready to point out that the Bible is "our book," the "book of the church," relatively few Catholics read and study the Bible regularly. Relatively few know as well as many other Christians do what "our book" teaches. Hence, the challenge to Catholics today in this area is twofold.

First, we must *know the Word of God* so that we will "always be prepared to make a defense to any one who calls you to account for the hope that is in you…with gentleness and reverence" (1 Peter 3:15). Second, Catholics must *live the Word of God.* Our salvation depends on being "doers of the word, and not hearers only, deceiving [ourselves]" (James 1:22). These two challenges, of course, are related because we cannot live God's word unless we understand it and know what it really means.

The Second Vatican Council addresses the questions of what God's Word is and how it comes to us. The Council invites us to put the Word into practice in our daily lives. It is not surprising then that one of the four primary documents of Vatican II, called "constitutions," is the *Dogmatic Constitution on Divine Revelation.* The Latin title is simply *Dei Verbum* (often indicated by *DV* in citations): "The Word of God." Let's examine what this document has to say as it addresses some important questions often asked about God's revelation.

Why do we need God's Word?

This document stresses that the main purpose of God's revelation is not to deliver commands from on high, nor is it to provide important information about God or about the universe. God has chosen to reveal himself to the human race in order to invite us into a personal relationship of friendship and fellowship with himself (see *Dei Verbum,* 2).

What a tremendous offer! Out of God's pure, unmerited love, he desires to share his life with us and to make us his friends and even members of his family. God reveals himself that we might accept his invitation to life, thus becoming daughters and sons of God and brothers and sisters of the Son of God who became man, Jesus Christ.

We can come to know of God's existence indirectly through nature or creation. But through the sacred Scriptures we can come to know God "with ease, with solid certitude, and with no trace of error" (no. 6).

What God reveals about himself is life-giving and life-changing. The Old Testament teaches that "man does not live by bread alone, but…by everything that proceeds out of the mouth of the LORD"

(Deuteronomy 8:3). The New Testament records Jesus' teaching: "The words that I have spoken to you are spirit and life" (John 6:63). Jesus promises his followers, "If you continue in my word, you are truly my disciples, and you will know the truth, and the truth will make you free" (John 8:31-32). In God's Word we find truth, freedom and life. Why settle for anything less?

Is there any new revelation?

Jesus Christ, who is God's eternal Word made flesh, is the final and fullest revelation to humanity of God's own nature and identity. In Jesus, God has made with us a "new and definitive covenant, [which] will never pass away, and we now await no further new public revelation before the glorious manifestation [the Second Coming] of our Lord Jesus Christ (cf. 1 Tim. 6:14 and Tit. 2:13)" (*Dei Verbum*, 4).

Jesus is the climax of God's revelation of himself—because he is the very image of the Father (see Colossians 1:15), in whom all the fullness of God was pleased to dwell. This is why Catholics cannot accept non-Christian religions as revelations of God equal to that found in Christ. Catholics reject the additions by Mormons, the New Age movement and others that clearly have no root or basis in the public revelation of Christ in the first century. The Catholic Church, along with many other Christian traditions, believes that this privileged period of public revelation ended with the death of the last apostle of Jesus.

What is our response to God's revelation?

God has totally given himself and revealed himself to us in Jesus Christ. The only fitting response on our part is to believe fully in his revelation and to give ourselves totally to God. As *Dei Verbum* states: "'The obedience of faith' (Rom. 16:26; cf. 1:5; 2 Cor. 10:5-6) must be given to God who reveals, an obedience by which man entrusts his whole self freely to God...freely assenting to the truth revealed by Him" (no. 5).

As Jesus promised, when we come to believe in him, we "will know the truth, and the truth will make [us] free" (John 8:32). In obedience to God, we discover true freedom.

How does the Bible come to us?

God revealed himself to the ancient Hebrew people and later came among us in fullness in Jesus Christ. It is reasonable to ask how we can know with certainty what actually happened thousands of years ago.

Catholics believe that all the books in the Old and New Testaments were written under the inspiration of the Holy Spirit and hence have God as their author. The writers of the sacred Scripture, though, are also true authors of the Bible. God used their human talents and abilities, along with their limited cultural backgrounds, to communicate the truths he wanted written down (*Dei Verbum*, 11). The Bible is truly "the Word of God in human words."

We have this unique set of writings, preserved two thousand to three thousand years after their composition, because they have been safeguarded and handed on to us by the Hebrew people of the old covenant and by the church of the new covenant. We can outline the steps by which the New Testament has come down to us (see *Dei Verbum*, 7, 8).

1.   Christ commissioned the apostles to preach to all people. They faithfully handed on, by word of mouth and example, all that they had received from Christ or through the prompting of the Holy Spirit.

2. The apostles and those who worked with them wrote down this revelation, under the inspiration of the Holy Spirit. Letters of the apostles and various Gospels, which are orderly collections of the oral and written teaching about Jesus (see Luke 1), were circulated among the local communities of the early church.

3. The apostles left bishops as their successors. The apostles were "handing over their own teaching role to the bishops," as Saint Irenaeus explained in the second century, so that the truth would be preserved until the end of time.

4. The bishops of the early church developed official lists ("canons") of inspired writings. They believed these writings expressed God's revelation most fully and faithfully. Although slightly different canons emerged in the early church, by the Middle Ages a consensus had been reached that the forty-six writings of the Old Testament and the twenty-seven writings of New Testament that comprise the present "Catholic Bible" were all inspired by the Holy Spirit and are God's revelation for all time.

Is the Bible alone God's Word?

The Bible is God's Word, but Catholics do not believe that God's revelation is limited to the Bible. What was it that the apostles handed on to the churches they founded? The heritage of the apostles includes not only those things that eventually were written down in the sacred Scripture but "everything which contributes to the holiness of life, and the increase in faith of the People of God." From the example of the apostles, the Second Vatican Council concludes, "the Church, in her teaching, life, and worship, perpetuates and hands on to all generations all that she herself is, all that she believes" (*Dei Verbum*, 8).

Catholics believe that God desires to hand on to us not only an inspired *written* Word but a whole way of life and worship that includes all that the church is and believes. This includes, for example, how Christians are to worship God communally and beliefs about morality, especially moral issues not directly spoken of in Scripture.

These truths "handed on" within the church are known as "sacred Tradition." The word *tradition* simply means "something that has been passed on or handed on." The capital *T* in "sacred Tradition" designates those traditions in the church that are an essential part of God's revelation. They are not liable to change over time. Many other "traditions" in the church may change and often reflect a particular culture, time or circumstance.

For example, sacred Tradition includes such things as the basic form of the eucharistic liturgy, which dates back to the primitive church, and the teaching authority of ecumenical or worldwide councils of the church's leaders. In the moral sphere it includes the condemnation of abortion, infanticide and homosexual practices. For centuries Christians have upheld these matters and others like them, so Catholics consider them part of God's inspired and unchangeable word to his church. God has not only given his church a written Word but a way of life that needs to be presented, taught and handed on. This is sacred Tradition.

Traditions (with a small *t*) that are liable to change include particular regulations for fasting and abstinence, the language and other outward forms of the liturgy, the wearing of veils or other conventions of dress that are often determined by the culture. These traditions are good and often necessary for a particular place and time but not for all places and times. Celibacy is a requirement, for example, for priesthood in the Latin Rite Catholic Church but not for all priests in Catholic churches of the Eastern rite. Thus it is an honored Catholic practice and tradition, though not part of sacred Tradition.

What is the relationship between Scripture and Tradition?

Dei Verbum explains that the word of God is made up of both sacred Scripture and sacred Tradition and that there is a close connection and communication between the two:

> For both of them, flowing from the same divine wellspring, in a certain way merge into a unity and tend toward the same end. For sacred Scripture is the word of God inasmuch as it is consigned to writing under the inspiration of the divine Spirit. To the successors of the apostles, sacred Tradition hands on in its full purity God's word, which was entrusted to the apostles by Christ the Lord and the Holy Spirit.... Consequently, it is not from sacred Scripture alone that the Church draws her certainty about everything which has been revealed. Therefore both sacred Tradition and sacred Scripture are to be accepted and venerated with the same sense of devotion and reverence. (no. 9)

Is sacred Tradition unchanging?

Sacred Tradition is not static and unchanging, like the canon of Scripture. Sacred Tradition develops through the guidance of the Holy Spirit, who is constantly leading the church into a fuller and deeper understanding of the truth.

The church grows in its understanding as its members study and pray over the truths handed down and seek to live them faithfully. There is also a deepening understanding of these truths through the preaching and teaching of the church's leaders, particularly the bishops "who have received...the sure gift of truth" (*Dei Verbum*, 8). Indeed, the Council assures us that the church is constantly moving forward to a fuller grasp of divine truth until the Lord brings history to a close.

One example of deeper insights into God's truth discovered over the centuries concerns the *dignity of the human person*. The development of Christian teaching and social action regarding human rights is expressed in the church's stand against slavery. In the area of *religious freedom,* the church teaches against coercion in religious matters, including bigoted religious intolerance and wars of religion. This is why Catholics strongly oppose racial discrimination and are seeking an end to religious wars such as the prolonged conflicts in Northern Ireland and in the Middle East.

Who decides the authentic meaning of Scripture and Tradition?

While biblical scholars, historians and other experts can provide important insights into the meaning of God's word, Catholics believe that God has given the charism (gift) and office of interpreting the authentic meaning of God's revelation to the successors of the apostles—the bishops in union with the successor of Peter, the pope. These are the official teachers or magisterium of the Catholic Church.

In the history of our church, the universal body of bishops has always made the crucial decisions about God's word. They first decided which ancient writings were truly God's revelation for all time: that is, they determined the "canon" of Scripture. They decided what Scripture actually meant, especially when disputes arose, as they met in councils seeking the guidance of the Holy Spirit. And they have acted as the official teachers of the Christian faith in each age, as successors of Jesus' apostles.

Dei Verbum beautifully explains the role of the magisterium and the close relationship of sacred Scripture, sacred Tradition and the magisterium. One point made very clear is that the teaching office or magisterium of the Catholic Church "is not above the word of God, but serves it, teaching only what has been handed on, listening to it devoutly, guarding it scrupulously, and explaining it faithfully by divine commission and with the help of the Holy Spirit; it draws from this one deposit of faith everything which it presents for belief as divinely revealed" (no. 10).

Like a tripod, which cannot stand without each of its legs, the Word of God cannot come to Christians in its purity and completeness without these three channels of God's truth: the Bible, sacred Tradition and the teaching authority of the living church.

Is the Bible free from all error?

Why has God revealed himself to us? So that he may bring us into a relationship of love with himself, through which we are saved from our sin and brought to eternal salvation—life with God forever in heaven. Hence, Catholics believe in biblical inerrancy. We believe that the Bible—every word and line of it—is without error in revealing those truths that pertain to salvation. *Dei Verbum* states "that the books of Scripture must be acknowledged as teaching firmly, faithfully, and without error that truth which God wanted put into the sacred writings for the sake of our salvation" (no. 11; also see no. 6).

In other words, sacred Scripture cannot err as it teaches us God's truth, which he has revealed for the sake of our salvation. When the Bible speaks of God, the nature of human persons, God's will for them, the relationship of God to humanity and how we are to relate to him and to each other, there can be no error.

What is the relationship between the Old and New Testaments?

This relationship is well expressed in article 16 of *Dei Verbum*. In short, God's design is that "the New Testament is hidden in the Old and the Old is made manifest in the New."

What should be our attitude toward biblical scholarship?

This constitution instructs Catholics to interpret sacred Scripture with reference to three major sources. First, sound scholarship attempts to ascertain the author's intention in writing. The scholar does this by studying the literary forms used (prophecy, poetry, didactic story, history and so on), the prevailing *styles* of writing and narrating and the *customs* of the time. All of these shed light on what God intends to say to us through the sacred writer (no. 12).

Second, the scholar studies how each writing fits into the unity of the whole of Scripture and how it has been interpreted in the living tradition of the church, since "holy Scripture must be read and interpreted according to the same Spirit by whom it was written" (no. 12).

Third, the teaching office *(magisterium)* of the church is the final judge of the meaning of Scripture by virtue of its "divine commission and ministry of guarding and interpreting the word of God" (no. 12).

Does this mean that Catholics must be scholars in order to read the Bible correctly and profitably?

No. Catholics must respect and be open to learning from the insights of scholars. But Joseph Ratzinger (Pope Benedict XVI) once pointed out that Vatican II's recommendation of sound biblical scholarship was not intended to make the Bible a "closed book," accessible only to experts. He noted that the foundational elements of our faith are not based upon the recent discoveries of biblical studies "but on the Bible *just as it is* [his emphasis], as it has been read in the Church since the time of the Fathers until now. It is precisely the fidelity to this reading of the Bible that has given us the saints, who were often uneducated and, at any rate, frequently knew nothing about exegetical contexts. Yet they were the ones who understood it best."[1]

Reading the Bible in a spirit of faith and prayer as one well-instructed in the doctrine of the Catholic Church normally would be an adequate safeguard against false interpretations. Study of the church's tradition of interpreting Scripture and using good scholarly resources enhances and deepens a person's understanding of God's Word. Various daily reading guides for Catholics (such as *The Word Among Us* and *God's Word Today*) are helpful resources for the layperson. Short Catholic commentaries, such as the series published by Liturgical Press in Collegeville, Minnesota, may also be helpful, although the quality and accuracy of individual commentaries differ in such series. Background articles in larger scholarly commentaries, such as *The Jerome Biblical Commentary,* may be useful to the academically inclined reader.

Should we fear reading the Bible "too literally"?

The constitution does not answer this question directly. However, it affirms the "historical character" of the four Gospels. The Council explains that while the authors of the Gospels compiled and edited their sources and shaped their writings to meet the situations of their churches, they did this "always in such fashion that they told us the honest truth about Jesus" (no. 19). We can conclude that the Gospels have a historical basis (that is, they are neither myths nor fabricated stories).

Should we beware of "fundamentalists" or "liberal" interpreters of the Bible?

Certainly we should avoid labeling people as "fundamentalist" or "liberal" unless they themselves embrace these terms. *Dei Verbum* presents a carefully balanced approach to interpreting the Bible. It asserts the inerrancy of Scripture and the historical character and truth of the Gospels, while also urging the use of some modern methods of biblical scholarship to help us understand more fully what God and the sacred author intended to communicate.

The Council values the findings of scholars yet reminds us that it is the God-given task of the church's teaching office to finally determine the authentic meaning of sacred Scripture if disputes or questions arise. By defining what interpretations of the Bible are unacceptable, the magisterium fixes limits within which scholars or readers are free to discover various interpretations and meanings of God's Word that are valid and profitable for Christian life.

Catholics must reject any interpretation of the Bible that denies either its human or divine character. As "the Word of God in human words," Catholics must recognize and obey the divine truth the Bible teaches. Yet we should also respect and employ sound scholarship that studies how God used the various modes of thinking and writing of the human authors to communicate the truth he wished to reveal for the sake of our salvation.

What place should reading and studying the Bible have in our lives?

Vatican II teaches that through the Bible, the heavenly Father "meets His children with great love and speaks with them" (*Dei Verbum*, 21). It speaks of the Word of God as a source of strength, spiritual life and food. Catholics should have "easy access to sacred Scripture" in "suitable and correct translations" (no. 22).

All the faithful, especially clergy and religious, are urged "to learn by frequent reading of the divine Scriptures the 'excelling knowledge of Jesus Christ' (Phil. 3:8)." Also, "prayer should accompany the reading of sacred Scripture, so that God and man may talk together" (no. 25).

Since the close of Vatican II, many Catholics have participated in a resurgence of reading and study of Scripture, which the Council recommended and encouraged with a variety of new aids to Bible study and meditation. This is certainly a continual challenge that the Second Vatican Council lays before Catholics today. If the Bible is truly "the book of the Church," Catholics should love it, study it and know it well.

Dei Verbum exhorts us in its closing section:

> In this way, therefore, through the reading and study of the sacred books, let "the word of the Lord run and be glorified" (2 Th. 3:1) and let the treasure of revelation entrusted to the Church increasingly fill the hearts of men. Just as the life of the Church grows through persistent participation in the Eucharistic mystery, so we may hope for a new surge of spiritual vitality from intensified veneration for God's word, which "lasts forever" (Is. 40:8; cf. 1 Pet. 1:23-25). (no. 26)

Dei Verbum and the *Catechism of the Catholic Church*

There are seventy-seven references to the *Dogmatic Constitution on Divine Revelation* in the *Catechism of the Catholic Church*. Nearly all of these are from the beginning of Part I, Section I, which discusses in chapter two "The Revelation of God" (art. 1), "The Transmission of Divine Revelation" (art. 2) and "Sacred Scripture" (art. 3).

Recent Magisterial Documents Relating to God's Word

Pontifical Biblical Commission. "The Interpretation of the Bible in the Church." *Origins* 23, no. 29 (January 6, 1994).

Pope John Paul II. "Faith Can Never Conflict with Reason." *L'Osservatore Romano* (English Edition), no. 44 (1264) (November 4, 1992).

Favorite Quotes from *Dei Verbum*

Through…revelation, therefore, the invisible God…out of the abundance of His love speaks to men as friends…and lives among them…so that He may invite and take them into fellowship with Himself. (no. 2)

The task of authentically interpreting the word of God, whether written or handed on, has been entrusted exclusively to the living teaching office of the Church, whose authority is exercised in the name of Jesus Christ. This teaching office is not above the word of God, but serves it, teaching only what has been handed on, listening to it devoutly, guarding it scrupulously, and explaining it faithfully by divine commission and with the help of the Holy Spirit.… It is clear, therefore, that sacred tradition, sacred Scripture, and the teaching authority of the Church, in accord with God's most wise design, are so linked and joined together that one cannot stand without the others, and that all together and each in its own way under the action of the one Holy Spirit contribute effectively to the salvation of souls. (no. 10)

God, the inspirer and author of both testaments, wisely arranged that the New Testament be hidden in the Old and the Old be made manifest in the New. (no. 16)

The Church has always venerated the divine Scriptures just as she venerates the body of the Lord, since from the table of both the word of God and of the body of Christ she unceasingly receives and offers to the faithful the bread of life, especially in the sacred liturgy.… Easy access to sacred Scripture should be provided for all the Christian faithful. (nos. 21, 22)

This sacred Synod earnestly and specifically urges all the Christian faithful…to learn by frequent reading of the divine Scriptures the "excelling knowledge of Jesus Christ" (Phil. 3:8). "For ignorance of the Scripture is ignorance of Christ [Saint Jerome]." (no. 25)

CHAPTER SIX

The Church: A Mystery and the People of God

"The Mystery of the Church" is the title of the opening chapter of Vatican II's *Dogmatic Constitution on the Church (Lumen Gentium)*. But why is the church called a "mystery"?

I have encountered Catholics who are convinced that the church is really not mysterious at all. They hold that it can be understood fully in sociological, political and anthropological categories, just like any other human institution. Some have even said that the church could be improved by eliminating any remaining "mysterious" elements and its outmoded hierarchical structure, with the aim of modeling it after a modern political democracy. (I have even heard Catholics say that Vatican II calls for this change!)

These views neglect the fact that the church is *not* a purely human reality or product; it is fundamentally a work of God! Thus Catholics must discover and respect the nature of the church as God has established it. We cannot re-create or restructure the church according to our own wisdom or resources. The church is a mystery because it is, like Jesus Christ and sacred Scripture, a union of the divine and the human. It can never be reduced to a merely human organization.

Further, the church is a mystery because its membership includes not only followers of Jesus Christ on earth but also all those who have died in union with Christ: Mary and the saints in heaven and the souls in purgatory. There is more to the church than meets the eye, more than is visible. The church is a "communion of saints" that spans heaven and earth. The reported appearances of Mary and the saints throughout Christian history are reminders of the transcendent or "vertical" dimension of the church. As Catholics today rediscover the place of the angels and saints as they encounter the Lord himself in prayer and in the liturgy, they are rediscovering the reality of the mystery of the church.

This challenging concept is followed up by Vatican II's presentation of the church as the "People of God" in chapter two of *Lumen Gentium*. The church is a divine mystery, but on earth it appears as a group of ordinary people who are brought together and united in Jesus Christ, just as the first followers of Jesus were. The image of the church as the people of God tells us that "the church" is not just a building, nor is it limited to priests, religious sisters and brothers or the pope. *All* the faithful, including the laity, are equally members of God's people, the church.

This realization that "*we* are the church," including equally each baptized member, was a great contribution of the Second Vatican Council to our understanding. Though our roles and tasks may differ, we who have been baptized into Christ have been baptized into one body and made one people. As Saint Paul reminds us, we are "individually members one of another" (Romans 12:5; see also 1 Corinthians 12:27; Ephesians 4:25).

The Second Vatican Council challenges us to discover who we are. The church is *the* central topic of the Council. The four constitutions of Vatican II, which embody the Council's foundational teaching, all have to do with the church: the sources of its beliefs, its nature, its worship and its place and mission in the modern world.

The *Dogmatic Constitution on the Church* (*Lumen Gentium* in Latin, meaning "Light of the Nations") presents in modern terms the Catholic Church's understanding of herself, her own nature. This constitution is like the hub of a wheel because it sets forth the fundamental doctrine of the church in a number of areas, which are treated in more detail by other Council documents. In fact, no less than nine or ten of the sixteen Council documents have their basic teaching set forth in the *Dogmatic Constitution on the Church*.

For the sake of study, this constitution may be divided into three sections. The first two chapters deal with the nature of the church. The middle chapters describe specific ministries and vocations within the church. The last two chapters focus on the invisible and eschatological aspects of the church, especially the church as the communion of saints, with Mary as the church's model and mother.

Let's pose some questions that capture the essence of each section.

What is the nature of the church?

It is not coincidental that the first chapter of the *Dogmatic Constitution on the Church* is entitled "The Mystery of the Church." As we have seen, the church is a *work of God* that cannot be reduced to a merely human reality, a mystery that cannot be adequately explained in sociological, anthropological or political terms.

There are many reasons why the church is a mystery, but primarily it is because it is founded upon the work of Jesus Christ and the mystery of his cross and resurrection. Jesus is God's love present in human history. The church is the universal "sacrament of salvation," which makes God's love present in all ages and draws people into communion with him.

Jesus proclaimed the kingdom of God. The church represents the breaking forth of that kingdom on earth—not yet in its completed form but like a seed budding and slowly growing amid the trials and adversity of this world (see *Lumen Gentium*, 5). It is the mystery of a holy church made up of sinners always in need of purification and renewal, yet always striving to announce to the world the cross and death of the Lord until he comes (see *Lumen Gentium*, 8; 1 Corinthians 11:26).

The reality is so rich that it is impossible to *define* precisely all that the church is. You can't define a mystery! We would do better to study the many images of the church found in the Old and New Testaments that describe various aspects of the church's nature, as the different facets of a precious stone show forth its rich beauty. The church is a "sheepfold," a "field," the "edifice of God," his temple, the "Jerusalem which is above," the bride of Christ and the spouse of the spotless Lamb (no. 6), just to mention a few biblical images.

Modern secular people have difficulty with the concept of mystery. We are uncomfortable if we can't define or explain something fully in rational terms. But the reality of the church reminds us that God is greater than our human intellect. The love he has shown in sending his only Son to redeem us and to make us his own people, his church, exceeds anything we could expect or imagine.

How is the church a communion?

Communion comes from the Greek word *koinonia*, which can mean "community," "fellowship" or "unity." Acts 2:42 lists this oneness as one of the central characteristics of the church. The first Christians experienced this fellowship or unity in their relationships with each other and with God.

The goal of the life of the church, as well as its richest fruit, is to build this close unity or fellowship among believers. Communion is not an emotion but the realization of our oneness with God and with each other in Jesus Christ, which transcends all our differences and puts them in the proper perspective.

The Extraordinary Synod of Bishops of 1985 taught that this idea of communion is the key to understanding the church. The church is a communion with God through Jesus Christ and in the Holy Spirit. We *enter* this communion of the church through baptism, which is the foundation of our unity in Christ. Partaking in the Eucharist visibly expresses unity and mysteriously makes us one through the power of God. Unity is also expressed in our common faith and beliefs.

The fact that we are in communion with each other in Christ also explains our relationships within the church better than an organizational chart showing "who does what." Even though there are many diverse roles and ministries in the church and some members exercise authority in their leadership roles in the church, the basic reality is that the church is a communion of believers in Jesus Christ sharing his life with each other and finding their unity in him (Synod, 52).

What image does Vatican II use to describe the church?

In different ages church leaders have chosen particular biblical images that epitomize how Catholics should look at the church. For centuries after the Council of Trent, the church often was viewed as the "perfect society," with clear teaching, structure and order. In 1943 Pope Pius XII's encyclical letter on the mystical body of Christ shifted the focus away from the external structure and order and to a new sense of a living body of people founded by Christ. Members of the "body of Christ" are bound together in unity and charity, contributing their various gifts for the upbuilding of this body, as Saint Paul taught.

The *Dogmatic Constitution on the Church* does discuss the hierarchical structure of the church (chap. 3) and the church as the body of Christ (no. 7). However, the chief image that the constitution presents for understanding the church today is that of the "people of God." First Peter 2:9-10 states, "You are a chosen race, a royal priesthood, a holy nation, God's own people.... Once you were no people but now you are God's people; once you had not received mercy but now you have received mercy."

The "people of God" image stresses the fact that God has called us together through an act of his mercy and has given us a new identity as his people. Furthermore, the *Dogmatic Constitution on the Church* challenges our individualistic concept of salvation, as expressed in the question, "Have you been saved?" This document declares, "It has pleased God, however, to make men holy and save them not merely as individuals without any mutual bonds, but by making them into a single people, a people which acknowledges Him in truth and serves Him in holiness" (no. 9).

God calls us to follow him as a people. The Council also reminds us that we are a "pilgrim people of God" who are never fully at home or "comfortable" in this world but are ever striving to bring about and to enter God's kingdom. Our life on earth is a pilgrimage to God's eternal city—heaven. "For here we have no lasting city, but we seek the city which is to come" (Hebrews 13:14; see *Lumen Gentium,* 9).

Is the church still viewed as a hierarchy?

A common occurrence since Vatican II is that of Catholics down-playing or rejecting the hierarchical structure of the church or the church as the mystical body of Christ, because they think that these images are outmoded or incompatible with the church as the "people of God." However, the *Dogmatic Constitution on the Church* makes it clear that the people of God is a hierarchically ordered people. All the images of the church are biblical and complementary, not in conflict or mutually exclusive. We must remember that Vatican II *builds* upon past Catholic traditions and teachings rather than invalidates them.

Jesus Christ, who possessed both a divine and a human nature, is the model for his body on earth. By virtue of God's indwelling, the church is also composed of both divine gifts and graces and the human structures and forms necessary to organize and live in this world as a society. The organizational structure of the church is not merely a "power structure" but serves the Spirit of Christ, just as Christ's humanity served his divine nature. As we shall see later, offices in the church are intended to serve God and his people, not to "lord over" others nor exalt those in office.

Who belongs to the people of God?

The *Dogmatic Constitution on the Church* makes a number of points related to this question that are at the heart of the Council's teaching. First, "*All…are called to belong to the new People of God*" (no. 13, emphasis added). Membership in the church is open to all. The church is truly universal (catholic)—embracing all of humanity, for God "desires all men to be saved and to come to the knowledge of the truth" (1 Timothy 2:4). Note that God's *desire* to save does not mean that all *will* be saved, nor does the statement that the church is *open* to all people mean that all will join the church.

Second, the church of Christ "constituted and organized in the world as a society, subsists *[subsistit]* in the Catholic Church, which is governed by the successor of Peter and by the bishops in union with that successor, although many elements of sanctification and of truth can be found outside of her visible structure" (*Lumen Gentium*, 8). The word *subsists* is very important here. One scholar says that more ink has been spilled over the word *subsists* than over any other word in the Council documents!

In the past it was common for Catholics to say that the Catholic Church is the true church of Jesus Christ. This simple identification left no possibility of other Christian groups or bodies having *any* share in the church of Christ. At the Second Vatican Council the bishops rejected this notion.

The word *subsists* means literally "to stand still, to stay, to continue, to remain." This particular word was chosen to indicate that the church Jesus founded has continued and will continue to exist in the Catholic Church until the end of time, with all the essential marks of the church present (one, holy, catholic and apostolic) and all the means of salvation available within her.[1]

Catholics, then, believe that only the Catholic Church possesses the *fullness* of the church of Christ: all of the truth and all the means of salvation that Christ has entrusted to the church he founded (see also *Lumen Gentium*, 14). We read in this document: "They *are fully incorporated* into the society of the Church who, possessing the Spirit of Christ, accept her entire system and all the means of salvation given to her, and through union with her visible structure are joined to Christ, who rules her through the Supreme Pontiff and the bishops" (no. 14, emphasis added).

The Catholic Church is "linked" in many ways to other Christian churches and ecclesial bodies who possess many of the "elements of sanctification and truth" that belong to the church of Christ. These elements may include sacred Scripture, common beliefs, the sacraments, the office of bishop, the Eucharist, devotion to Mary and numerous other devotions and beliefs. Hence it is possible to say that these Christians belong to the people of God, yet in an incomplete or imperfect way, since they "do not profess the faith in its entirety or do not preserve unity of communion with the successor of Peter" (*Lumen Gentium,* 15). When we discuss the *Decree on Ecumenism* in chapter twelve, more will be said about other Christians and our relationship with them.

Finally, although they do not belong to the people of God, Vatican II says that God's plan of salvation includes those who, through no fault of their own, do not yet know or embrace the gospel of Christ in whatever way it comes to them (no. 16). This refers to many who are not Christian. To the extent that these embrace some aspects of the truth about God and respond to the grace of Christ, they are related to the new people of God, although they are not members of it because they do not believe in Jesus Christ and have not been baptized into Christ and his church. In chapter eleven on the missionary dimension of the church, we will discuss more fully the Council's teaching on non-Christians.

Are only Roman Catholics members of the Catholic Church?

Those who formally call themselves "Roman Catholics" belong to the Roman or Latin Rite of the Catholic Church. Within the Catholic

Church there are a number of rites. These individual churches all submit to the pastoral guidance and authority of the pope, although they differ somewhat in liturgy, ecclesiastical discipline and spiritual heritage.

The Roman or Latin Rite is by far the largest rite in terms of numbers and geographical extent, but the Second Vatican Council devoted a document to the Catholic churches of the various Eastern rites. The *Decree on Eastern Catholic Churches (Orientalium Ecclesiarum)* declared that *all* rites of the Catholic Church are "of equal dignity, so that none of them is superior to the others" (no. 3).

The existence of these different rites adds to the richness and beauty of the Catholic Church. The Extraordinary Synod of 1985 called attention to the great esteem that all Catholics hold for the Eastern rite churches because of the richness of their traditions, which date back to the apostles and come to us through the great Eastern theologians and fathers of the church (Synod, 55). For instance, among the events that were most moving and instructive for the bishops at the Second Vatican Council were the celebrations of the Mass in different rites. In one liturgy the principal celebrant entered with a large hat shaped like a beehive. How surprised the Council fathers were when the celebrant bent down and a deacon removed the offertory gifts from the headpiece! Instances such as this reminded the bishops just how diverse and rich are the rites and cultural expressions of the Catholic Church.

The Eastern Catholic churches are a sensitive issue for many Orthodox Christians, who view the existence of these *uniate* ("in union" with Rome) churches as an obstacle to Christian unity. They fear that Orthodox union with Rome would mean a loss of Orthodox identity and heritage.

The Catholic Church, however, believes that these Eastern rite Catholic churches have a special role to play in *promoting* Christian unity (see *Orientalium Ecclesiarum*, 24). These churches demonstrate the fact that practices that differ greatly from the Latin Rite are compatible with belonging to the Catholic Church.

The *Decree on Eastern Catholic Churches* lists a number of ways that will make it easier for Eastern Catholics and Orthodox Christians to relate to each other. For example, the decree facilitates marriages between Catholics and Orthodox. But the regulations that prohibit full intercommunion between Catholics and Orthodox Christians must still be respected, until the day when the Lord brings us into full unity.

Since Catholics have the fullness of truth, do we have a ticket to heaven?

No. The Catholic Church possesses this fullness, but not every Catholic takes full advantage of all that God offers to us in the church. Article 14 of this constitution explains that a Catholic can be a member of the church in an external manner but not "in his heart." We are warned that even a person with external membership in the church will not be saved if he or she does not persevere in charity.

The Council also warns against inflated Catholic pride or "triumphalism," reminding us that whatever good resides within the church is solely due to the special grace of Christ. Moreover, Catholics will be judged more severely than others on the last day. They have a responsibility to utilize fully in thought, word and deed the grace and the means of grace that God has generously showered upon the Catholic Church.

I tremble when I consider the extent to which Catholics in the West are neglecting many of the traditional means of receiving God's grace and growing in holiness: the sacraments, especially the sacrament of reconciliation and the Eucharist; prayer and fasting; almsgiving and works of mercy; and supporting one's parish through money, service and active participation! God's judgment "*will* begin with the household of God" (1 Peter 4:17). Jesus himself instructed us: "Every one to whom much is given, of him much will be required" (Luke 12:48).

Can only Catholics be saved?

The *Dogmatic Constitution on the Church* states that because Christ founded the Catholic Church in order to save humanity, "Whosoever, therefore, knowing that the Catholic Church was made necessary by God through Jesus Christ, would refuse to enter her or to remain in her could not be saved" (no. 14).

The key word here is *knowing.* God judges us according to whether we act on what we *know* as revealed by our conscience. If a person knows or recognizes that God made the Catholic Church necessary for salvation, he or she must act according to that knowledge by remaining in or joining the Catholic Church. Reasons of pride, fear, inconvenience, loss of friends or social prestige might prevent a person from acting according to what he or she knows is right. The Council warns people that in a matter of salvation, one must act decisively regardless of the obstacles.

This teaching is very unpopular today because in Western culture we commonly view membership in a church as a matter of personal preference or convenience. But God's perspective is that belonging to his people is a matter of life and death—a matter of salvation.

Also we must understand that in rejecting the church, one is really rejecting Jesus, since Christ identifies himself with his body, the church. The Lord told his disciples, "He who hears you hears me, and he who rejects you rejects me, and he who rejects me rejects him who sent me" (Luke 10:16).

We need to distinguish this belief from the erroneous one that only Catholics will be saved. Vatican II's teaching clearly deals only with those who *know* or recognize that Christ founded the Catholic Church and made her necessary for salvation. Even in the 1950s a Catholic priest from Boston, Leonard Feeney, was excommunicated for teaching that only Catholics can be saved.

How does God make his people holy?

The *Dogmatic Constitution on the Church* draws special attention to the sacraments (no. 11), to the proclamation of the Word of God (no. 12) and to the "charismatic" gifts of the Holy Spirit (listed in 1 Corinthians 12) as particular ways that the Holy Spirit, the sanctifier, makes God's people holy. The constitution devotes an entire chapter to "The Call of the Whole Church to Holiness" to emphasize that holiness is for *everyone*. This holiness is *expressed* in somewhat different ways according to one's call as a single person, married person, priest, deacon or vowed religious.

The document praises the practice of the "evangelical counsels" of poverty, chastity and obedience as a particular way in which holiness shines forth. In the midst of a world marked by materialism, obsession with sex and rebellion against authority (even in the milder form of "do your own thing"), these practices are a more powerful witness to Christ than ever.

Holiness is a gift from Christ and a fruit of the grace of the Holy Spirit in a person's life. Our task is to give our lives fully to God and to the service of our neighbor. This document teaches us that "*all* the faithful of Christ...are called to the fullness of the Christian life and to the perfection of charity. By this holiness a more human way of life is promoted even in this earthly society" (no. 40).

The Extraordinary Synod of 1985 urged all Catholics to pursue holiness, which is an invitation to conversion and full participation in the life of God. Today many people experience an emptiness that only God can fill. The church offers the only solution: discovering God through prayer, penance, adoration, sacrifice, self-giving, charity and justice. It is the saints who have always led the way in the renewal of the church in the most difficult periods of its history. Today is no different. "Today, we have a tremendous need of saints, for whom we must assiduously implore God" (Synod, 47). But through the Second Vatican Council we understand more clearly that holiness is for everyone.

We are all called to be saints! It is the purpose of human life, the end or goal for which God created each of us. The greatest challenge to Catholics, in this age and in every age, is to respond to this call to holiness.

How do we reflect the life of Jesus and share his mission?

The church carries on the threefold ministry of Jesus as priest, prophet and king. The first section of the *Dogmatic Constitution on the Church* discusses how the church as a whole, as a "priestly people," continues this ministry of Jesus. All of God's people are called to offer themselves to God as a "living sacrifice" (Romans 12:1) in union with Jesus Christ.

The constitution notes a distinction between this priesthood of the faithful and the ministerial priesthood. Jesus and the church set apart certain people to *lead* the people of God in their prayer and offering of themselves. This ordained priesthood and the priesthood of the faithful are different but complementary ways of participating in the sacrificial priesthood of Christ, the great High Priest. The second major section of the constitution elaborates on how ordained leaders, the laity and those in the religious state uniquely exercise the threefold ministry of Christ.

Why does the church place so much emphasis on ordained leaders?

Actually, the *Dogmatic Constitution on the Church* doesn't discuss the hierarchy of the church until the third chapter, *after* speaking of the mystery of the church and the people of God.

The Catholic Church values the role of the ordained leaders because Jesus himself spent much time training and equipping his own apostles and then commissioned them in a special way to continue his ministry and to represent him as servants of their brethren—just as Christ came not to be served but to serve and to lay down his life for his sheep. The document states that it is Jesus' will that the apostles' successors, "namely the bishops, should be shepherds in His Church even to the consummation of the world," with the successor of Peter as "a permanent and visible source and foundation of unity of faith and fellowship" (no. 18). (The role of these ordained leaders is spelled out in detail in three Vatican II documents that will be discussed later.)

Why isn't there a separate document on the pope?

The papacy in the modern world was a focus of the First Vatican Council from 1869 to 1870, which promulgated the decree on the pope's primacy (as the church's chief pastor) and infallibility. Vatican II basically repeats what Vatican I taught concerning the pope's infallibility and jurisdiction, except that it speaks at greater length about the pope's unity with the "college" or body of bishops, of which he is both the head and a member. The pope and the bishops are joined into one body as Peter and the apostles were (no. 22). However, as Vicar (representative) of Christ, and pastor of the whole church, the pope has "full, supreme, and universal power over the Church. And he can always exercise this power freely" (no. 22).

I have heard critical comments about the pope's intervening in the affairs of the church in a diocese, as if this were contrary to the Council. Jesus Christ himself gave special authority to Peter (see Matthew 16:18-19) and appointed him shepherd of the whole flock (see John 21:15-17). The pope must be ready to exercise that Petrine authority for the good of the church. The constitution says that the office of the pope shows forth the *unity* of the church, gathered around one head, while the bishops represent the variety and universality of God's people (no. 22).

How does Vatican II define "papal infallibility"?

Article 25 of the constitution explains that infallibility is God's gift to insure that the deposit of divine revelation that he has entrusted to the church in matters of faith and morals will be faithfully preserved, interpreted and handed on.

The Council presents three ways in which the church can propose a belief as infallibly true. First, repeating the teaching of the First Vatican Council, the pope can define a doctrine infallibly regarding faith and morals when he proclaims this by a definitive act in his capacity as chief shepherd and teacher of all the faithful—that is, when he defines a doctrine *ex cathedra* (from the chair of Peter).

Second, the universal body of bishops, teaching in union with the pope, can speak infallibly when "gathered together in an ecumenical council, they are teachers and judges of faith and morals," or even when, scattered around the world, "they concur in a single viewpoint as the one which must be held conclusively" (no. 25).

Third, the whole church can recognize a doctrine concerning faith or morals as infallibly true when through a supernatural sense of the faith *(sensus fidei),* "'from the bishops down to the last members of the laity' [St. Augustine], it shows universal agreement" (no. 12).

All of this flows from the promise of Jesus to send his Holy Spirit to teach his followers all things and guide them into the fullness of truth (see John 14:25-26; 16:12-15).

We must adhere to what the church defines as infallibly true with the submission of faith. We *must* believe in such teachings, because they are certainly true and direct our understanding of Christianity and our worship of God.

Some examples of doctrines formally defined by the church and considered infallible include the divinity of Jesus Christ, fully equal to the Father in the Godhead (Council of Nicea, A.D. 325); the divinity of the Holy Spirit, co-equal to the Father and the Son in Godhead (Council of Constantinople, A.D. 381); that Jesus Christ is fully God and fully human (Council of Chalcedon, A.D. 451); that Mary is rightly called the "Mother of God" because she truly gave birth to Jesus Christ, the Son of God (Council of Ephesus, A.D. 431); that Mary was conceived without sin (the Immaculate Conception, Pope Pius IX, 1854) and was assumed body and soul into heaven (the Assumption, Pope Pius XII, 1950).

But what about those things that do not fall into the category of infallible statements? This, the vast majority of the teaching of the pope and our bishops, includes teachings on the application of the gospel to the economy, social life and politics. It includes practical directives on fasting, support of Catholic education and so on. The *Dogmatic Constitution on the Church* states that Catholics must accept the ordinary teaching of the bishops in matters of faith with "a religious assent of soul" and adhere to the pope's "non-infallible" teaching with the same attitude of "religious submission of will and of mind" (no. 25).

In other words, by virtue of the pope's and the bishops' offices as teachers of the faithful, Catholics are to heed their ordinary teaching with a disposition of assent. This is true even if we know that this teaching is not infallible.

Some Catholics wonder whether there are different levels of authority or importance among the many different teachings of the pope. There are. The constitution notes that the mind of the pope and the degree of solemnity or importance attached to his statements may be ascertained "chiefly either from the character of the documents, from his frequent repetition of the same doctrine, or from his manner of speaking" (no. 25).

In other words, all papal teaching, and to a lesser extent that of bishops and priests teaching in union with the pope, should be accepted by Catholics with an attitude of religious assent, but only matters formally defined by the church as infallibly true must be held with full submission as official doctrines of our faith. When the pope repeats a doctrine frequently, emphasizes a teaching as particularly important or includes a doctrine in an encyclical letter or other more solemn mode of teaching, a Catholic knows that this teaching is very significant, even though not formally defined.

The teaching of the magisterium of the Catholic Church, when not presented as infallible truth, is intended to form our consciences and help to conform them to the mind of Christ. That is why a disposition of assent, even toward teachings that are not infallible, is so important for Catholics. Later we will discuss how this understanding affects theological pluralism and the issue of dissent in the church.[2]

Wasn't "collegiality" a major theme of Vatican II?

Yes, collegiality was an important theme of the Council, and it is discussed most fully in chapter three of the *Dogmatic Constitution on the Church*. The theme of collegiality was important because Vatican I—forced to close early by a war—was unable to present a full picture of the Catholic hierarchy that included the bishops and priests. Vatican II's *Dogmatic Constitution on the Church* completes this picture by showing how bishops work together, along with their priests, in union with the pope.

The document explains that the apostles were formed by Jesus as a "college" or fixed group, with Peter singled out as head of this college under Christ himself (see no. 19). To ensure that the mission of the apostles would continue until the end of the world, the apostles appointed successors, who also formed a "college"—the college of bishops, with the successor of Peter, the pope, as their head under Christ.

As evidence for this collegiality, the document mentions first "the very ancient practice by which bishops…were linked with one another and with the Bishop of Rome by bonds of unity, charity, and peace." Second, councils of bishops, especially ecumenical (worldwide) councils "made common judgments about more profound matters." The full authority of the college of bishops over the church "is exercised in a solemn way through an ecumenical council." Third, the document mentions "the practice, introduced in ancient times, of summoning several bishops to take part in the elevation of someone newly elected to the ministry of the high priesthood" (no. 22). All of these are time-proven expressions of collegiality that continue in the church today.

The college of bishops, working together, "expresses the variety and *universality* of the people of God," but the college *always* must act in union with the head of the college, the pope, who represents and preserves the *unity* of the flock of Christ.

Is there a section devoted to permanent deacons?

Vatican II opened the door for the restoration of the ancient office of permanent deacon. Over the course of centuries, the office of deacon in the Catholic Church became almost exclusively a stage in becoming a priest. Vatican II called for the restoration of ordination to the diaconate as a unique, permanent ministry of service in the church, as it had been in the first centuries of Christianity.

The institution of the permanent diaconate is left to the discretion of the bishops of each territory. As explained in the *Dogmatic Constitution on the Church,* this diaconate is "to be conferred upon men of more mature age, even upon those living in the married state" (no. 29). Single men who are ordained to the diaconate must remain single and celibate in exercising their ministry as deacons.

What about the role of the laity in the church?

Another revolutionary aspect of the Second Vatican Council is that it is the first council to directly address the ministry of the lay faithful, those neither ordained nor embracing religious vows. At the Council Cardinal John J. Wright of Pittsburgh said, "The faithful have been waiting for 400 years for a positive conciliar statement on the place, dignity and vocation of the layman."[3] In addition to a chapter of this constitution, an entire document is devoted to the laity, entitled the *Decree on the Apostolate of the Laity* (see chapter ten of this book). Vatican II truly ushered in the "age of the laity" in the Catholic Church.

What is the role of the laity? In short, they are to carry out the mission of the church in the world of temporal or secular affairs. The laity carry out the mission of Christ and his church in the home and in the marketplace.

The constitution states, "The laity, by their very vocation, seek the kingdom of God by engaging in temporal affairs and ordering them according to the plan of God." The laity "work for the sanctification of the world from within" like leaven. They make Christ known to others, "especially by the testimony of a life resplendent in faith, hope, and charity." Their call is to order earthly affairs of every sort according to the mind of Christ (no. 31).

The church commissions the lay faithful for this apostolic ministry, but so does the Lord himself, through the call and grace he gives them, especially through baptism, confirmation and the Eucharist (no. 33). The constitution notes that the laity are sometimes the *only* ones who can bring the gospel of Christ into certain places or circumstances. They must respond generously to this call.

Finally, the laity "are in their own way made sharers in the priestly, prophetic, and kingly functions of Christ" (no. 31). This will be described fully in the chapter on the challenge to the laity.

What about the calling of religious in the church?

Religious are not to be distinguished primarily by the way they dress or by their title "brother," "sister" or "father" but by the fact that they embrace a singular way of life within the church. They vow themselves to live out the evangelical counsels of poverty, celibate chastity and obedience in a religious community or according to a particular rule that describes and guides their way of life.

The document notes that the religious life "is not an intermediate one between the clerical and lay states," but it includes both clerics and laypeople who have heard and responded to God's call to follow Christ by living according to those counsels of Christian holiness (no. 43). The faithful living of these evangelical counsels is a sign that witnesses to the priority of the values of God's kingdom. Thus religious inspire all Christians to live out their own calling more fully.

The Council called for a renewal of religious life through a return to the ideals and spirits of the founders. Religious life must also be adapted in some ways to better serve the needs of people of this time. The Vatican II *Decree on the Appropriate Renewal of the Religious Life* develops these themes in detail.

How do we prepare for the second coming of Christ?

With the sending of the Holy Spirit, the restoration of all things in Christ has begun. Thus the *Dogmatic Constitution on the Church* teaches, "The final age of the world has already come upon us" (no. 48). We are living in the "end times," the "last days." This final age of the world is the time between Jesus Christ's first coming as a man and his glorious second coming to judge the living and the dead.

Although God's reign on earth has already begun, it has yet to come to completion. The pilgrim church now lives in this world promoting the growth and values of God's kingdom, while looking forward with expectation and hope for Christ to return and bring his work to final fulfillment (see Colossians 1:15-20; 3:4). The church is not passively waiting for Christ's return but is striving to do his will in order "to please the Lord in all things (cf. 2 Cor 5:9)," and is engaged in spiritual warfare against Satan. "We put on the armor of God that we may be able to stand against the wiles of the devil and resist on the evil day (cf. Eph 6:11-13)" (*Lumen Gentium*, 48). These things, done in watchfulness as the Lord commanded, will enable us to stand with confidence before the judgment seat of Christ.

Somehow many Catholics have gotten the impression that Vatican II does not teach about or the Catholic Church does not believe in the end times—the second coming of Christ and the last judgment—or in Satan and the need to war against him. This notion certainly is not supported by this document, which confirms all of these truths, as they have also been taught by two of our most recent popes, Paul VI and John Paul II.

Are those who have died part of the church?

The *Dogmatic Constitution on the Church* presents another dimension of the nature of the church. Until Christ returns in glory, the church not only includes those who are faithfully following Christ on earth but also the "invisible Church": those who "have finished with this life and are being purified"—the souls in purgatory—and those in glory, the saints in heaven. The constitution stresses that these three states of the church are united "in the same love for God and neighbor, and all sing the same hymn of glory to our God." In fact, the constitution asserts that the union between those in the church on earth and those who have died in Christ is actually "*strengthened* through the exchanging of spiritual goods" (no. 49, emphasis added). In Christ we are clearly united to each other.

This mystery of the union of all who are in Christ is known as the "communion of saints." Those in the "church militant" on earth are "fighting the good fight of faith." Those in the "church suffering" in purgatory are experiencing the final cleansing or purification from venial sin and the effects of sin before entering heaven. Those in the "church triumphant" are enjoying the fullness of God's presence in heaven.

How does the communion of saints interact?

To summarize, the *saints in heaven* primarily help the church as they powerfully *intercede*. Their prayer draws its strength from their close union with Christ. Their lives also provide an *inspiration* and an *example* for those in the church on earth. We, the church on earth, honor and venerate the saints—especially Mary the Mother of God, the apostles, the martyrs—and the holy angels, and we ask for their prayers. We can strengthen and assist those in purgatory by praying for them, for "'it is a holy and wholesome thought to pray for the dead that they may be loosed from sins' (2 Mach. 12:46)" (*Lumen Gentium,* 50).

The visible and invisible church is bound together most closely in communion when we on earth gather to praise and worship God, especially in the sacred liturgy and the sacraments. In the Mass we call to mind the presence of the saints in heaven and our union with them in worship. We also remember and pray for the dead, uniting our prayer for them with the one perfect sacrifice of Christ on Calvary (see *Lumen Gentium,* 50).

Each liturgy is a foretaste of the liturgy of consummate glory, which will occur when Christ returns (see *Sacrosanctum Concilium,* 8). Each liturgy reminds us that all in the vast communion of saints, whether in heaven, on earth or in purgatory, are joined together in Christ and in worshiping God the Father through Christ and in the Holy Spirit.

Don't devotions to the saints detract from worship of God?

Lumen Gentium reminds Catholics that authentic devotion to the saints "consists not so much in the multiplying of external acts, but rather in the intensity of our active love" (no. 51). What really counts is not how many devotions to the saints we have or prayers we say but how well we follow their example of love of God and neighbor.

The constitution explains that our devotion to the saints does not weaken our worship of God but "more thoroughly enriches the supreme worship we give to God the Father, through Christ, in the Spirit" (no. 51). God is glorified in his saints. When we honor them, we honor God and God's work in them. When we ask for their prayers, we recognize God's work in and through them, because he hears the prayers of those who love him and have been faithful to him. God alone is to be worshiped, but the Father in heaven rejoices when he sees his children honoring and praying for each other.

Why is Mary called the Mother of the church?

A lively debate occurred at the Second Vatican Council over whether a separate document should be devoted to Mary because of her importance in God's plan of salvation. Finally, the Council fathers decided to place the teaching on Mary in the *Dogmatic Constitution on the Church* to underscore the fact that Mary is a part or a *member* of the church. The chapter on Mary is placed last in the document because truly Mary is a living summary or model of all that the church is. Mary is a member of the church but certainly the preeminent one.

God formed a new covenant people, the church, as a culmination of his plan to save the human race by gathering a people of faith, to whom he would send a Savior, the Messiah. Mary represents the "New Israel," the new people of God, because she was the first to receive the Messiah by consenting to bear him in her own body. Not only was Mary the first to receive the eternal Word of God, Jesus; she also opened herself to receive every word he spoke. She is a model of faithful discipleship.

Mary is the model of the church as the people who believe in Jesus and who welcome and treasure his words and actions and live according to them. Pope John Paul II in his encyclical letter on Mary, *Redemptoris Mater (Mother of the Redeemer),* took for his theme Luke

1:45: "Blessed is she who believed that there would be a fulfillment of what was spoken to her from the Lord."

The *Dogmatic Constitution on the Church* presents a fully biblical treatment of Mary and her role in salvation. The constitution is not giving a complete doctrine on Mary nor deciding any "questions which have not yet been fully illuminated by the work of theologians" (no. 54).

What is Mary's role with regard to the church?

The constitution describes Mary as a *member* of the church, a *model* for the church, *mother* of the church and *mediatrix* for the church, praying to Christ for the church on our behalf. Mary is "hailed as a preeminent and altogether singular *member* of the Church, and as the Church's *model* and excellent exemplar in faith and charity. Taught by the Holy Spirit, the Catholic Church honors her with filial affection and piety as a most beloved *mother*" (no. 53, emphasis added).

Who intercedes more effectively for her children than a mother? And so the constitution also speaks of Mary as an intercessor or mediatrix for the church but emphasizes that her mediation does not obscure or diminish the unique mediation of Christ (see 1 Timothy 2:5-6). Rather her prayers "rest on His mediation, depend entirely on it, and draw all their power from it" (no. 60).

In recommending the title of "mediatrix" for Mary, the constitution compares the use of this title with the use of "priest" to describe Christ. Christ is the one great High Priest for Christians (see Hebrews 4:14-15), and he shares this priesthood with both the ministers of the church and, in a different way, the laity. In a similar way the work of Christ, the one Mediator, is shared in fullness with his mother, who opens the door to all graces by her prayer, and with all Christians and the saints, who can pray to God through Christ for one another and for those in need (no. 62).

God has richly blessed the church with a unique *member* who is a *model* of its virtues, a *mother* who cares for the church's needs and forever a *mediatrix* of grace through her powerful prayers on behalf of her children.

Don't some Catholics exaggerate Mary's role?

In the section on devotion to the Blessed Virgin Mary (nos. 66, 67), the constitution acknowledges this danger but notes that the honor given to Mary and the saints is essentially different from adoration, which Catholics offer only to God. The document then goes on to warn against the two extremes of exaggerating Mary's role in God's plan and of neglecting her (see *Lumen Gentium*, 67). The document exhorts Catholics to study sacred Scripture and the fathers, doctors and liturgies of the church, guided by the church's teaching office, in order to understand Mary's role more fully.

The constitution mentions that the Catholic teachings about Mary "are always related to Christ, the Source of all truth, sanctity, and piety" (no. 67). The document's section on Mary attempts to explain and clarify misconceptions about Mary's immaculate conception (nos. 53, 55), her role as model disciple and mother (no. 58), her assumption into heaven and queenship (no. 59), her intercessory role as "mediatrix" (nos. 60, 61), her virginity (no. 63) and her presence in heaven as a sign of hope and solace for God's people (no. 68). All of these teachings are related to Christ and his plan of salvation.

The Second Vatican Council recommends that all past teaching of the church about Mary be faithfully observed and that all error or exaggeration be avoided: "Let the faithful remember moreover that true devotion consists neither in fruitless and passing emotion, nor in a certain vain credulity. Rather, it proceeds from true faith, by which we are led to know the excellence of the Mother of God, and are moved to a filial love toward our mother and to the imitation of her virtues" (no. 67).

We also remember that Mary "unites and mirrors within herself the central truths of the faith. Hence when she is being preached and venerated, she summons the faithful to her Son and His sacrifice, and to love for the Father" (no. 65).

How can the church be called both a "virgin" and a "mother"?

In the same way that Mary was. By her single-hearted devotion to the Lord, "the Church herself is a virgin, who keeps whole and pure the fidelity she has pledged to her Spouse.... She preserves with virginal purity an integral faith, a firm hope, and a sincere charity" (no. 64). The church becomes a mother "by accepting God's word in faith. For by her preaching and by baptism she brings forth to a new and immortal life children who are conceived of the Holy Spirit and born of God" (no. 64).

Conclusion

Vatican II calls Catholics today to recognize that *each* person— whether single, married, lay, religious or ordained—is a full member of the church, the people of God. Each is called to holiness.

Unfortunately, we still witness in the church those who are dissatisfied and those who think that they cannot contribute fully to the life of the church unless they are ordained or involved in a particular ministry. Such attitudes not only harm the individual but perpetuate a false "clericalism" or other distorted understandings of the church. Mary, a woman of faith and prayer, remains the ultimate model for the church—a model whom all can imitate in our quest for holiness.

The *Dogmatic Constitution on the Church* reflects Saint Paul's vision of a church with many members possessing different gifts and ministries, *all* of which contribute to the building up of the body.

Paul's warnings about dissension, disunity and party spirit are also very timely today. These oppose the Spirit of God and the true nature of the church.

We are presented with a vision of a church which is rich and diverse: a church on earth longing for its home in heaven; the people of God possessing both divine gifts and a human form and structure; a church called to holiness with many ways of expressing and attaining it; a church including members in this world and in the next, united in a bond of love and service that transcends even death.

When is the church most fully what God has made her? It is in prayer, especially when her members gather around the eucharistic table to re-present Jesus' sacrifice, which has made us one people of the new covenant in his blood. As we prepare to study the liturgy of the church in the next chapter, let us recall the words of Pope John Paul II: "The Council saw in the liturgy an epiphany of the Church: It is the Church at prayer. In celebrating divine worship, the Church gives expression to what she is: one, holy, catholic and apostolic."[4]

Lumen Gentium and the Catechism of the Catholic Church

There are nearly three hundred references to the *Dogmatic Constitution on the Church* in the *Catechism* (296 to be exact). This document is the most oft-cited of Vatican II (or of any document, other than the Bible) in the *Catechism*.

Although these references are present throughout the *Catechism*, they are especially to be found in the presentation of the article of the Creed: "I believe in the Holy Catholic Church" (nos. 748-975) and in the discussion of the liturgy and sacraments of the church in Part II of the *Catechism*.

Recent Magisterial Documents

Congregation for the Doctrine of the Faith. "Dominus Iesus: On the Unicity and Salvific Universality of Jesus Christ and the Church." August 6, 2000.

Congregation for the Doctrine of Faith. "Letter to the Bishops of the Catholic Church on Some Aspects of the Church Understood as Communion." May 28, 1992.

Pope John Paul II. "Ad Tuendam Fidem." May 18, 1998. *Origins*. 28, no. 8 (July 16, 1998).

Pope John Paul II. *Redemptoris Mater* (Encyclical Letter *Mother of the Redeemer*). March 25, 1987.

Favorite Quotes from *Lumen Gentium*

The Church, "like a pilgrim in a foreign land, presses forward amid the persecutions of the world and the consolations of God" [Saint Augustine], announcing the cross and death of the Lord until He comes (cf. 1 Cor. 11:26). By the power of the risen Lord, she is given strength to overcome patiently and lovingly the afflictions and hardships which assail her from within and without, and to show forth in the world the mystery of the Lord in a faithful though shadowed way, until at the last it will be revealed in total splendor. (no. 8)

It has pleased God, however, to make men holy and save them not merely as individuals without any mutual bonds, but by making them into a single people, a people which acknowledges Him in truth and serves Him in holiness. (no. 9)

Favorite Quote from *Orientalium Ecclesiarum*

Individual [Catholic] Churches, whether of the East or of the West, although they differ somewhat among themselves in what are called rites (that is, in liturgy, ecclesiastical discipline, and spiritual heritage) are, nevertheless, equally entrusted to the pastoral guidance of the Roman Pontiff, the divinely appointed successor of St. Peter in supreme governance over the universal Church. They are consequently of equal dignity, so that none of them is superior to the others by reason of rite. (no. 3)

CHAPTER SEVEN

Touching Eternity: The Call to Worship

It is easy to fall into a purely "horizontal" existence, constantly involved with the affairs of the world. But worship is the "vertical" dimension that reveals the meaning of all our earthly activity and gives our lives depth and purpose. God calls us daily to cease from our activity and to return to the source of our life, lifting our minds and hearts to him, the living God.

In the last chapter we spoke of the church as the "communion of saints." When Christians worship, we join our prayer with the myriad of angels and all the saints in heaven who ceaselessly sing, "Holy, holy, holy, is the Lord God Almighty, who was and is and is to come!" (Revelation 4:8).

Worship is the subject of the Second Vatican Council's *Constitution on the Sacred Liturgy* (*Sacrosanctum Concilium*). Since worship is the only adequate response to God's revelation of himself and is the highest activity of the church, it is appropriate now to consider the liturgy.

The church is primarily a worshiping community—a people called by God to be his own, full of adoration, praise and thanksgiving for who he is and what he has done. This is not self-evident, though. If one were to ask a Catholic today what is the most important activity of the church, some responses might be feeding the hungry, caring for the sick and the dying, proclaiming the gospel to the unchurched, overturning unjust social structures or simply loving your neighbor.

Each of these is an important way of living the gospel, but the *Constitution on the Sacred Liturgy* affirms that the liturgy is "the summit toward which the activity of the Church is directed; at the same time it is the fountain from which all her power flows. For the goal of apostolic works is that all who are made sons of God by faith and baptism should come together to praise God in the midst of His Church, to take part in her sacrifice, and to eat the Lord's supper" (no. 10).

Let us now consider why the church considers worship in the liturgy so important and how we are to suitably worship God as his people.

How is the liturgy the summit of all our works?

What is the liturgy? Literally, the word *liturgy* means "work of the people." It is the work of the people to offer to God all that we are and all that we do, in union with Jesus Christ.

The liturgy, therefore, is connected with our apostolic works, such as service of the poor, evangelism, love of neighbor and the works of justice. These efforts reach their fulfillment and find their true meaning when they are offered as sacrifices to the Father in union with the one perfect sacrifice of Christ on Calvary. In other words, it is only in the context of worship that all the other things we do as Catholic Christians make any sense and find their true meaning. For example, the great charitable work of Mother Teresa and the Missionaries of Charity, as well as that of countless other lay and religious communities, finds its fulfillment and source of power in prayer and the Eucharist.

We *all* come to worship God in the liturgy, bringing to him as our offering our whole selves and everything we do for love of him and our neighbor, just as Jesus Christ offered to the Father his whole life and all his works at the Last Supper and on Calvary. Saint Paul writes, "I appeal to you therefore, brethren, by the mercies of God, to present your bodies as a living sacrifice, holy and acceptable to God, which is your spiritual worship" (Romans 12:1).

How is this "living sacrifice" actually offered to God? The *Dogmatic Constitution on the Church* says the laity exercise their share in Christ's priesthood by offering their lives to God each day:

> For all their works, prayers, and apostolic endeavors, their ordinary married and family life, their daily labor, their mental and physical relaxation, if carried out in the Spirit, and even the hardships of life, if patiently borne—all of these become spiritual sacrifices acceptable to God through Jesus Christ (cf. 1 Pet 2:5). During the celebration of the Eucharist, these sacrifices are most lovingly offered to the Father along with the Lord's body. Thus, as worshipers whose every deed is holy, the laity consecrate the world itself to God. (no. 34)

At the Offertory of the Mass, each Catholic can offer his or her troubles, joys and every aspect of life to the Father in union with Jesus' perfect offering of himself.

How is the liturgy "the fountain" from which the church's power flows?

The church's power to carry out its mission in the world and the power to make its own members holy comes from Jesus Christ. Jesus comes to us most fully in the liturgy of the Eucharist, in which we receive his own body and blood. Indeed, the *Constitution on the Sacred Liturgy* says that through the liturgy the faithful "are given access to the stream of divine grace which flows from the paschal mystery of the passion, death, and resurrection of Christ, the fountain from which all the sacraments and sacramentals draw their power" (no. 61).

Hence, even though the liturgy is a fountain, the grace of the liturgy and the sacraments ultimately flows from the font of the cross of Jesus Christ. The liturgy and sacraments have no power or life of their own; they are channels of the grace of Christ.

Pope John Paul II wrote in *Vicesimus Quintus* that from the liturgy and the sacraments "the faithful draw abundantly the water of grace which flows from the side of the Crucified Christ. To use an image dear to Pope John XXIII, it is like the village fountain to which every generation comes to draw water ever living and fresh" (no. 22).

While Catholics come to the liturgy ready to repent of their sins and to offer to God the sacrifices of their lives, they receive much more than they give. The Word of God and Christ's body and blood nourish and strengthen the faithful to go forth and live and work for God's kingdom.

To be nourished in this way, Catholics must listen attentively to the Word of God proclaimed and preached. They must receive the Lamb of God in the Eucharist with faith and a desire to be guided, healed and strengthened by him.

Are there any other reasons why the liturgy is so important?

Yes. The church basically exists to worship God. Worship is the one activity of the church that will never end. The constitution says that the earthly liturgy we celebrate is a foretaste and a sharing in "that heavenly liturgy which is celebrated in the holy city of Jerusalem [above] toward which we journey as pilgrims" (no. 8). All other activities of the church will pass away, but worship of God lasts forever (see Revelation 22:3-5).

Isn't this an exaggerated view of the importance of the liturgy?

The *Constitution on the Sacred Liturgy* states that sacred liturgy "does *not* exhaust the entire activity of the church" and that, before people come to the liturgy, "they must be called to faith and to conversion."

Important tasks of the church are, therefore, to preach faith and repentance, to prepare people for the sacraments, to teach them to obey God's law and to "win them to all the works of charity, piety, and the apostolate" (no. 9).

The liturgy does not exist in a vacuum. It is now a commonly recognized problem that many Catholics have been "sacramentalized but not evangelized." They receive the sacraments of the church without a full faith in and commitment to Jesus Christ. It is possible to participate in the liturgy without living out its grace and teaching in everyday life.

The constitution warns that "in order that the sacred liturgy may produce its full effect, it is necessary that the faithful come to it with proper dispositions, that their thoughts match their words, and that they cooperate with divine grace lest they receive it in vain" (no. 11).

An important theological point is made here. God always gives grace in the sacraments and the liturgy. But any person may block the work of grace in his or her own life through lack of faith, rejection of God through serious sin or other obstacles. In fact, Saint Paul warned that whoever "eats the bread or drinks the cup of the Lord in an unworthy manner will be guilty of profaning the body and blood of the Lord.... For any one who eats and drinks without discerning the body eats and drinks judgment upon himself" (1 Corinthians 11:27, 29).

The *Constitution on the Sacred Liturgy* also teaches that one who prays with the Christian community in the liturgy "must also enter into his chamber to pray to the Father in secret (cf. Mt. 6:6); indeed...he should pray without ceasing (cf. 1 Th. 5:17)" (no. 12). Personal prayer is a necessary foundation for engaging in the prayer of the church. Pope Benedict XVI once wrote: "Eucharist presupposes personal prayer, prayer in the family, and extra-liturgical prayer in community."[1]

What's the purpose of Vatican II's reform of the liturgy?

The constitution states that the aim of this restoration of the liturgy is "the full, conscious, and active participation" of all the faithful in liturgical celebrations. The word translated "active" here more accurately means "real" participation—participation from the heart, which could include silence as well as activity.

The Extraordinary Synod of Bishops of 1985 noted, "The active participation, so happily increased after the Council, does not consist only in external activity, but above all in interior and spiritual participation.... It is evident that the liturgy must favor the sense of the sacred and make it shine forth. It must be permeated by the spirit of reverence, adoration and the glory of God" (Synod, 52). Realizing that we are in the presence of God as a people in the liturgy, joined in worship with all the saints, Catholics should participate fully with attitudes of gratitude, joy and prayerful reverence.

How was the renewal of the sacred liturgy to come about?

The constitution recognized that the hoped-for renewal of the liturgy required that *pastors* first become "thoroughly penetrated with the spirit and power of the liturgy, and become masters of it" (*Sacrosanctum Concilium,* 14). From there could come the education of future priests in seminaries and the instruction of the laity. Pope John Paul II stressed that the future of the renewal of the liturgy still depends on the "biblical and liturgical formation of the People of God, both pastors and faithful" (*Vicesimus Quintus,* 15).

What were some of the major elements of this renewal?

These elements are familiar to most people today, since "the liturgical renewal is the most visible fruit of the whole conciliar effort,"

(Synod, 52), beginning with "turning the altar around so that the priest faces the people" (which was not mentioned in Vatican II but certainly not forbidden). The Council distinguished between the unchangeable elements of the liturgy and those subject to change (*Sacrosanctum Concilium*, 21). Among the many changes called for or permitted by the Council were

○ streamlining rites so that they would be marked by "a noble simplicity," avoiding needless repetition and respecting people's power of comprehension;

○ emphasizing reading from holy Scripture and advocating sermons drawing their content mainly from Scripture and liturgical sources;

○ the introduction of the vernacular language by the competent ecclesiastical authorities (usually the bishops) where they deemed this helpful in encouraging the faithful to understand the rites;

○ involvement of different members (servers, lectors, commentators, musicians where appropriate) and the establishment of liturgical commissions in parishes and dioceses;

○ revisions of liturgical books and rites for the Mass and various sacraments;

○ introduction of prayers that would increase the participation of the faithful, such as the "Prayer of the Faithful";

○ concelebration of Mass as directed by the local bishop;

○ restoration of the catechumenate for adults as in the early church (the RCIA);

○ "Extreme Unction" renamed the "Anointing of the Sick" and administered to those in danger of death, not only at the point of death;

○ new emphasis on praying the "Liturgy of the Hours" (the Divine Office) by laypeople and in parishes, as well as by clergy and religious;

○ revision of the calendar of the liturgical year, with special emphasis on Sunday, the Lord's Day, as "the foundation and nucleus of the whole liturgical year" (no. 106);

○ changes in laws regarding fast and abstinence, placing more responsibility on the individual;

○ adaptation of the liturgy, within some specified boundaries, to different cultures;

○ revisions and some new directions for sacred music, sacred art and sacred furnishings.

Do we understand the presence of Christ in the liturgy any differently as a result of the Council teachings?

Before the Second Vatican Council, many Catholics would only think of Christ's presence at Mass in terms of the *Eucharist* at Holy Communion and in the tabernacle and perhaps in the *priest*, who represents Christ. In addition to these modes of Christ's presence, this constitution reminds the faithful that Christ is also present in the *other sacraments*, such as baptism, in *God's Word*, which is proclaimed, and in *his people* gathered to pray and sing.

"[Jesus] promised, 'Where two or three are gathered together for my sake, there am I in the midst of them' (Mt. 18:20)" (*Sacrosanctum Concilium*, 7). Pope John Paul II has said that this presence of Christ in the Christian assembly gives it a unique character, with the consequent duties of brotherly welcome, forgiveness (see Matthew 5:23, 24) and dignity in behavior, gesture and song (see *Vicesimus quintus*, 7).

What does the constitution say about the Mass as a sacrifice?

Certainly the death of Christ on the cross is the one sacrifice that redeems the human race. This constitution declares that at the Last Supper Jesus instituted the eucharistic sacrifice of his body and blood "in order to *perpetuate* [that is, to continue or to 're-present'] the sacrifice of the Cross throughout the centuries until He should come again" (emphasis added). The church is entrusted with "a memorial of His death and resurrection: a sacrament of love, a sign of unity, a bond of charity, a paschal banquet in which Christ is consumed, the mind is filled with grace, and a pledge of future glory is given to us" (no. 47).

The Eucharist perpetuates and makes present to us in sacramental form the one eternal sacrifice of Christ on Calvary. In this sense the Eucharist is a *memorial* of Jesus' death and resurrection. But it is also a *living* memorial in which the one being remembered is actually present to us under the appearance of bread and wine. Jesus is not re-sacrificed, but the event of Christ's one sacrifice, which transcends time, is made present to us, and his body and blood are really given to us in sacramental form.

Pope John Paul II recognized the reenactment of the paschal mystery of Christ in the liturgy as the central topic of this constitution, especially Christ's presence in the Eucharist. He urged pastors to teach frequently about the real presence of Christ in the Eucharist in their catechetical instructions, called the faithful to live it out and encouraged theologians to expound on it. Pope John Paul II also urged: "Faith in this presence of the Lord involves an outward sign of respect toward the church, the holy place in which God manifests himself in mystery (cf. Ex 3:5), especially during the celebration of the sacraments: holy things must always be treated in a holy manner" (*Vicesimus quintus*, 7).

Was the teaching on the Word of God in the liturgy a major change?

Yes. Although the reading of sacred Scripture has always been part of the sacred liturgy, Vatican II underscores that the Liturgy of the Word and the Liturgy of the Eucharist are *both* the bread of life for God's people (*Dei Verbum*, 21). They "are so closely connected with each other that they form but one single act of worship" (*Sacrosanctum Concilium*, 56).

The *Constitution on the Sacred Liturgy* insists that if the renewal of the sacred liturgy is to be achieved, a "warm and living love for Scripture" must be promoted (no. 24). "There is to be more reading from holy Scripture, and it is to be more varied and suitable" (no. 35; see also no. 51). Further, the sermon should draw its content mainly from scriptural and liturgical sources, and Bible services should be encouraged (no. 35).

In 1988 Pope John Paul II noted that Catholics now know the Word of God better, but there are new challenges: the need for faithfulness to the authentic meaning of the Scriptures, especially in good translations; proclaiming the Word of God as truly *God's* Word; prayer and study of Scripture for ministers of the Word and homilists; and an effort on the part of the faithful to seek out God's Word, to pray and study it, in order to discover Christ (see *Vicesimus quintus*, 8).

The pope also warned: "Since the liturgy is totally permeated by the word of God, any other word must be in harmony with it, above all in the homily, but also in the various interventions of the minister and in the hymns which are sung. No other reading may supplant the Biblical word, and the words of men must be at the service of the word of God without obscuring it" (*Vicesimus quintus*, 10).

How do popular devotions fit into this understanding?

While most popular devotions are "warmly commended," they are subordinate to the liturgy. As the prayer of the whole church, "the liturgy by its very nature far surpasses any of them" (*Sacrosanctum Concilium,* 13). Pope John Paul II was more cautious in his evaluation of popular devotions, speaking of a need for them to become ever more mature and authentic acts of faith. In general, popular devotions are to be welcomed and encouraged. "The Liturgy will build upon the riches of popular piety, purifying and directing them towards the Liturgy as the offering of the peoples" (*Vicesimus quintus,* 18).

Has the renewal of the liturgy been successful?

Pope John Paul II wrote in his letter on the Eucharist (*Dominicae Cenae*): "A very close and organic bond exists between the renewal of the liturgy and the renewal of the whole life of the Church."[2]

Although the reform of the liturgy has encountered many difficulties and has not yet been fully accomplished, I would agree with Pope John Paul II's observation that the vast majority of pastors and Christian people have accepted the liturgical reform in a spirit of obedience and indeed joyful fervor. He noted that "for many people the message of the Second Vatican Council has been experienced principally through liturgical reform" (*Vicesimus quintus,* 12).

What has been the greatest concern regarding liturgical renewal?

The greatest concern among church leaders such as Cardinal Ratzinger and many of the bishops at the Extraordinary Synod is this: Has the church experienced a loss of the sense of the sacred in the liturgy and a loss of the sense of the mystery of God present in the church?

The Extraordinary Synod, in its *Final Report*, speaks of a secularism that denies the dimension of mystery. But the Synod notes:

> Signs of a return to the sacred also exist. Today, in fact, there are signs of a new hunger and thirst for the transcendent and divine. In order to favor this return to the sacred and to overcome secularism, we must open the way to the dimension of the "divine" or of mystery and offer the preambles of faith to mankind today.... Does not the spread of sects perhaps lead us to ask whether we have sometimes failed to sufficiently manifest the sense of the sacred? (nos. 44-45)

The Synod states that the liturgy always must favor the sense of the sacred and make it shine forth, permeated by the spirit of reverence, adoration and the glory of God (see no. 52).

Why does the liturgy seem to have lost its sense of "sacredness"?

There are various opinions about this. Some think that the shift of the language to the vernacular made the liturgy too familiar or common. The Council never mandated the abolition of the Latin language but allowed the introduction of the vernacular at the discretion of the bishops. Most bishops and episcopal conferences, of course, elected to change to the vernacular in order to promote the full, conscious and active participation of the faithful, which was the primary goal of the liturgical renewal.

The then Cardinal Joseph Ratzinger insisted that we must preserve the beauty of sacred music, reminding us that the liturgy is not a show or a spectacle to be made by men and women but consists in solemn repetitions. "It cannot be an expression of what is current and transitory, for it expresses the mystery of the Holy."[3]

Some of the difficulties with the liturgy resulted from experimentation and innovations in violation of article 22 of the *Constitution on the Sacred Liturgy,* which prohibits anyone but the bishop or the pope from changing anything in the liturgy on his or her own authority. Many Catholics have experienced abuses, such as having parts of the canon of the Mass modified. Pope John Paul II explained that liturgical celebrations "are not private acts, but 'celebrations of the Church,' the 'sacrament of unity.'" This is why no priest or group is permitted to add, subtract or change anything in the liturgy. The pope specifically taught that no one is allowed to compose eucharistic prayers or substitute other readings for sacred Scripture. These actions are in direct contradiction to the genuine reform of the liturgy and "deprive the Christian people of the genuine treasures of the Liturgy of the Church." Pope John Paul called for bishops to root out such abuses (*Vicesimus quintus,* 10, 13).

What can be done to restore the "sacredness" of the liturgy?

The liturgy is a gift of God to the church, as well as the "work of the people." We observe many people flocking to Christian churches or fellowships that emphasize in some way the sacred and divine aspects of Christianity, such as the transcendence of God, the holiness of the Word of God and the gifts of God. Sadly, we also see people seeking spiritual experience in cults like New Age religions, which promise initiation into the sacred but which actually counterfeit true religion—or may even be demonic.

Yet the Catholic Church offers in her liturgy the real presence of the one true God, as well as the worship he desires, centered on the paschal mystery of Jesus Christ, the Son of God and our Savior. This is a major reason why so many people are attracted to the Catholic Church: God and Christ are truly present there and given authentic worship. As a cardinal, Pope Benedict XVI once observed that the liturgy "does not come from what *we do* but from the fact that something is *taking place* here that all of us together cannot 'make.' In the liturgy there is a power, an energy at work which not even the Church as a whole can generate: what it manifests is the Wholly Other."[4]

For this reason Catholics do not need to worry about losing the sacredness of the liturgy. This sacredness can be obscured, or even effaced, if the liturgy is distorted in such a way that it is no longer the prayer of the church, as the pope has warned. But if what is celebrated is truly the prayer of the church, it is sacred because Christ is present there in all the ways we have described.

In order for those who participate in the liturgy to discern the presence of God and to benefit from the graces available there, they must come with the appropriate attitudes and dispositions of heart and mind. God will not force his way into anyone's heart. Therefore, the faithful must be instructed and called to approach the liturgy with faith, repentant hearts and a desire to worship.

You might say, then, that we don't have to change the liturgy; the liturgy needs to change us! And it will, if our hearts are open. The mighty, loving, all-holy God is present there. This is why the *Constitution on the Sacred Liturgy* stresses that Catholics must be properly *instructed* in the meaning of the liturgy, so they can approach God with reverence.

For example, we will never appreciate the liturgy fully if our focus is on how much we are being uplifted, or worse, entertained. Our focus should be on worshiping God, placing ourselves in his presence through prayer and seeking to gain as much as we can from the celebration and the homily.

On the other hand, the Council stresses the need for the celebrants, ministers and those who plan and lead the liturgy to make God's presence as accessible and evident as they can. They need to prepare well and conduct themselves with authentic reverence and respect for the mysteries they are celebrating and proclaiming. These efforts are not to be equated with the sacredness of the liturgy, since that depends on God's presence. However, these efforts certainly can enhance the beauty and majesty of the liturgy. They will help the faithful enter into worship more easily.

What are some directions for the ongoing renewal of the liturgy?

The basic challenge for Catholics today is to continue to implement the authentic teaching of the constitution in ways and areas where it has not yet been fully carried out. Every Catholic could benefit personally from more instruction in the liturgy and greater effort to participate in the liturgy and sacraments of the church. We all need to deepen our personal prayer and family prayer, which enrich the liturgical worship of the church community.

Pope John Paul II, in 1988, suggested some directions and areas for future renewal of the liturgy in the church. These include:

- ○ "A new and intense education, in order to discover all the richness contained in the new liturgy" (*Dominicae Cenae,* 9).

- ○ Ongoing biblical and liturgical formation programs for seminarians, for priests throughout their ministries and for laypeople (*Vicesimus quintus,* 15).

- ○ The adaptation of the liturgy to different cultures, welcoming expressions that are compatible with the authentic spirit of the liturgy, with respect for the substantial unity of the Roman Rite. "Cultural adaptation also requires conversion of heart and even, where necessary, a breaking with ancestral customs incompatible with the Catholic Faith" (*Vicesimus quintus,* 16).

○ A response in liturgical renewal to new problems, such as "the exercise of a diaconate open to married men; liturgical tasks in celebrations which can be entrusted to laypeople; liturgical celebrations for children, for young people and the disabled" and so on (*Vicesimus quintus,* 17).

It is still true, as John Paul II said, that the time has come to renew that spirit of worship that was so powerful at the time of the Council. "The seed was sown; it has known the rigors of winter, but the seed has sprouted, and become a tree. It is a matter of the organic growth of a tree becoming ever stronger the deeper it sinks into the soil of tradition" (*Vicesimus quintus,* 23). Truly this renewal will bear fruit, for worship is a gift of God to the church, a gift that will endure and continue forever in heaven.

Just as the Second Vatican Council challenged Catholics to a new level of participation in worship, so too it has challenged us to a new intensity of participation and involvement in the modern world. Through the liturgy, Catholics are strengthened in their worship of God to do the will of God. They are sent forth with the commission: "Go in peace, to love and serve the Lord." Through the nourishment that the liturgy and prayer provide, Catholics should desire to go forth to transform the world for Christ. The next chapter, on the *Pastoral Constitution on the Church in the Modern World,* presents the church with the direction and guidance it needs to undertake this challenging mission.

Sacrosanctum Concilium and the *Catechism of the Catholic Church*

The *Constitution on the Sacred Liturgy* is referred to eighty-eight times in the *Catechism of the Catholic Church.* Not surprising, most of these references are in Part II, section 1, which focuses on the liturgy (nos. 1066-1209). It is cited also in the sections on the sacraments (nos. 1210-1666), sacramentals (nos. 1667-1679) and Christian funerals (nos. 1680-1690).

Recent Magisterial Documents

Pope John Paul II. *Dies Domini, (On Keeping the Lord's Day Holy).* May 31, 1998.

Pope John Paul II. *Ecclesia de Eucharistia,* (Encyclical Letter *On the Eucharist in its Relationship to the Church).* April 17, 2003.

Pope John Paul II. *Spiritus et Sponsa, (Apostolic Letter for the Fortieth Anniversary of Vatican II's* Constitution on the Sacred Liturgy). December 4, 2003. *Origins* 33, no. 32 (January 22, 2004).

Favorite Quotes from *Sacrosanctum Concilium*

In the earthly liturgy, by way of foretaste, we share in that heavenly liturgy which is celebrated in the holy city of Jerusalem toward which we journey as pilgrims, and in which Christ is sitting at the right hand of God. (no. 8)

Nevertheless the liturgy is the summit toward which the activity of the Church is directed; at the same time it is the fountain from which all her power flows. For the goal of apostolic works is that all who are made sons of God by faith and baptism should come together to praise God in the midst of His Church, to take part in her sacrifice, and to eat the Lord's supper. (no. 10)

Mother Church earnestly desires that all the faithful be led to that full, conscious, and active participation in liturgical celebrations which is demanded by the very nature of the liturgy. Such participation by the Christian people as "a chosen race, a royal priesthood, a holy nation, a purchased people" (1 Pet. 2:0; cf. 2:4-5), is their right and duty by reason of their baptism. (no. 14)

CHAPTER EIGHT

How Should a Catholic Act in the World?

As the third millennium begins, monumental issues regarding the dignity and rights of individual persons and the future of the world itself press upon us. Will regional wars and terrorism continue to cause worldwide instability and anxiety? Will a nuclear conflagration engulf us? Will the opening of the communist world lead to a flourishing of spiritual and human values and conversion to Christ or to the decadence, materialism and secularization that has infected the West? Will world poverty and hunger increase? Will the global assault against human life continue through the plagues of abortion, euthanasia and other flagrant violations of human rights and dignity? What new moral questions will emerge with advances in genetic engineering?

Catholics know that they cannot escape these issues. We need to decide where and how to respond to them. For example, how does a Christian respond when the law of the land continues to allow abortion on demand? Should one picket, petition, support pro-life politicians, block abortion clinic entrances, pray, contribute to right-to-life organizations or march on Washington, D.C.?

Perhaps I am painting too bleak a picture. There are positive signs that the consciences of people throughout the world are awakening. The longings of the human heart for peace, justice and the preservation of human life are rising as people begin to work together for those goals.

Pessimism or optimism? Which marks the Catholic's view of the modern world? In studying the Second Vatican Council's *Pastoral Constitution on the Church in the Modern World*, the answer emerges that Catholics are to be neither optimists nor pessimists about the world but are to possess a *realism marked by Christian hope.* This document presents the condition of the world with a stark realism. Yet the last word—the word of hope—is that Jesus Christ is present and has redeemed the world.

Christ and his Holy Spirit offer us specific guidance, through the church, about how we should view the modern world and act within it so that God's kingdom will break forth here more fully. The challenge to Catholics is to seek and to hear God's guidance and wisdom and then to *act* according to it in the world.

The *Pastoral Constitution on the Church in the Modern World* is a unique document in many ways. The preparatory commissions and the pope initially had no plans for such a document. "Schema 13" emerged from the floor of the Council at the urging of Bishop Helder Camara of Brazil, with the support of Cardinal Leon-Josef Suenens of Belgium and Cardinal Montini (Pope Paul VI). They thought it incredible that a Council that hoped to place the church in touch with the modern world would fail to issue a document on how Catholics were to view and respond to the actual conditions of modern society. Their concern certainly was in keeping with the purpose and vision Pope John XXIII set for the Council, even though he had not explicitly called for such a document. Thus this constitution was born.

This is the only constitution explicitly addressed to the whole world and not only to Catholics. It is the only "pastoral" constitution issued. This longest document of the Council is divided into two parts: the first sets forth the *principles* of the Catholic understanding of the modern world and involvement in it; the second discusses *specific areas* where the church is challenged today to become involved, providing leadership and guidance. This chapter will deal with the first part. What are the guiding principles and values that this constitution presents for a Catholic understanding of the modern world and Catholic involvement in it?

Are Catholics to identify with the modern world?

The document begins with the understanding that Catholics are to *identify* themselves with the modern world because they are part of it and share its life. "The joys and the hopes [hence the Latin title, *Gaudium et spes*], the griefs and the anxieties of the men of this age, especially those who are poor or in any way afflicted, these too are the joys and hopes, the griefs and anxieties of the followers of Christ. Indeed, nothing genuinely human fails to raise an echo in their hearts" (no. 1).

What is the reason for getting involved?

Catholics have a specific understanding of the nature of humanity and the world, which is the foundation for all their involvements. The constitution says that "the pivotal point of our total presentation will be *man himself*, whole and entire, body and soul, heart and conscience, mind and will" (no. 3, emphasis added). This truth about humanity also includes what Catholics know through divine revelation. Christians see the world "as created and sustained by its Maker's love, fallen indeed into the bondage of sin, yet emancipated now by Christ. He was crucified and rose again to break the stranglehold of personified Evil [Satan], so that this world might be fashioned anew according to God's design and reach its fulfillment" (no. 2).

So the church offers its assistance to foster the true meaning and brotherhood of all people. The people of God carry on the mission of Christ: to seek and to save those who are lost. "Inspired by no earthly ambition, the Church seeks but a solitary goal: to carry forward the work of Christ Himself under the lead of the befriending Spirit. And

Christ entered this world to give witness to the truth, to rescue and not to sit in judgment, to serve and not to be served" (no. 3).

This is the heart of the "mission of Catholics"—and we believe, of all Christians—in the modern world.

How do we evaluate the present condition of society?

In order to know specifically how to act in different circumstances, the church has the duty of "scrutinizing the signs of the times and of interpreting them in the light of the gospel" (*Gaudium et Spes,* 4). Too often people unthinkingly follow whatever trend of thought or behavior is currently popular. Catholics need to discern and test these things according to the standard of the gospel of Jesus Christ.

In discerning the "signs of the times," the constitution noted a number of disturbing imbalances and paradoxes. Never have wealth, resources and economic power been greater, yet a huge proportion of the world's population is starving and illiterate. Never has the world been so keenly aware of freedom, yet new forms of social, psychological and economic slavery continually appear. Never has humanity been so aware of the unity of the human race, the "global village," yet wars and conflicts continue to abound. Ironically, "man painstakingly searches for a better world, without working with equal zeal for the betterment of his own spirit" (no. 4). These imbalances reflect what Blaise Pascal termed "the greatness and wretchedness of man."[1]

After the constitution describes these challenges and choices that face human freedom today, it notes that these difficulties are linked with "that more basic imbalance rooted in the heart of man. For in man himself many elements wrestle with one another" (no. 10). As Saint Paul described so well in Romans 7, the root of humanity's struggle lies within each human heart.

People are again asking themselves the most basic questions: What is humanity? Why do we suffer? What is the purpose of our efforts toward progress? What can people offer to human society, and what can they hope to receive? What happens to us after death?

The introduction of this constitution ends with the word of hope: The church believes that Christ "can through his Spirit offer man the light and the strength to measure up to his supreme destiny" (no. 10). Jesus is the ultimate answer to all our questions and struggles.

What about the nature of the human person?

Many humanists and even atheists agree with Christians that "all things on earth should be related to man as their center and crown" (no. 12). But not all agree about the nature of humanity. The first chapter of the *Pastoral Constitution on the Church in the Modern World* presents an excellent summary of basic Christian teaching about the human person. Topics include our goodness and dignity; the reality of sin, which has corrupted human nature and cast us into "a dramatic struggle between good and evil, between light and darkness"; and the hope that humanity has in the redemption of Christ, who "came to free and strengthen man, renewing him inwardly and casting out the prince of this world (cf. Jn. 12:31) who held him in the bondage of sin" (no. 13).

The presentation hinges around the inherent goodness and dignity of the human person, who "by his interior qualities, outstrips the whole sum of mere things." Far from being just a meaningless speck in a vast universe, the human person is loved by God and possesses an immortal soul. A single human person is more precious and valuable in God's eyes than the sum of all merely material things in the universe put together. Christ died to save each individual person. This is the root of the Catholic understanding of the dignity of the human person and explains why Catholics are opposed to any activity that unjustly and needlessly threatens or destroys human life, such as abortion, euthanasia, wars of aggression and the like. God calls each person, from the moment of conception, to the fullness of life in this world and to eternal life and joy in heaven.

The constitution teaches that God created each person as good and precious to him. The evil and rebellion that stirs within us due to sin does not negate the dignity of the person but indicates that each person must strive to resist sin and evil and "glorify God in his body" (no. 14).

The constitution illustrates the dignity of the person by describing his or her various attributes: the dignity of the *mind,* which can grasp truth and seek wisdom (no. 15); the dignity of the *moral conscience,* which can detect God's law within (no. 16); the dignity of the *will,* which is free to choose good or evil. We will examine some of these aspects of human dignity in more detail, since they are foundational to the Catholic understanding of the person in the modern world.

What do we mean by "conscience"?

The constitution calls conscience a person's "most secret core and sanctuary," where he "detects a law which he does not impose upon himself, but which holds him to obedience. Always summoning him to love good and avoid evil, the voice of conscience can when necessary speak to his heart more specifically: do this, shun that. For man has in his heart a law written by God. To obey it is the very dignity of man; according to it he will be judged" (no. 16).

Conscience guides all people to "objective norms of morality" that have God as their source and are "fulfilled by love of God and neighbor" (no. 16). Everyone, Christian and non-Christian alike, is bound to follow the dictates of conscience.

However, part of human dignity is to seek to *form* our consciences by seeking truth and goodness. Can conscience err? Yes, but God does not condemn us for this error if we are genuinely seeking the truth. "The same cannot be said of a man who cares but little for truth and goodness, or of a conscience which by degrees grows practically sightless as a result of habitual sin" (no. 16).

Do people really possess "free will"?

Despite the contentions of some behavioral scientists and despite the Calvinistic view that all things are determined by God, the Catholic Church continues to teach that the human person possesses authentic freedom of choice. The pastoral constitution explains that there can be no real human goodness without genuine freedom to choose the good. This freedom is a sign of the image of God in each man and woman. In sum, "man's dignity demands that he act according to a knowing and free choice" (no. 17).

Normally the greatest limitation on the freedom of a person is due to sin, which blinds us and inhibits our ability to freely choose the good. Only with the help of God's grace can freedom be restored and exercised fully. Because we are truly free, each person is responsible for his or her own decisions and actions. "Before the judgment seat of God each man must render an account of his own life, whether he has done good or evil" (no. 17; see also 2 Corinthians 5:10).

It seems to me that this *responsibility* that flows from human freedom is very important to understanding the church in the modern world today. Many modern people are not taught to accept the responsibility that goes with freedom. We desire freedom, but will we take responsibility for the effects of our free choices? Any parent knows that as children grow they desire greater freedom to choose and act. But they must be taught to take responsibility for their choices and to accept the consequences of them, for good or ill.

Why do we have to suffer?

The Council views the suffering of the world largely as a result of humankind's own free choices based upon sin, not something inflicted by our good Creator (see no. 13). Death is a mystery that presents the greatest challenge to human existence. Far from evading the question of death, Christianity faces it squarely and answers that death is the result of sin. "Man has been created by God for a blissful purpose beyond the reach of earthly misery." Jesus Christ won the victory over death when he rose to life, "since by His death He freed man from death" (no. 18).

Given the reality of suffering, is atheism a more realistic belief than Christianity? The ultimate question is not whether atheism or Christianity is more attractive or "realistic" but which view is *true*. Atheism cannot explain suffering and death, because it supposes there is no goal or meaning to life other than that which we create. Christians believe that suffering and death have a purpose in God's plan that can be discovered.

The constitution acknowledges that Christians whose faith is weak or in error, or whose conduct contradicts their faith, can cause Christianity to appear untrue or less desirable than atheism or other religious systems when faced with the mystery of death. Nonetheless, the church strongly rejects atheism and proposes that the best response to it is a proper presentation of the church's teaching and the authentic life of the church and her members. "What does the most to reveal God's presence...is the brotherly charity of the faithful who are united in spirit...and who prove themselves a sign of unity" (no. 21).

The church professes that all people must work together for the betterment of the world. While working prudently with atheists, the church "courteously invites atheists to examine the gospel of Christ with an open mind." The message of the gospel is in harmony with the deepest desires of the human heart. Far from diminishing man, it "brings to his development light, life, and freedom" (no. 21). As

Saint Augustine wrote after many years of searching for God, "You have made us for yourself, and our heart is restless until it rests in you."[2]

What is the ultimate key to understanding the human person?

Jesus Christ. "The truth is that only in the mystery of the incarnate Word does the mystery of man take on light" (no. 22). The first part of the *Pastoral Constitution on the Church in the Modern World* is so structured that the end of each chapter explains how Jesus Christ is the ultimate key to understanding the mystery of the human person (chap. 1), the communal nature of humanity (chap. 2), human activity in the world (chap. 3) and the role of the church in the modern world (chap. 4). Thus the whole constitution is centered on the person and work of Jesus Christ, who is the "new man"—the model and goal of redeemed humanity.

Don't we need to avoid a false "individualism"?

The *Pastoral Constitution on the Church in the Modern World* noted that one of the most striking features of the modern world is that people are increasingly recognizing their interdependence—that is, the actions of a part of the world's peoples often affect the whole world, for good or ill (no. 23). The constitution points out that this reality is rooted in God's plan for the human race. God wills that we live together in society in order to lead each other to salvation. God's law governing all of human interaction can be boiled down to this: "You shall…'love your neighbor as yourself'" (Romans 13:9-10; see also 1 John 4:20).

The basic message of the gospel speaks of God's saving us as a people (not merely as individuals) and stresses that this salvation depends on how we treat and relate to one another. Hence, Catholics cannot understand their lives and salvation in a purely individualistic manner. God has joined us together in human society and in the church in order that we might love and serve each other and thus attain salvation together.

Does society exist for the good of the person?

Yes. Because the individual person is a social being, created by God to live in society, Catholics insist that the good of the person and the good of society as a whole are interrelated. In terms of priority, however, "the subject and the goal of all social institutions is and must be the human person, which for its part and by its very nature stands completely in need of social life" (no. 25).

Social life is essential to human nature, yet society exists for the good of the person and not vice versa. Catholics, therefore, must reject Marxism and any view of society that claims that the individual ultimately exists for the good of the state, as a replaceable "cog" in the great, all-important "machine" of human society.

Some social entities are absolutely essential for human welfare, such as the family and the political community. Other social groups originate and develop from free decisions of persons. All of these social groups have a great impact on forming the persons who belong to them.

Shouldn't individuals and social groups promote the "common good"?

The constitution acknowledges that individuals and groups "must take account of the needs and legitimate aspirations of other groups, and even of the general welfare of the entire human family" (no. 26). Yet the constitution insists that the "common good" cannot be in violation of the basic rights and dignity of the human person, "since he stands above all things, and his rights and duties are universal and inviolable" (no. 26).

You cannot, for example, destroy innocent human life in order to advance or protect the "quality of life" or the "common good" of other persons. If the lives of some innocent persons are threatened, then *everyone* in society is endangered, at least in principle, and the common good is thereby hindered, not advanced.

The constitution concludes that the social order must always work to the benefit of the human person "and not contrariwise, as the Lord indicated when He said that the Sabbath was made for man, and not man for the Sabbath" (no. 26).

What are the rights of each person?

The Council explicitly lists

○ everything necessary for leading a life truly human, such as food, clothing and shelter,

○ the right to choose a state of life freely and to found a family,

○ the right to education,

○ to employment,

○ to a good reputation,

○ to respect,

○ to appropriate information,

○ to activity in accord with the upright norm of one's own conscience,

○ to protection of privacy and

○ to rightful freedom in matters religious (no. 26).

Does the constitution condemn certain practices that are opposed to human life and dignity?

Yes. One of the strongest and most explicit denunciations of evil contained in *any* Catholic conciliar document is found in the *Pastoral Constitution on the Church in the Modern World:*

> Furthermore, whatever is opposed to life itself, such as any type of murder, genocide, abortion, euthanasia, or willful self-destruction, whatever violates the integrity of the human person, such as mutilation, torments inflicted on body or mind, attempts to coerce the will itself; whatever insults human dignity, such as subhuman living conditions, arbitrary imprisonment, deportation, slavery, prostitution, the selling of women and children; as well as disgraceful working conditions, where men are treated as mere tools for profit, rather than as free and responsible persons; all these things and others of their like are infamies indeed. They poison human society, but they do more harm to those who practice them than those who suffer from the injury. Moreover, they are a supreme dishonor to the Creator. (no. 27)

Note that the constitution says that in the moral order, these crimes harm the perpetrators more than the victims. The innocent victims will suffer pain or even physical death in this life. But those who willfully carry out these crimes (knowing that they are evil either through the church's teaching or their own conscience), unless they repent, become hardened and less human. Such persons will suffer the just punishment of God for their sin after death.

How should we treat those who commit such evil acts?

Rather than judging them or returning evil for evil, the constitution urges Catholics to "speak the saving truth to all men," including those who practice evil, and to "distinguish between error, which always merits repudiation, and the person in error, who never loses the dignity of being a person, even when he is flawed by false or inadequate religious notions. God alone is the judge and searcher of hearts; for that reason He forbids us to make judgments about the internal guilt of anyone" (no. 28).

In other words, we can judge the action as evil but not the person. We must hate the sin but love the sinner. We must forgive even our enemies and those who persecute us. That is what is distinctive about being a follower of Christ: "The teaching of Christ even requires that we forgive injuries, and extends the law of love to include every enemy, according to the command of the New Law: 'You have heard that it was said, "Thou shalt love thy neighbor, and shalt hate thy enemy." But I say to you, love your enemies, do good to those who hate you, and pray for those who persecute and calumniate you' (Mt. 5:43-44)" (no. 28).

Are there any other "social sins" that are condemned?

This document asserts the basic equality of all people and states that "every type of discrimination, whether social or cultural, whether based on sex, race, color, social condition, language, or religion, is to be overcome and eradicated as contrary to God's intent" (no. 29). An example is given of "a woman who is denied the right and freedom to choose a husband, to embrace a state of life, or to acquire an education or cultural benefits equal to those recognized for men" (no. 29). Some Catholics may not be aware that the Second Vatican Council spoke out so strongly to procure these basic rights for women!

Isn't such a view of social responsibility challenging?

Yes. The constitution exhorts Catholics to break from "a merely individualistic morality." Instead we are to consider it a "sacred obligation to count social necessities among the primary duties of modern man, and to pay heed to them" (no. 30).

This document notes how easy it is to ignore the needs of others around us, to be "drugged by laziness" and hence fail to contribute to the common good of society and of other people according to our resources and abilities. There are also those who profess "grand and rather noble sentiments" but "nevertheless in reality live always as if they cared nothing for the needs of society" (no. 30).

Can any of us identify with these failings? (I can!) One can have great aspirations to serve or to give money but just never get around to doing it.

The call is for *participation* by Catholics in the life of society for the good of others. We must overcome obstacles such as poverty, which can focus people almost exclusively on their own needs, and affluence, by which a person "indulges in too many of life's comforts and imprisons himself in a kind of splendid isolation" (no. 31). The constitution also praises those nations whose policies "allow the largest possible number of citizens to participate in public affairs with genuine freedom" (no. 31). My mother, for example, was involved for years with the League of Women Voters, which encouraged citizens to vote and to become more knowledgeable about public affairs.

"God did not create man for life in isolation, but for the formation of social unity" (no. 32). Jesus Christ most fully demonstrates this truth. He took flesh in order to share in our human condition, preached the necessity of treating one another as brothers and founded "a new brotherly community," the church, in which we might learn how we should love one another as he has loved us. Our responsibilities as members of the global community should first be shown and practiced by how we conduct ourselves and relate as members of the community of Jesus Christ, the church (see no. 32).

How does the church look upon human efforts to shape the world?

The third chapter of the *Pastoral Constitution on the Church in the Modern World* is devoted to human activity in the world. Some major points include the fact that Christians do not see any necessary opposition between human activity and God's power and freedom. Rather we are "convinced that the triumphs of the human race are a sign of God's greatness" (no. 34). In fact, the gospel binds Christians to build up the world and to care for the needs of others through our activity.

Yet the greatest value of human activity, as we have noted, is not that a person alters things and society but that the person develops himself or herself. "A man is more precious for what he *is* than for what he *has* [or *does*]" (no. 35, emphasis added). Constructive activity enhances and promotes the dignity of the person who performs it.

This is a major theme of Pope John Paul II's encyclical letter *On Human Work (Laborem Exercens)*, issued September 14, 1981. The pope writes, "The Christian vision of reality focuses on man and his dignity as a person created in God's image." This means that the person is the first priority in work: that work is for the person and not the person for work. This is a hard saying for "workaholics" and those constantly working just to "get ahead." The final goal of any kind of work is always the benefit of the person.

The Holy Father concludes: "Man is the axis around which the entire organization of work must move. Work is a great thing. But man is incomparably greater. Man is sacred. And this sacredness is inviolable" (*Laborem Exercens*, 6).

The *Pastoral Constitution on the Church in the Modern World* summarizes that the norm of human activity is: first of all, to promote the genuine good of the human race according to God's plan; and second, to enable people to pursue and fulfill the vocation that God has given them, so that they may live a truly human life.

Who best exemplifies the meaning and dignity of work?

We see the dignity of work in Jesus, who was born into the home of a carpenter and worked in his father's trade until age thirty, when he began his public ministry of preaching and teaching about the kingdom of God. The Son of God was both a skilled laborer and a teacher.

His mother Mary, the most exalted of all women, spent her days making a home and caring for her family and later for the church. Her ministry, too, was one of work in the home, prayer and service to God's people.

Could combining work and religion threaten the rightful independence of human affairs and science?

The pastoral constitution speaks of the "autonomy of earthly affairs," which means that God has created things to exist and to operate with "their own stability, truth, goodness, proper laws, and order" (no. 36). Religion does not interfere with methodical investigations that seek to understand how and why things exist and work as they do. There is then no such thing as "Christian chemistry" or "Christian physics" per se, except that a Christian may apply and implement his or her findings in a different way than others, according to authentic moral standards.

The "autonomy of earthly affairs" does *not* mean that "created things do not depend on God, and that man can use them without any reference to their Creator" (no. 36). To the contrary, understanding how things and people are made can show us that they have proper and improper uses and behavior. A true understanding of people and things can even lead individuals to discover God, as he is manifest in his works (see Romans 1:19-20).

Is there a "dark side" to human activity and progress?

Yes. The constitution recognizes that human activity is also caught up into the "monumental struggle against the powers of darkness [that] pervades the whole history of man" (no. 37). This war began at the origin of the world and will continue until the end of history, at the day of Christ's return in glory (no. 37).

Although human progress *can* serve the true happiness of humanity, it has also been infected and corrupted by sin: "Hence if anyone wants to know how this unhappy situation can be overcome, Christians will tell him that all human activity, constantly imperiled by man's pride and deranged self-love, must be purified and perfected by the power of Christ's cross and resurrection" (no. 37).

All human activity reaches its perfection through the power of God present in the paschal mystery of Christ's passion, death and resurrection. Through the work of the Holy Spirit, God purifies our activity from sin, gives us a vision of God's will and arouses a desire for the age to come, when all sin will be wiped away. Only then will all our human activity and achievements be brought to perfection in Christ.

Is it possible to build the kingdom of God on earth?

This constitution states, "Earthly progress must be carefully distinguished from the growth of Christ's kingdom. Nevertheless, to the extent that the former [earthly progress] can contribute to the better ordering of human society, it is of vital concern to the kingdom of God" (no. 39).

In short, people cannot directly build Christ's kingdom, but we can cooperate with God's work of establishing his kingdom by ordering society according to God's will and plan. For example, working through political means to establish a just society does not bring about the kingdom of God. Even if that just society were attained perfectly, the kingdom of God in its fullness is always greater and more magnificent than anything we could accomplish on earth. However, a just society would be a sign of God's reign that can hasten the coming of God's kingdom, and it would be a fulfillment of the Lord's prayer, "Thy kingdom come, thy will be done on earth as it is in heaven."

How would you summarize the relationship between the church and the world?

The church is in the world and so experiences everything that is common to humanity. Thus the church and the world penetrate each other. There are various ways that the church can serve the world and in which the world can contribute to the church. The church can feed the poor, encourage constructive scientific research, promote justice and peace and, most importantly, tell the world the meaning and purpose of human existence, which is revealed in its fullness in Jesus Christ.

The world contributes to the church the richness of its diverse cultures, its endeavors and findings that promote the welfare of humanity and various means of spreading the gospel of Jesus Christ more effectively, such as modern mass media. The relationship between the church and the world is like a soul to a body, as the "Letter to Diognetus" observed in the second century. The *Pastoral Constitution on the Church in the Modern World* also states that the church is "a leaven" and "a kind of soul for human society as it is to be renewed in Christ and transformed into God's family" (no. 40).

How does the church serve individuals?

The church primarily serves individuals by shedding light on the meaning of their existence and proclaiming that only God meets and fulfills the deepest longings of the human heart. The church also proclaims and seeks to safeguard the dignity and value of each human person (see no. 41), as we see in her efforts against human rights violations, poverty, social injustice, abortion, infanticide, euthanasia and so on.

How does the church serve society?

"Christ, to be sure, gave His Church no proper mission in the political, economic, or social order. The purpose which He set before her is a religious one" (*Gaudium et Spes*, 42). However, the religious mission of the church provides a light and energy for human society that can help us live together according to the law of God. God's law ultimately applies to all human life and relationships, including social, political and economic realms.

For instance, all people of good will recognize the value of peace among peoples and promote relations among nations based upon justice, forthright mutual agreements and reconciliation where needed. These are all aspects of God's will and his law.

The church is also to be a model and source of *unity* for the world. Because the church is not identified with any particular culture or social system, she is able to bring together different human communities and nations.

How does the church contribute to human activity?

A hallmark of the Second Vatican Council is the teaching of *Gaudium et Spes* that Christians cannot shirk their earthly responsibilities because they are seeking a heavenly kingdom. The pastoral constitution declares that the "split between the faith which many profess and their daily lives deserves to be counted among the more serious errors of our age" (no. 43). There is to be no false dichotomy between activity and life in society and religious life. The constitution even goes so far as to state that "the Christian who neglects his temporal duties neglects his duties toward his neighbor and even God, and jeopardizes his eternal salvation" (no. 43).

A strong statement! Being a Catholic Christian does not only include "religious activities" but also means engaging in a Christlike manner in fulfilling one's duties in the affairs of the world. The constitution proceeds to discuss the role of laypeople, whose main arena of activity is the world. Bishops, priests and others set apart for religious service should also be concerned about how their lives witness to Christ's presence in the world.

Hasn't the church fallen short of fulfilling this mission?

The pastoral constitution honestly admits that "among her members, both clerical and lay, some have been unfaithful to the Spirit of God during the course of many centuries. In the present age, too, it does not escape the Church how great a distance lies between the message she offers and the human failings of those to whom the gospel is entrusted" (no. 43).

This document encourages Catholics to be aware of those failings and to work to correct those that still exist. Also it speaks of a "ripening which comes with the experience of centuries," by which the church is growing in her understanding of God's will and the proper relationship between the church and society. We do not have all the answers, but we trust that the Holy Spirit will continue to guide the church into all truth.

Does the church have anything to gain from the world?

Another major advance of Vatican II is the recognition of all that the church has gained and learned from the history of humanity. The church is indebted to the "ideas and terminology of various peoples" in expressing the message of Christ. For example, the Greek philosophical expression *homoousios* is used to help define Christ's full divinity. The church also makes use of the "wisdom of philosophers" in understanding and clarifying this message (*Gaudium et Spes*, 44).

Nonetheless, all that the modern world has to offer to the church must be discerned by the help of the Holy Spirit. A crucial task of the entire people of God, especially pastors and theologians, is "to hear, distinguish, and *interpret* the many voices of our age and to judge them in the light of the divine Word" (no. 44, emphasis added).

This discernment of what is good and helpful from our age, and what is harmful to or incompatible with Christian faith, remains one of the greatest challenges to Christians in relationship to the modern world. The final chapter of this book, for example, discusses the need for discernment in using the mass media. Good and evil are certainly admixed to a striking degree in this area, as they are in other areas of business, politics and commerce to name a few.

What then is the goal of the church in relationship to the modern world?

The heart of the promise of Vatican II in the modern world is the call "to unite all things in him, things in heaven and things on earth" (Ephesians 1:10). We wish to exalt Jesus Christ, the light of the world, the Alpha and the Omega. In the words of the constitution, "the Church has a single intention: that God's kingdom may come, and that the salvation of the whole human race may come to pass.... The Lord is the goal of human history, the focal point of the longings of history and of civilization, the center of the human race, the joy of every heart, and the answer to all its yearnings" (no. 45).

This chapter has examined the principles for understanding the life and mission of the church in the modern world. The next chapter will explore some specific challenges that confront the church in the world today.

Gaudium et Spes, Part I, and the *Catechism of the Catholic Church*

The first part of the *Pastoral Constitution on the Church in the Modern World* (general principles) is cited exactly one hundred times in the *Catechism of the Catholic Church*. These references appear first in the discussion of original sin, the Fall and death in Part I, but the greatest concentration of references is in Part III ("Life in Christ"), in the discussion of the "Dignity of the Human Person" (sec. 1, chap. 1) and the "Human Community" (chap. 2). The latter includes articles on the person and society, participation in the life of society and social justice.

Recent Magisterial Documents

Pope John Paul II. *Centesimus Annus* (Encyclical Letter *On the 100th Anniversary of* Rerum Novarum). May 1, 1991.

Pope John Paul II. *Laborem Exercens* (Encyclical Letter *On Human Work*). September 14, 1981.

Pope John Paul II. *Novo Millennio Ineunte (At the beginning of the New Millennium)*. January 6, 2001.

Pope John Paul II. *Sollicitudo Rei Socialis* (Encyclical Letter *On the Twentieth Anniversary of* Populorum Progressio). December 30, 1987.

Pope John Paul II. *Veritatis Splendor* (Encyclical Letter *On the Splendor of Truth*). August 6, 1993.

Favorite Quotes from *Gaudium et Spes*, Part I

The Church believes that Christ, who died and was raised up for all, can through His Spirit offer man the light and the strength to measure up to his supreme destiny. Nor has any other name under heaven been given to man by which it is fitting for him to be saved. She likewise holds that in her most benign Lord and Master can be found the key, the focal point, and the goal of all human history.

The Church also maintains that beneath all changes there are many realities which do not change and which have their ultimate foundation in Christ, who is the same yesterday and today, yes and forever. Hence in the light of Christ, the image of the unseen God, the firstborn of every creature, the Council wishes to speak to all men in order to illuminate the mystery of man and to cooperate in finding the solution to the outstanding problems of our time. (no. 10)

Man is not wrong when he regards himself as superior to bodily concerns, and as more than a speck of nature or a nameless constituent of the city of man. For by his interior qualities he outstrips the whole sum of mere things. (no. 14)

The truth is that only in the mystery of the incarnate Word does the mystery of man take on light. (no. 22)

Man, who is the only creature on earth which God willed for itself, cannot fully find himself except through a sincere gift of himself. (no. 24)

CHAPTER NINE

Specific Challenges Confronting the Church in the Modern World

Does Christianity, and the Catholic Church in particular, address the really "tough" issues that fill the media and the ones that we encounter personally every day? What does the church have to say about the pain of divorce and the break-up of families?…about the disintegration of Christian culture in the West and the great diversity of other cultures that influence us in our "global village"?…about politics and economics as we face difficult choices and the stark reality of poverty around us? And how do we even begin to attain and maintain peace in a world lapsing continually into war and conflict?

While the first part of the *Pastoral Constitution on the Church in the Modern World* presented some foundational principles for a Catholic's approach to the modern world, the second part confronts the issues with some direct and practical applications of these principles.

One important goal of the Second Vatican Council was to put the Catholic Church in touch with modern needs and problems. The Extraordinary Synod of 1985 clarified that bringing the church "up-to-date" *(aggiornamento)* does not mean "an easy accommodation [to the modern world] that could lead to the secularization of the Church"; rather it calls Catholics to "a missionary openness for the integral salvation of the world." "Integral salvation" means the defense of all truly human values (such as the dignity of the human person; fundamental human rights; peace; freedom from oppression, poverty and injustice), realizing that these efforts must be "further elevated through grace" and lead to "familiarity with God, through Jesus Christ, in the Holy Spirit" (Synod, 63).

In other words, the church does not promote authentic human values as a social program carried out by purely human efforts but seeks to promote these values through the power and guidance of God, in order to lead the world ultimately to the fullness of salvation in Jesus Christ and in his Holy Spirit.

Let us then examine this document's discussion of the salvific work of the church in these important areas of modern life.

How does the Catholic Church view marriage in the modern world?

This pastoral constitution recalls the basic reasons why God instituted marriage and why Jesus confirmed it as a sacrament of the church. These reasons are, first, for the good of the spouses through the mutual giving of their whole selves to each other (conjugal love) and secondly for the procreation and education of children, which is a main purpose and even the "ultimate crown" of marriage and conjugal love (no. 48). The constitution states clearly that "children are really the supreme gift of marriage" (no. 50).

The constitution teaches that "authentic married love is caught up into divine love and is governed and enriched by Christ's redeeming power and the saving activity of the Church" (no. 48). Married love cannot survive and flourish without the grace of God given through Christ and his church. "For this reason, Christian spouses have a special sacrament by which they are fortified" to live their married lives fully and faithfully (no. 48).

The need for this sacramental grace is especially evident in the West, where traditional social supports to the unbreakable bond of marriage are rapidly disappearing. It becomes increasingly difficult to live "total fidelity" and to grow into deeper unity day by day, even among those who recognize the importance of this both for the good of their spouse and for their children.

In sum, the Second Vatican Council reaffirms the sanctity of marriage and the indissolubility of a true Christian marriage. It points to the grace of the sacrament of matrimony as sufficient and necessary to preserve the couple's conjugal love and unity and to strengthen the couple for the bearing and rearing children.

What does Vatican II say about the responsibility of Christian parents to have children?

Children are a gift of God. This pastoral constitution affirms that although there are other purposes of marriage, the bearing and raising of children is the proper mission and task of Christian couples. In it they cooperate with the love of God the Creator.

In determining how children should be added to the family, the constitution calls for "human and Christian responsibility" based on reverence toward God and his law (as presented by the church's teaching office) and with consideration of the material and spiritual conditions of the times and the family. In other words, the regulation of birth is a matter of conscience but "a conscience dutifully conformed to the divine law itself, and…submissive toward the Church's teaching office" (no. 50).

In article 51 the pastoral constitution provides a brief preliminary outline of the reasons behind the Catholic Church's teaching on the regulation of birth, which Pope Paul VI explained more fully in his encyclical letter of 1968, *On the Regulation of Birth (Humanae Vitae)*. The church accepts only natural means of birth regulation that do not artificially obstruct or interfere with the normal sexual process of reproduction. As the document states beautifully, "the acts themselves which are proper to conjugal [married] love and which are exercised in accord with genuine human dignity must be honored with great reverence" (no. 51).

This teaching is based on the presupposition "that human life and the task of transmitting it are not realities bound up with this world alone" (no. 51). Human beings are not the creators of human life; they are cooperators with God in his plan for the life and destiny of persons. For this same reason the Catholic Church demands that "from the moment of its conception life must be guarded with the greatest care, while abortion and infanticide are unspeakable crimes" (no. 51).

The constitution readily points out that even couples who are unable to have children can experience the beautiful gift of mutual love, support and communion in marriage. Nonetheless, this document makes "special mention" of couples who have chosen, with wise deliberation and gallant hearts, to bring up "even a relatively large family" (no. 50). The large family is still praiseworthy in the eyes of the Catholic Church!

What does Vatican II say about the role of the family in the modern world?

The *Pastoral Constitution on the Church in the Modern World* calls the family "the foundation of society" and a "school of deeper humanity" (no. 52). However, the family will only succeed in leading members to deeper humanity if

○ the family *prays* together;

○ the parents *educate* their children (especially in religion) and give a good example (no. 48);

○ the father is *actively present* in their formation, and the children, especially the younger ones, receive the care of the mother at home (no. 52);

○ the mother's *domestic* role is preserved and respected, "though the legitimate social progress of women should not be under-rated on that account" (no. 52).

Children too contribute to the family by obeying their parents, responding to their parents' kindness "with sentiments of gratitude, with love and trust" and standing by their parents in hardship and old age (no. 48).

Preserving and rebuilding marriage and family life is a high pri-ority for the whole of society today. The constitution insists, "Public authority should regard it as a sacred duty to recognize, protect, and promote their authentic nature, to shield public morality, and to favor the prosperity of domestic life. The right of parents to beget and educate their children in the bosom of the family must be safe-guarded" (no. 52).

Obviously, there is much work to be done here. In his apostolic exhortation *On the Role of the Christian Family in the Modern World (Familiaris Consortio),* Pope John Paul II gave further help for Catholics and others who are concerned for the preservation of mar-riage and family life.

What does the church have to say about the proper development of culture?

Culture affects our daily lives, personalities and living environments. Wherever they live, Catholics must become aware of both the posi-tive and negative elements of their cultural environment. Unfortunately, there are elements of any world culture that do not promote full human existence and dignity. In the West, for example, the culture supports egocentrism, materialism and hedonism. It pro-motes a life that is centered on self, money and possessions, enjoy-ment and sex.

While culture does form each of us, we are the creators of culture! The second chapter of part two of this constitution encourages Catholics to form culture according to true human and Christian values. It notes that we are in a historical period in which new forms of culture are emerging because of a more unified world, the advances of science and technology and a growing common awareness of humanity's responsibility to build a better world based upon truth and justice (no. 56).

How does our Catholic faith affect our role in the development of culture?

Christians are on a pilgrimage toward a heavenly city. This *increases* the weight of our responsibility to work with others in constructing a more human world (no. 57). Through the incarnation of his Son, we know that God takes seriously the affairs and transformation of the world. We will be judged according to how we live in the world.

Catholics are to oppose elements of culture that contradict the truths that we know by faith, such as the belief that science and reason are the *only* means of discovering the truth. The church is not bound to any one culture. She seeks to confirm and purify the truth to be found in any cultural expression. The constitution summarizes the approach of Catholics to culture:

> The good news of Christ constantly renews the life and culture of fallen man. It combats and removes the errors and evils resulting from sinful allurements which are a perpetual threat. It never ceases to purify and elevate the morality of peoples. By riches coming from above, it makes fruitful, as it were from within, the spiritual qualities and gifts of every people and of every age. It strengthens, perfects, and restores them in Christ. Thus by the very fulfillment of her own mission the Church stimulates and advances human and civic culture. By her action, even in its liturgical form, she leads men toward interior liberty. (no. 58)

May the faithful, therefore, live in very close union with the men of their time. Let them strive to understand perfectly their way of thinking and feeling, as expressed in their culture. Let them blend modern science and its theories and the understanding of the most recent discoveries with Christian morality and doctrine. Thus their religious practice and morality can keep pace with their scientific knowledge and with an ever-advancing technology. Thus too they will be able to test and interpret all things in a truly Christian spirit. (no. 62)

The Catholic Church praises all that is good and true in the cultures of the world and seeks to purify and perfect these elements by the fullness of truth found in Jesus Christ and his teaching.

What does the church teach about the economic realm?

Scripture warns against the love of money and the serving of money instead of God (see 1 Timothy 6:10; Matthew 6:24). Money should serve the dignity and total vocation of the human person, promoting the welfare of society as a whole. The constitution points out certain abuses, such as letting money become the dominant concern of one's life.

The unjust distribution of wealth results in a shocking disparity between the comfortable prosperity of a small proportion of the world's population and the grinding poverty of the majority. This contrast "is becoming more serious day by day" (no. 63). Jesus' parable about the rich man and the beggar, Lazarus, is being realized on a worldwide scale.

What can be done about this situation? The *Pastoral Constitution on the Church in the Modern World* advocates technical and economic development that is directed by, and directed to assist, the greatest number of people. The constitution equally condemns the extremes of capitalism, "which obstruct(s) the necessary reforms in the name of a false liberty," and of socialism or communism, "which subordinates the basic rights of individual persons and groups to the collective organization of production" (no. 65). Pope John Paul II has taught more fully on the shortcomings of both capitalism and communism in his encyclical letter *Sollicitudo Rei Socialis.*

What does the constitution have to say about the role of workers?

Workers must be treated as persons and not as mere tools of production (no. 66). Jesus himself illustrated the dignity of work through his own years as a laborer. Those who work must be paid sufficiently to provide for their own material, social, cultural and spiritual needs and those of their dependents. Productive work should be adapted to the requirements of a person's life, above all, his or her family life. "Such is especially the case with respect to mothers of families" (no. 67).

What other economic themes are discussed?

In his apostolic letter *Laborem Exercens,* Pope John Paul II reflected on the nature and dignity of human work. This pastoral constitution also discusses the right of workers to found labor unions and to participate in the running of business enterprises; the responsibility of management and labor to seek peaceful settlements to disputes; the Christian duty to give to the poor "and to do so not merely out of their superfluous goods" (no. 69); the investment of money and goods to provide "employment and sufficient income for the people of today and of the future" (no. 70); and the importance of private ownership and private control of material goods so that people can express their personalities and exercise their legitimate role in society and the economy (no. 71).

The position of the Council on the socio-economic realm is summarized by this exhortation from the *Pastoral Constitution on the Church in the Modern World:*

Christians who take an active part in modern socio-economic development and defend justice and charity should be convinced that they can make a great contribution to the prosperity of mankind and the peace of the world. Whether they do so as individuals or in association, let their example be a shining one. After acquiring whatever skills and experience are absolutely necessary, they should in faithfulness to Christ and His gospel observe the right order of values in their earthly activities. Thus their whole lives, both individual and social, will be permeated with the spirit of the beatitudes, notably with the spirit of poverty.

Whoever in obedience to Christ seeks first the kingdom of God will as a consequence receive a stronger and purer love for helping all his brothers and for perfecting the work of justice under the inspiration of charity. (no. 72)

Does Vatican II explain the "preferential option for the poor" or the "theology of liberation"?

The Second Vatican Council called attention to the church's mission in service to the poor, the oppressed and the outcast and urged a prophetic denunciation of every form of poverty and oppression. This denunciation was based on a recognition of the fundamental and inalienable rights of the human person. It included defense of human life "from the time of its very beginning" (Synod, 65-66).

The "preferential option for the poor" points out the biblical truth that God has a special love and care for the poor. Christians may participate in their own special concern for and service to the poor. The Extraordinary Synod affirmed and praised this preferential option for the poor but noted that it does not exclude care and concern for those who are not poor, nor is it limited to the alleviation of material poverty to the neglect of spiritual poverty.

The Synod reminds us, "The salvific mission of the Church in relation to the world must be understood as an integral whole. It must involve both the spiritual and the temporal (earthly) needs of mankind." There is certainly a clear distinction—but not a separation—between the natural and the supernatural aspects of the church's mission. The Synod calls Catholics to "put aside the false and useless oppositions between, for example, the Church's spiritual mission and *diaconia* (service) for the world" (p. 66).

The "theology of liberation," as taught and practiced over the past years, has led to a more careful examination of how the preferential option for the poor is to be properly understood. Clearly the church must oppose unjust and oppressive social structures as part of its service to the poor. But the methods of this opposition must be in accordance with the teaching of Jesus. The spiritual needs of God's people cannot be neglected or seen as less important than temporal needs.

In order to clarify the Catholic Church's position on the theology of liberation, the Sacred Congregation on the Doctrine of the Faith has issued *Instruction on Certain Aspects of the "Theology of Liberation,"* August 6, 1984, and *Instruction on Christian Freedom and Liberation,* March 22, 1986. The reader might want to consult these for further study.

How are Catholics to participate in political life?

The Catholic Church is not bound to any political system or party (*Gaudium et Spes,* 76). Yet Catholics are to be active in political life in order to safeguard personal rights and promote the common good. The political order exists for the promotion and protection of personal rights such as "the rights of free assembly, of common action, of expressing personal opinions, and of professing a religion both privately and publicly" (no. 73). In fact, these personal rights are necessary conditions for the free and active participation of citizens in government.

Today there is a growing recognition of the importance of promoting the rights of *all* citizens, not just a privileged few. The public
authority of the political community exists to foster these rights and
the common good of all its citizens "exercised within the limits of
morality." Citizens are expected to obey public authority, although
"it is lawful for them to defend their own rights and those of their
fellow citizens against any abuse of this authority, providing that in
so doing they observe the limits imposed by natural law and the
gospel" (no. 74).

The normal ways that Catholics participate in the political order
are by exercising their right to vote, by presenting their views of how
the government should be run, by observing their duty to their
country and service to the advancement of the common good and by
serving in political office, a task that the church praises (nos. 75-76).
Christians should be loyal to their countries "but without any nar-
rowing of mind. In other words, they must also look simultaneously
to the welfare of the whole human family" (no. 75).

The Catholic Church does not place her hopes in the privileges
conferred by civil authority. She even stands ready to renounce her
political rights if their exercise raises doubt about the sincerity of her
witness. The duty of the church is "to preach the faith with true freedom, to teach her social doctrine" and "to pass moral judgments,
even on matters touching the political order, whenever basic personal rights or the salvation of souls makes such judgments necessary" (no. 76).

The church and its members (especially its politicians) must
speak out boldly when basic human rights, or the right to human life
itself, is attacked or threatened in any way. There is no distinction
made by the Council between one's personal moral beliefs and what
one promotes in the political arena. If Catholics do not speak out *as
Christians,* political communities inevitably will reflect values and
pass legislation indifferent or inimical to Christian values, even to
the most basic human rights and values. If we who live in democratic
political communities are displeased with the legislation passed and

judicial decisions made, we must first ask ourselves whether we have fully accepted the challenge of the Second Vatican Council to actively engage in the political life of our country.

How does the Council view efforts toward world peace?

Christ himself has called his followers to be peacemakers, and he declares them "blessed" (Matthew 5:9). The constitution focuses on the unification of the world community of nations in the quest for peace. Despite the tremendous obstacles and risks involved, Christians must assume leadership in working for unity and peace in response to Christ's call.

What is peace? How is it to be achieved?

The constitution makes its plea for peace founded on a question for justice: "Peace is not merely the absence of war. Nor can it be reduced solely to the maintenance of a balance of power between enemies. Nor is it brought about by dictatorship. Instead, it is rightly and appropriately called 'an enterprise of justice' (Is. 32:7). Peace results from that harmony built into human society by its divine Founder, and actualized by men as they thirst after ever greater justice" (no. 78).

The efforts made for economic equality and full political participation for all, discussed earlier, have significant bearing upon the attainment and maintenance of world peace.

A striking aspect of chapter five, section one of this constitution is the vehement denunciation of the arms race and of wars that indiscriminately kill combatants and noncombatants alike. Concerning warfare, the constitution declares, "Any act of war aimed indiscriminately at the destruction of entire cities or of extensive areas along with their populations is a crime against God and man himself. It merits unequivocal and unhesitating condemnation" (no. 80).

The arms race is called "an utterly treacherous trap for humanity, and one which injures the poor to an intolerable degree. It is much to be feared that if this race persists, it will eventually spawn all the lethal ruin whose path is now making ready" (no. 81). The Council ultimately urges the banning of all war (no. 82).

What is the path to peace? The Council teaches: "Peace must be born of mutual trust between nations rather than imposed on them through fear of one another's weapons. Hence everyone must labor to put an end at last to the arms race, and to make a true beginning of disarmament, not indeed a unilateral disarmament, but one proceeding at an equal pace according to agreement, and backed up by authentic and workable safeguards" (no. 82).

The constitution also praises those who practice nonviolence. It urges governments to protect the rights of those who for reasons of conscience refuse to bear arms and to provide them with alternative service to the human community (nos. 78, 79).

The closing sections of the *Pastoral Constitution on the Church in the Modern World* focus on some practical suggestions and approaches to achieving peace: urging citizens of all nations to work for peace with their government officials (no. 82), eliminating primary sources of war such as excessive economic inequalities and the quest for power (*conversion* is needed here!), cooperation between advanced and developing nations, the international coordination and stimulation of economic growth and the support of organizations promoting such international cooperation and accountability, such as the United Nations. Christians are called and challenged to "collaborate willingly and wholeheartedly in establishing an international order involving genuine respect for all freedoms and amicable brotherhood between all men" (no. 88).

Continuing the tradition of the great Catholic social encyclicals on peace; such as Pope John XXIII's *Peace on Earth (Pacem in Terris)*, every January 1 the pope addresses the nations with a message on this theme. Let us heed and respond to the call of Jesus Christ, the

Prince of Peace, as it comes to us through his gospel and the church. We should also pray fervently for peace.

Conclusion

The *Pastoral Constitution on the Church in the Modern World* outlines many principles governing the church's response to the pressing and urgent needs of the world today. Who will take up these challenges to work for peace, economic justice, political communities guided by human and Christian values, the restoration of culture based upon the dignity and gifts of the person and the preservation and restoration of married and family life according to God's will?

The lay members of the church are especially called by God to live and work in the world so that it reflects God's truth and values. Our next chapter will explore the essential role of the laity in meeting this challenge.

Gaudium et Spes, Part II, and the *Catechism of the Catholic Church*

There are sixty-seven references in the *Catechism* to the various "problems of special urgency" discussed in Part II of the *Pastoral Constitution on the Church in the Modern World.* These references appear mainly where the *Catechism* addresses issues of marriage and family life (nos. 1601-1666; 2360-2387); rights of ownership and economic justice (nos. 2401-2442); participation in the political life of society (nos. 1897-1927; 2238-2246) and safeguarding peace (nos. 2302-2330).

Recent Magisterial Documents

Pope John Paul II. *Evangelium Vitae* (Encyclical Letter *The Gospel of Life*). March 25, 1995.

Pope John Paul II. *Familiaris Consortio (Role of the Christian Family in the Modern World)*. November 22, 1981.

Pope John Paul II. "Letter to Families." February 2, 1994.

Favorite Quotes from *Gaudium et Spes*, Part II

The intimate partnership of married life and love has been established by the Creator and qualified by His laws.... Thus a man and a woman, who by the marriage covenant of conjugal love "are no longer two, but one flesh" (Mt. 19:6), render mutual help and service to each other through an intimate union of their persons and of their actions.... For this reason, Christian spouses have a special sacrament by which they are fortified and receive a kind of consecration in the duties and dignity of their state. By virtue of this sacrament, as spouses fulfill their conjugal and family obligations, they are penetrated with the spirit of Christ. This spirit suffuses their whole lives with faith, hope, and charity. Thus they increasingly advance their own perfection, as well as their mutual sanctification, and hence contribute jointly to the glory of God.

As a result, with their parents leading the way by example and family prayer, children and indeed everyone gathered around the family hearth will find a readier path to human maturity, salvation, and holiness. (no. 48)

Peace is not merely the absence of war. Nor can it be reduced solely to the maintenance of a balance of power between enemies. Nor is it brought about by dictatorship. Instead, it is rightly and appropriately called "an enterprise of justice" (Is. 32:7). Peace results from that harmony built into human society by its divine Founder, and actualized by men as they thirst after ever greater justice. (no. 78)

CHAPTER TEN

The Laity: A Call to Full Membership in the Church

A s a lay Catholic, the call to the laity presented by the *Decree on the Apostolate of the Laity (Apostolicam Actuositatem)* has special meaning for me. It is noteworthy that the first document ever issued by an ecumenical council that deals solely with the laity should be issued in our lifetime. It is exciting to live in an age in which lay Catholics are being called to assume greater responsibility and leadership in the church and its mission.

By way of example, it is extraordinary that my own lay apostolate simultaneously includes three different areas in my life: my *individual* vocation as a lay theologian in the church; my vocation as a husband and father *whose family* is part of the apostolate and mission of the church; and my vocation to be an active member of my *parish,* which is committed to carrying out actively the mission of the church.

Vatican II rightly has been called the "Council of the Laity." As we have seen, the modern world poses a variety of monumental and perilous challenges. God particularly calls the laity to confront these issues and to "seek the kingdom of God by engaging in temporal affairs and by ordering them according to the plan of God" (*Lumen Gentium,* 31). To equip laypersons to confront these issues, the Council presents the beginnings of an official Catholic theology of the laity for modern times.

What are some of the important points of this "lay theology"?

First, the Council's focus on the church as "the people of God" makes it clear that the laity *is* the church, equal in membership with those ordained and vowed to religious life. Each baptized Catholic is as fully a member of the church as the pope. The laity are not "second class citizens" in the church.

Through their baptism and reception of the Eucharist, the lay faithful share fully in the life of Christ and his church. Each layperson has a specific vocation or call from God, a particular way to follow Jesus Christ and to share in the church's life. Each layperson has an "apostolate." Christ sends each one of us to carry on his priestly, prophetic and kingly ministries and to participate in the church's mission in a unique way.

Finally, Christ equips laypeople with the particular gifts and graces they need to fulfill their vocations and their apostolates successfully.

Catholics have traditionally prayed for vocations to the priesthood and religious life. Now we see the need to pray for vocations to the lay apostolate as well, so that the world might be more fully and effectively transformed and sanctified from within, as leaven makes a lump of dough rise. As the Council notes, modern conditions demand that the lay apostolate be broadened and intensified and that laypersons carry out their tasks with great zeal.

Due to population growth and scientific and technical progress, there are many places and professional fields—such as in business and science—in which only laypeople are capable of making a Christian witness and instilling godly values. Without this witness, there is the real danger of "a certain withdrawal from ethical and religious influences and a serious danger to Christian life" (*Apostolicam Actuositatem*, 1). However, the Holy Spirit is unmistakably at work to make the laity ever more conscious of their responsibilities, to inspire them everywhere to serve Christ and the church.

Let us now examine some of the aspects of the vocation and apostolate of the laity.

How do laypeople carry out Jesus' ministry as priest, prophet and king?

Priest. As members of God's "royal priesthood" (1 Peter 2:9), laypeople offer all their daily work, family life and other activities to the Father as "spiritual sacrifices acceptable to God through Jesus Christ (cf. 1 Pet. 2:5)" (*Lumen Gentium*, 34).

Prophet. Catholic laypersons must proclaim Jesus Christ by both *word* and *deed* as prophets of the gospel. The laity "go forth as powerful heralds of...faith...provided they steadfastly join to their profession of faith a life springing from faith. This evangelization, that is, this announcing of Christ by a living testimony as well as by the spoken word, takes on a specific quality and a special force in that it is carried out in the ordinary surroundings of the world" (*Lumen Gentium*, 35).

King. The laity establishes the kingship of Christ first in their own lives, "that by self-denial and a holy life they might conquer the reign of sin in themselves (cf. Rom. 6:12)." Second, the laity brings the kingdom into the lives of others by leading them with humility and patience to accept Christ as their king. Third, guided by a Christian conscience, the laity works to establish God's kingdom and the values of that kingdom in all the affairs of the world. "For even in secular affairs there is no human activity which can be withdrawn from God's dominion" (*Lumen Gentium*, 36).

What do you mean by the word *apostolate*?

The first chapter of the *Decree on the Apostolate of the Laity* explains that the church was founded to spread the kingdom of Christ every-where, so that the whole world might be brought into relationship with Christ and share in his saving redemption. The decree says that "since it is proper to the layman's state in life for him to spend his days in the midst of the world and of secular transactions, he is called by God to burn with the spirit of Christ and to exercise his aposto-late in the world as a kind of leaven" (no. 2).

All activity of the church directed to this goal is called the "apos-tolate," which is carried on in various ways by all the church's mem-bers. The Christian vocation is necessarily a call to the apostolate, a call to carry out the mission of Christ in the world. All lay Catholics receive a common call to share in this mission. Christ calls each of us to exercise his or her own particular lay apostolate—that is, to advance the gospel with the unique gifts and in the area that God has apportioned.

Whenever the decree speaks of the particular way the laity carries out this apostolate, two dimensions are included: first, bringing to all people the message and the grace of Christ, which will lead them to holiness; and second, renewing the temporal order by "penetrating and perfecting the temporal sphere of things through the spirit of the gospel" (nos. 2, 5).

How is the laity equipped for this apostolate?

Each layperson is assigned to the apostolate by Jesus Christ himself through baptism and then strengthened by the power of the Holy Spirit through confirmation. Also "the [other] sacraments, especially the most holy Eucharist, communicate and nourish that charity which is the soul of the entire apostolate" (*Apostolicam Actuositatem,* 3).

The Council stresses that it is God's love, poured into our hearts through the Holy Spirit (see Romans 5:5), that impels us to promote the spread of God's kingdom so that all will come to know "the only true God, and Jesus Christ," whom God sent (John 17:3). "On all Christians," the Council declares, "is laid the splendid burden of working to make the divine message of salvation known and accepted by all...throughout the world" (no. 3). Laypeople are equipped for the apostolate since they themselves are filled with the love of Christ and desire to spread the good news about him to everyone. This can be carried out through the apostolate of married and family life, evangelization, political involvement, ecumenical endeavors and many other expressions of lay involvement aimed at spreading the message of Christ and advancing his kingdom.

Doesn't it seem that many Catholics lack this love and zeal?

Yes, and that is why this decree teaches that "the success of the lay apostolate depends upon the laity's living union with Christ. For the Lord has said, 'He who abides in me, and I in him, he bears much fruit: for without me you can do nothing' (Jn. 15:5)" (no. 4).

Without a living union with Jesus Christ, there is no lay apostolate worth speaking of. Pope John Paul II took this same parable of the vine and the branches as the central theme of his apostolic letter *On the Lay Members of Christ's Faithful People (Christifideles Laici)*. He stresses that the fruitfulness and growth of the lay apostolate depend upon the communion or unity of the laity with Jesus Christ.

Another way of saying this is that laypeople must be holy. As John Paul II states in the letter, holiness is "a fundamental presupposition" and "an irreplaceable condition" for everyone to fulfill the saving mission of the church. "The Church's holiness is the hidden source and the infallible measure of the works of the apostolate and of the missionary effort. Only in the measure that the Church, Christ's spouse, is loved by Him and she, in turn, loves Him, does she become a mother fruitful in the Spirit" (no. 17). Thus holiness is absolutely essential in carrying out the lay apostolate.

Is it realistic to expect that laypeople can grow in holiness?

It is true that most laypeople cannot have the same *type* of spiritual life as priests or religious, but laypeople can and must grow in holiness, for this is the call of God to all Christians (see *Lumen Gentium*, chap. 5). The *Decree on the Apostolate of the Laity* mentions some elements of an authentic "lay spirituality" by which laypeople can grow in holiness.

First, laypeople are "nourished by spiritual aids which are common to all the faithful, especially active participation in the sacred liturgy" (no. 4). Through the sacraments and other forms of prayer and devotion that are accessible to all, laypeople can develop an intimate union with God in prayer.

Second, the decree notes that by fulfilling their normal duties in life according to God's will, laypeople grow in union with God and progress in holiness. This includes "trying prudently and patiently to overcome difficulties" (no. 4). "Neither family concerns nor other secular affairs should be excluded from their religious program of life" (no. 4). We can do all things for God and offer all things to him in thanksgiving (see Colossians 3:17).

Third, faith and meditation on God's Word enable laypeople to seek God's will in all things and to make correct judgments.

Fourth, the decree affirms that the type of spirituality or religious life that a layperson pursues will depend on the person's specific state in life, career, vocation, health and other factors. The layperson's spiritual life will take its particular form according to whether one is married, widowed or single and from one's condition of health, profession, social status and so on. Whatever those may be, the layperson should seek to develop the unique talents God has given and "make use of the gifts which he has received from the Holy Spirit" (no. 4).

How do the gifts of the Holy Spirit equip the laity for their apostolate?

The decree states that the Holy Spirit gives *each* person a charism (gift) or charisms for the building up of the church and the service of humanity (see no. 3). Thus the lay apostolate is not carried out by human effort or talent alone but by the exercise of the gifts of the Holy Spirit.

> To each is given the manifestation of the Spirit for the common good. To one is given through the Spirit the utterance of wisdom, and to another the utterance of knowledge according to the same Spirit, to another faith by the same Spirit, to another gifts of healing by the one Spirit, to another the working of miracles, to another prophecy, to another the ability to distinguish between spirits, to another various kinds of tongues, to another the interpretation of tongues (1 Cor. 12:7-10; cf. 1 Cor. 12:4-6, 28-31; Rom. 12:6-8; 1 Pt. 4:10-11). (*Christifideles Laici,* 24)

It should be noted that possession of spiritual gifts (and other human talents) is not an indicator of holiness. God gives these gifts freely to whomever he wills for the upbuilding of the church, not as a mark or sign of the holiness of the individual who possesses the gift. Hopefully Catholics will use their gifts to give glory to God and to foster their own dedication to Christ, as well as to build up the church.

John Paul II stressed that the gifts of the Holy Spirit are to be received with gratitude by the individuals who exercise them and by the whole church, since "they are in fact a singularly rich source of grace for the vitality of the apostolate and for the holiness of the whole body of Christ" (*Christifideles Laici,* 24). He also notes the need for a continual *discernment of the charisms* by the pastors of the church to see that they are used rightly.

Pope John Paul II and the Council insisted that the laity has both a "right and duty" to exercise charisms "in the Church and in the world for the good of mankind and for the upbuilding of the Church. In so doing, believers need to enjoy the freedom of the Holy Spirit who 'breathes where he wills' (Jn. 3:8)" (*Apostolicam Actuositatem*, 3).

What does Vatican II say about specific "lay ministries"?

Based upon the gifts of the Holy Spirit, there emerge various *ministries* or services (in Greek, *diakonia*) for the upbuilding of the church. Some ministries are recognized and confirmed through ordination to the priesthood or entrance into different types of religious communities or commitments. By virtue of their varied gifts of the Spirit, laypeople too have ministries of service in the church.

Some of these, as Pope John Paul II observed, are connected with the church's liturgical celebration, which "is a sacred action not simply of the clergy, but of the entire assembly. It is, therefore, natural that the tasks not proper to the ordained ministers be fulfilled by the lay faithful" (*Christifideles Laici*, 23). The pope explained that this also opens the door for laypeople to exercise other services in the church, including "announcing the word of God and pastoral care" (*Christifideles Laici*, 23).

Through the gifts of the Holy Spirit, laypeople build up the body of Christ, serve the world and promote the spread of the gospel and the advance of God's kingdom. In light of this teaching, it should be common for laypeople today to be actively exercising these gifts and ministries in the church and in the world, in cooperation with their pastors. The typical Catholic parish has a wide variety of services in which laypeople exercise their gifts, including works of mercy (such as the St. Vincent de Paul Society), hospital visitation and visiting shut-ins, CCD and service to Catholic schools, extraordinary eucharistic ministers and lectors, liturgical music and a host of others.

But don't such ministries create tension between laypeople and their pastors?

At times. But the point here is not competition or tension but achieving and recognizing the complementarities between the gifts and ministries of laypeople and those of clergy and religious. We are all working together for the same goal: to advance the kingdom of Christ and spread his good news.

Vatican II distinguishes between the ministries of the laity and those of ordained clergy, noting that these are different ways of sharing in the priesthood of Christ (see *Lumen Gentium,* 10; *Apostolicam Actuositatem,* 2; *Christifideles Laici,* 22). "In the Church, there is diversity of service but unity of purpose" (*Apostolicam Actuositatem,* 2). Pope John Paul II stated that while laypeople can fulfill a variety of roles in the liturgy, in transmitting the faith and in the pastoral structure of the church, these should be exercised in a way appropriate to laypeople, which is different from that of the ordained ministers of the church (*Christifideles Laici,* 23).

The *Dogmatic Constitution on the Church* summarizes the mutual expectations that laity and clergy should have. The laity have the right to receive from their pastors the Word of God and the sacraments. Further, the constitution exhorts pastors to "recognize and promote the dignity as well as the responsibility of the layman in the Church. Let them willingly make use of his prudent advice. Let them confidently assign duties to him in the service of the Church, allowing him freedom and room for action. Further, let them encourage the layman so that he may undertake tasks on his own initiative" (*Lumen Gentium,* 37).

Pastors should expect laypeople to express their opinions about the church and their needs "in truth, in courage, and in prudence, with reverence and charity" (*Lumen Gentium,* 37). Nonetheless, pastors should also expect laypeople to *obey* them in their role as teachers and shepherds in the church and to *pray* for their pastors as those who will have to render an account for their souls (see Hebrews 13:17). As we can see, the laity are expected to do far *more* in the church than to "pray, pay and obey!"

Most importantly, laity and clergy are encouraged to get to know each other well and to converse frequently about issues and concerns, with the aim of promoting the good of the church (see *Lumen Gentium,* 37). This mutual cooperation and understanding is an expression of "co-responsibility" of laity and clergy for the life and mission of the church.

What is the unique goal of the lay apostolate?

Author George Sim Johnston astutely observed:

> Today, many Catholics (including some bishops) seem to think that Vatican II was about the role of the laity in the Church—eucharistic ministers, lectors, and so forth. But it was really about the role of the laity in the world. The true Catholic life is one of personal conversion and evangelization; it does not involve hanging around the sacristy. Recently, Francis Cardinal George of Chicago said that the biggest failure of the post-Vatican II Church was her failure to get out the council's message about the laity—who, after all, comprise 99 percent of the Church.[1]

The Council's message, as expressed in *Apostolicam Actuositatem,* is that the laity's primary mission is an *apostolate* (that is, being "sent out") to the world, not mainly performing services in church. The lay apostolate is threefold:

1. Proclaiming the gospel of Jesus Christ, by word and deed, in the world. The Council calls this "the apostolate of evangelization and sanctification."

   There are innumerable opportunities open to the laity for the exercise of their apostolate of making the gospel known and men holy. The very testimony of their Christian life, and good works done in a supernatural spirit, have the power to draw men to belief and to God; for the Lord says, "Even so let your light shine before men, in order that they may see your good works and give glory to your Father in heaven" (Mt. 5:16). (*Apostolicam Actuositatem*, 6)

2. "The laity must take on the renewal of the temporal order as their own special obligation. Led by the light of the gospel and the mind of the Church, and motivated by Christian love, let them act directly and definitively in the temporal sphere" (*Apostolicam Actuositatem*, 7).

3. Charitable works and social aid, "works of mercy," are a particular mark of the church:

   While [the church] rejoices in the undertakings of others, she claims works of charity as her own inalienable duty and right....

   Wherever there are people in need of food and drink, clothing, housing, medicine, employment, education; wherever men lack the facilities necessary for living a truly human life or are tormented by hardships or poor health, or suffer exile or imprisonment, there Christian charity should seek them out and find them, console them with eager care and relieve them with the gift of help. (*Apostolicam Actuositatem*, 8)

The final aspect and "crown" of the lay apostolate is the mission of charitable works.

What is the goal of Christian social action?

The decree highlights the importance of Christian social action, which must be carried out according to the principles of love and of justice. While charity is central, the document notes, "The demands of justice should first be satisfied, lest the giving of what is due in justice be represented as the offering of a charitable gift" (no. 8). Then we should provide charitable help, which goes beyond the demands of what is just and right.

For example, it is not charity to provide a just wage for a worker's labor. Nor is it charity to see that the poor of the world are provided the minimum standards of food, clothing and shelter. It is only just to provide these things that are abundant elsewhere.

In what fields do laypeople carry on their apostolate?

In Pope John Paul II's letter on the laity, he spoke of Jesus' image of the world itself as a field or vineyard in which people are sent to work and harvest. The whole world is the "field" of the lay apostolate!

Everyone is called to work in this field—now! We are in an *urgent* situation: "A new state of affairs today both in the Church and in social, economic, political and cultural life, calls with a particular urgency for the action of the lay faithful. If lack of commitment is always unacceptable, the present time renders it even more so. It is *not permissible for anyone to remain idle*" (*Christifideles Laici*, 3, emphasis added).

The church is also a field of the apostolate in which *all* the laity are called to work and contribute something. In fact, Vatican II warns that "the member who fails to make his proper contribution to the development of the Church must be said to be useful neither to the Church nor to himself" (*Apostolicam Actuositatem*, 2).

The decree on the laity lists as the more important fields of action church communities, especially the parish and the diocese, the family, the youth, the social environment and national and international affairs.

What about the laity's role in specific fields of the apostolate?

The involvement of the laity should not be limited to a few areas of the church's life and mission. Laypersons ought to be active "in *every* apostolic and missionary undertaking sponsored by their local parish" and should be ever ready to serve diocesan projects at their bishop's invitation (*Apostolicam Actuositatem*, 10, emphasis added).

The lay apostolate in the field of marriage and family life is strongly recommended since the majority of adult Catholics are married. The decree teaches that the "supreme task" of the apostolate of Christian couples today is threefold: to manifest "the unbreakable and sacred character of the marriage bond"; "to educate children in a Christian manner"; to "defend the dignity and lawful independence of the family" (*Apostolicam Actuositatem*, 11).

The decree proceeds to provide specific guidance for the family apostolate, encouraging the family to pray together both at home and in the liturgical worship of the church, to express mutual affection, to provide hospitality and to promote justice and good works for the benefit of those in need. Some specific examples of activities that can be carried out by families as their apostolate are

> the adoption of abandoned infants, hospitality to strangers, assistance in the operation of schools, helpful advice and material assistance for adolescents, help to engaged couples in preparing themselves better for marriage, catechetical work, support of married couples and families involved in material and moral crises, help for the aged not only by providing them with the necessities of life but also by obtaining for them a fair share of the benefits of economic progress. (no. 11)

A whole section (no. 12) is devoted to youth and their apostolate. Adults are encouraged to attract young persons to the apostolate by their example and their interest in young people. Pope John Paul II, in his exhortation on the laity, called youth "the hope of the Church" (*Christifideles Laici*, 46, 47).

Concerning the social environment, the decree speaks of "the apostolate of the social milieu." This refers to "the effort to infuse a Christian spirit into the mentality, customs, laws, and structures of the community in which a person lives." This duty especially rests upon the laity, since "it can never be properly performed by others." Laypersons can witness most effectively to others who share a common profession, common interests, residence in the same neighborhood and so on, which the decree calls "the apostolate of like toward like." They testify to Christ not only by their speech but also by their witness of a life committed to him (no. 13).

What are the methods of accomplishing this apostolate?

The Council speaks of the apostolate carried out by individuals and by various groups or associations. Every individual Christian is to be a witness to Christ in word and deed and to advance his kingdom through a life of charity. Individual laypersons can often reach places where lay groups and religious cannot. Pope John Paul II's letter on the laity speaks of "the absolute necessity of an apostolate exercised by the individual" (*Christifideles Laici*, 28). Unless each Catholic is committed to the apostolate, the mission of the laity as a whole will be weakened or even fail.

However, Vatican II prophetically called for groups of laypeople to join together in the apostolate, which reflects the communal nature of the church (*Apostolicam Actuositatem*, 18). It acknowledged the great variety of lay associations in the apostolate and recommended that "those [associations] which promote and encourage a closer harmony between the everyday life of the members and their faith must be given primary consideration" (no. 19).

Since the Council, there has been such a flourishing of lay associations, groups, communities and movements that Pope John Paul II spoke of "a new era of group endeavors of the lay faithful" (*Christifideles Laici,* 29). These groups include Communion and Liberation, Focolare, Cursillo, Regnum Christi, Opus Dei, Catholic charismatic prayer groups and covenant communities, to name but a few. These groups are very diverse, "so great is the richness and the versatility of resources that the Holy Spirit nourishes." Yet they have "a common purpose, that is, the responsible participation…in the Church's mission of carrying forth the Gospel of Christ" (*Christifideles Laici,* 29).

The *Decree on the Apostolate of the Laity* affirms that "the laity have the right to found and run such associations and to join those already existing" (*Apostolicam Actuositatem,* 19), as long as the associations maintain a proper relationship to church authorities. One chapter is largely devoted to explaining how laypeople and associations and the Catholic hierarchy may cooperate and maintain good relations. The apostolic exhortation *On the Lay Members of Christ's Faithful People* expands this teaching and presents some specific criteria for discerning how such associations may be properly formed (*Christifideles Laici,* 29-30). The most important criterion is to look at "the actual fruits" that the group shows in its organizational life and by the work it performs. "You will know them by their fruits" (Matthew 7:16).

Pope John Paul II noted the power of such groups to transform their surroundings and society. Equally important is the personal support they provide to fellow members in the midst of a secularized world. Such groups can offer Catholics "a precious help for the Christian life in remaining faithful to the demands of the Gospel and to the commitment to the Church's mission and apostolate" (*Christifideles Laici,* 29). Yes, we need such mutual support to keep that flame of the spirit of the gospel alive in us!

How are laypeople prepared to carry out their mission?

Too often we neglect the formation and training that laypeople need in order to spread the gospel of Christ in the world and transform human society according to the standard of the gospel. The final chapter of the *Decree on the Apostolate of the Laity* is devoted to discussing formation of lay Catholics for the apostolate.

Clearly this formation "takes its special flavor from the distinctively secular quality of the lay state and from its own form of spirituality" (*Apostolicam Actuositatem,* 29). It is *not* the same as formation for the priesthood or religious life. Some specific characteristics of this formation for the lay apostolate are mentioned.

1.   Each layperson should be *well-informed* about the modern world and should recognize and develop his or her own human talents and natural abilities.

2.   *Spiritual formation* is necessary, fostering a life based on strong faith in God and sensitivity to the movement of the Holy Spirit. "This formation should be deemed the basis and condition for every successful apostolate" (*Apostolicam Actuositatem,* 29).

3.   Solid *doctrinal instruction* in theology, ethics and philosophy, according to the situation and ability of each person, is necessary.

4.   Developing *the ability to relate well with people* is valuable, "especially the art of living fraternally with others, cooperating with them, and initiating conversation with them" (no. 29).

5.   Finally, the laity must learn "gradually and prudently" to *put all this into practice,* always with a view toward maturing in Christ and growing in one's understanding of the changing needs of the world.

The last article of the *Decree on the Apostolate of the Laity* (no. 32) speaks of many *aids* that are available to help laypeople acquire this formation. They are all directed toward developing a deeper knowledge of sacred Scripture and Catholic doctrine, nourishing a spiritual life, growing in an appreciation of world conditions and discovering and developing suitable methods for service.

When does this training begin?

The decree teaches that training for the apostolate begins with a child's earliest education, becoming more specific in adolescence and young adulthood. "The whole of family life, then, would become a sort of apprenticeship for the apostolate" (no. 30). Catholic family life is aimed not only at the Christian education of the young but at forming apostles for Jesus Christ! The young must understand that they are being trained and formed in order to *be sent out* into the world to spread the Good News of Jesus Christ and to work and pray for the transformation of society according to Christian values. Parents can foster this by praying and reading Scripture with their children in the home and discussing how this actually applies to everyday life. I have also found that reading and discussing the lives of the saints with my children motivates them to want to follow the Lord and do his will.

Example is another essential part of training for the lay apostolate. The biography of Catherine de Hueck Doherty, champion of the poor and foundress of the primarily lay Madonna House apostolate, relates how Catherine's parents prepared her for her apostolate. Although the de Huecks belonged to the Russian nobility, they frequently welcomed the poor into their home and shared meals with them. This memory deeply impressed young Catherine and launched her apostolate among the poor. We find this story repeated in the lives of many saints.

How is the laity challenged to carry out its apostolate today?

Many directives from the *Decree on the Apostolate of the Laity* are still very current, if not even more important, forty-five years after the document was issued. The document urges the laity especially to learn sound doctrine on subjects of controversy and to "provide the witness of an evangelical life in contrast to all forms of materialism" (no. 31).

Laypeople should "be instructed in the true meaning and value of temporal things, both in themselves and in their relation to the total fulfillment of the human person" (no. 31). How much we need this instruction, as the media bombards us daily with materialism and other false values! Christians today are challenged both to monitor their exposure to sources of false values, like movies that promote and glorify sex or violence, and to discuss openly with mature Christians both the truth and the error of what they see and hear in the media. The laity is also encouraged to learn the principles and conclusions of authentic Catholic moral and social teaching, so we will be able to advance this teaching in society and apply it correctly in individual cases.

More recently, Pope John Paul II challenged the Catholic laity, especially of the "first world," to undertake a great new effort of "re-evangelization" of their countries and cultures to Christ. He pointed to rising secularism, materialism or consumerism, atheism and "indifference to religion and the practice of religion devoid of true meaning," especially among the traditionally Christian countries of Europe and the West, as the reason for this call to re-evangelization. There is a growing number of "unchurched" people in the West who need to hear the Good News about Jesus Christ. Most of these people will never hear the gospel in church. They will hear it, if anywhere, from their Christian acquaintances, coworkers and friends.

Laypeople in the church are being called to carry out their own prophetic mission. First, we are called to evangelize those around us to Christ (even those within our parishes who do not know Christ personally or who fail to follow his teaching faithfully). Second, we are called to influence the broader culture and government toward a renewed belief in God and obedience to him. Hence *evangelization* is becoming a word that Catholics hear more frequently from the pope, our bishops and our priests.

But Catholics cannot give to others what they don't have themselves. The lay faithful must be fully alive in Christ and "know how to put the Gospel and their daily activities of life into a most shining and convincing testimony" (*Christifideles Laici*, 34). The "formation of mature ecclesial communities" and a new "systematic work in catechesis"—teaching the faith—are essential in this renewal of the laity. Then people can share that faith effectively with others and help renew the face of the earth.

Laypersons are not alone in this vocation. The whole church, in different ways, contributes to the basic Christian apostolate of leading others to faith and salvation in Jesus Christ and transforming the world into his image. In the next chapter we will explore how the Second Vatican Council instructs bishops, priests and those called to vowed religious life to understand their identity, mission and apostolate in the modern world.

Apostolicam Actuositatem and the *Catechism of the Catholic Church*

There are only fourteen references to the *Decree on the Apostolate of the Laity* in the *Catechism*. These relate especially to the apostolate (nos. 863-865) and evangelization (no. 2105), the transformation of culture (no. 2823) and social justice (no. 2446). The discussion in the *Catechism's* Part I (nos. 897-913) also refers to chapter four of *Lumen Gentium* on the laity.

Recent Magisterial Documents

Congregation on the Doctrine of the Faith. "Letter on the Collaboration of Men and Women," May 31, 2004. *Origins* 34, no. 11 (August 26, 2004).

Pope John Paul II. *Christifideles Laici (The Lay Members of Christ's Faithful People).* December 30, 1988.

Pope John Paul II. *Mulieris Dignitatem (On the Dignity and Vocation of Women).* August 15, 1988.

Vatican Congregations. "Instruction on Certain Questions Regarding the Collaboration of the Non-Ordained Faithful in the Sacred Ministry of the Priest." August 13, 1997.

Favorite Quotes from *Apostolicam Actuositatem*

An apostolate of this kind does not consist only in the witness of one's way of life; a true apostle looks for opportunities to announce Christ by words. (no. 6)

For this the Church was founded: that by spreading the kingdom of Christ everywhere for the glory of God the Father, she might bring all men to share in Christ's saving redemption; and that through them the whole world might in actual fact be brought into relationship with Him. All activity of the Mystical Body directed to the attainment of this goal is called the apostolate, and the Church carries it on in various ways through all her members. For by its very nature the Christian vocation is also a vocation to the apostolate. No part of the structure of a living body is merely passive but each has a share in the functions as well as in the life of the body.... So intimately are the parts linked and interrelated in this body that the member who fails to make his proper contribution to the development of the Church must be said to be useful neither to the Church nor to himself. (no. 2)

Since Christ in His mission from the Father is the fountain and source of the whole apostolate of the Church, the success of the lay apostolate depends upon the laity's living union with Christ. For the Lord has said, "He who abides in me, and I in him, he bears much fruit: for without me you can do nothing" (Jn. 15:5). (no. 4)

CHAPTER ELEVEN

The Challenge to Bishops, Priests and Religious

In the aftermath of the Second Vatican Council, the West experienced a dramatic decline in the number of vocations to the priesthood and religious life, as well as the departure of numerous priests and religious from their ordained ministries and vowed life. On the surface it appeared that priesthood and religious life were experiencing an "identity crisis." Or perhaps the identity proclaimed by the Council was no longer suitable to many present or prospective priests and religious in the West.

However, the Second Vatican Council did not precipitate this crisis so much as did other voices and forces in Western culture. These directly undermined priestly and religious life or seemed to provide attractive alternatives to them.

With regard to bishops, the Second Vatican Council devoted a great deal of attention to their collegial role in leading the church. Yet by 1985 controversy over the teaching and governing authority of national episcopal conferences had raised the issue of the nature and limits of the bishops' role.

Some studies downplay or overlook the Council's teaching concerning bishops, priests, priestly formation and religious life. This would be a serious mistake, especially in light of these pressing challenges today. Certainly the Council did not change the basic leadership structure of the Catholic Church, but it did present a fresh understanding of these roles and convey a new style or spirit, which opens the way for renewal among clergy and religious.

While the First Vatican Council focused on the primacy and the infallibility of the pope, an ecumenical council had not addressed the roles of bishops, priests and religious since the Council of Trent did so in the sixteenth century. The time was ripe for a fresh look at these ministries and vocations, especially since Vatican II set out to present a complete, up-to-date understanding of the church, its life and its purpose in the modern world.

If we could put in a nutshell the challenge presented to bishops and priests, some key words would be *communion, collegiality* and *imitating Christ the Good Shepherd* in their pastoral offices. For religious the challenge is to *rediscover* the call and charisms of their orders, as well as the basic charism and call of religious life, and then to *renew* these charisms in the situation of the modern world, adapting their original call and mission to the context of our own time.

First let us discuss the concepts of communion, collegiality and shepherding, as set forth in the *Decree on the Pastoral Office of Bishops in the Church (Christus Dominus)*, the *Decree on the Ministry and Life of Priests (Presbyterorum Ordinis)* and the *Decree on Priestly Formation (Optatum Totius)*.

What is the heart of the teaching about bishops and priests?

At the heart of the Council's teaching on bishops and priests and their formation is the concept of "communion," the deep unity and fellowship that believers have in Jesus Christ. The Extraordinary Synod of 1985 called it "the central and fundamental idea of the Council's documents." Communion focuses on our unity in the church—having a common identity, purpose and mission on earth, even having our eternal destinies bound up with each other.

The "communion of saints" not only refers to the saints in heaven but also to our communion with them and with each other on earth.

The early church speaks of the *koinonia* or close fellowship that Christians share in Christ, which was an essential mark of the church from its early years. This unity provides the foundation upon which all relationships in the church are to be built. We are truly one in Christ. The sacraments, especially baptism and the Eucharist, provide the grace and power from God for such unity.

The specific way that communion is expressed and lived out among the bishops, including the pope, is through *collegiality*. The secular equivalent of collegiality might be "teamwork" or "team spirit." For example, the bishops are called to show concern for the entire church throughout the world, not just for their own local churches or dioceses (see *Christus Dominus,* 6).

This collaboration among the bishops for the good of the whole church is expressed in many ways: sending missionaries and funds from one diocese to another in need, coordinating together the pastoral journeys of the pope, being involved in the Synod of Bishops and episcopal conferences, cooperating with the worldwide services of the Roman Curia and so on.

The fullest expression of collegial action is found in an ecumenical council, where *all* the bishops gather to decide issues affecting the entire church. Here it is most evident that the bishops work together as a "college" or a "team"—in a communion of faith and love.

How do the bishops work together with the pope?

The pope is a bishop, a member of the college or body of bishops, but he is also its head, just as Peter was both an apostle and the leader of the apostles. The pope represents Christ in a special way as the pastor of all the faithful, as Jesus appointed Peter to shepherd the whole flock of God (see John 21:15-19).

The bishops as a body, joined with the pope and never apart from him, share in the care and shepherding of all Christ's faithful people. They serve in the name and person of Christ as the church's primary leaders, priests and teachers. They faithfully pass on the message of the gospel the apostles entrusted to them.

The college of bishops can never act as a whole without the pope, since he is the head of this college. The pope is said to have "supreme, full, immediate, and universal authority" over the care of souls (*Christus Dominus*, 2). Each bishop possesses the "ordinary, proper, and immediate authority" needed to pastor a local church or diocese (*Christus Dominus*, 8). This means that the bishop is able to freely lead and teach the faithful in his diocese or jurisdiction, but the faithful are also immediately subject to the pope as the universal pastor and shepherd of all Christians.

Hence, it is true that the pope has the right and the authority as chief shepherd of the church on earth to pastor directly any situation in the Catholic Church in any part of the world. The pope is not overstepping his authority when he intervenes directly in the affairs of any diocese or local church. However, observing the spirit of collegiality, the pope usually works with the bishops in such a way as to strengthen their leadership and to express his communion with them. He observes Jesus' command to Peter to "strengthen your brethren" (Luke 22:32).

What are some ways this communion and collegiality is expressed?

In his pastoral service to the church, the pope makes use of the departments of the Roman Curia, as well as various papal representatives or legates. In response to Vatican II, the Roman Curia has been streamlined and internationalized to better represent the whole church. Also, the Council called for more bishops, especially at the diocesan level, to serve the pope as consulters and in Vatican departments in order to "more adequately apprise the Supreme Pontiff of the thinking, the desires, and the needs of all the churches" (*Christus Dominus*, 10).

A major step toward the collaboration of the pope and the bishops was the establishment of a synod, drawn from the bishops of the world with the charge to meet regularly to discuss specific issues affecting the whole church. They advise the pope of their discernment on important issues of the day. The Synod of Bishops is a specific way in which the bishops share in the responsibility of shepherding the universal church.

Since the close of the Council, the popes have held a number of regular synods, and one Extraordinary Synod of Bishops in 1985, to evaluate and promote the teaching of the Second Vatican Council. The popes have used the bishops' reports from the regular synods as the basis for apostolic exhortations on the topics discussed.

The pope also meets regularly with groups of bishops from around the world, both on his pastoral journeys to various countries and when the bishops of different regions travel to Rome for regularly scheduled *ad limina* visits. The latter "state-of-the-diocese" visits are made every five years by all bishops with responsibility for their own dioceses.

Isn't there controversy over episcopal conferences?

Episcopal conferences are national or territorial groupings of bishops who meet regularly to pastor and discuss issues affecting the church in their countries and to promote the church's apostolate there (see *Christus Dominus,* 38). The Council urged that such conferences be established throughout the world and meet together at fixed times, since existing conferences "have furnished outstanding proofs of a more fruitful apostolate" (*Christus Dominus,* 37).

Some questions have arisen, however, concerning the authority, especially the teaching authority, of episcopal conferences. Episcopal conferences in different countries have issued pastoral statements that appear to differ from each other in approach or even in content. How is the unity of the Catholic Church 's teaching to be preserved?

What right do individual bishops have to disagree with the decisions or pastoral statements of the episcopal conference to which they belong?

The Catholic Church's teaching is fairly clear on the authority of the *whole* college of bishops and of individual bishops in relationship to the pope and the whole college of bishops. But what about the teachings and pastoral authority of an episcopal conference? Could they sometimes reflect the beliefs of a "national church" on certain issues, rather than those of the universal church?

In response to the request of the Extraordinary Synod of 1985 that this issue be studied, Pope John Paul II issued an official document (called a *motu propio*) on May 21, 1998, to clarify this issue. In *Apostolos Suos (On the Theological and Juridical Nature of Episcopal Conferences)* the pope reaffirmed the importance of episcopal conferences in teaching the faith of the church. The document states:

> The concerted voice of the bishops of a determined territory, when, in communion with the Roman Pontiff, they jointly proclaim the catholic truth in matters of faith and morals, can reach their people more effectively and can make it easier for their faithful to adhere to the magisterium with a sense of religious respect.... The Bishops, assembled in Episcopal Conference, must take special care to follow the magisterium of the universal Church and to communicate it opportunely to the people entrusted to them. (no. 21)

However, the pope also noted that no episcopal conference can issue any teaching "as authentic teaching of the conference to which all the faithful of the territory would have to adhere" unless *all* the bishops of the conference agree with it and it is approved by the Apostolic See (the pope or his designated representative). The unanimous approval of all the bishops of the particular episcopal conference is necessary because the authority of the individual bishop to teach and govern is conferred by Jesus Christ, through the bishop's consecration, so that he can teach and pastor his own "local church" (diocese) in communion with the pope and with all the Catholic bishops of the world.

The pope concludes, "At present, Episcopal Conferences fulfill many tasks for the good of the Church. They are called to support, in a growing service, 'the inalienable responsibility of each Bishop in relation to the universal church and to his particular Church' and, naturally, not to hinder it by substituting themselves inappropriately for him" (*Apostolos Suos,* 24, quoting Synod, II, C).

Does each bishop need to have a concern for the whole church?

Yes. One thing that is evident in *Christus Dominus* is the care and sense of responsibility that each bishop has for the universal church. This would even include lands where the Word of God has not yet been proclaimed (no. 6). Therefore, bishops should be ready to promote works of evangelization, to support the missions and to aid in times of disaster and affliction as they are able.

Even within his own local diocese, the bishop is called to have a pastoral care not only for the Catholics of the diocese but for *everyone* who lives within that geographical area. Jesus himself expressed care for "sheep, that are not of this fold" and prayed for the day when there would be "one flock, one shepherd" (John 10:16). A bishop's pastoral concern and activity reaches out and extends to others in this way, especially to the poor, the sick and those most in need.

Far from exalting the merits of bishops or focusing on their privileges, this document is almost exclusively concerned with the duties and responsibilities of bishops, which includes care of some kind for every member of the church and society. A bishop's life is clearly one of sacrificial service—like Jesus Christ's.

What of other aspects of the bishops' pastoral office?

Christus Dominus also discusses how the bishop carries on Jesus' threefold ministry of priest, prophet and king. The bishop is a witness to Christ before all (no. 11). The teaching role is "a task which is eminent among the chief duties of bishops. They should, in the power of the Spirit, summon men to faith or confirm them in a faith already living" (no. 12). They must present Christian doctrine faithfully and yet "in a manner adapted to the needs of the times" (no. 13), especially through preaching and catechetical instruction. This instruction, which includes a new emphasis on the instruction of adult catechumens (RCIA), "is based on sacred Scripture, tradition, the liturgy, the teaching authority, and life of the Church" (no. 14).

In their priestly role "bishops enjoy the fullness of the sacrament of orders, and all priests as well as deacons are dependent upon them in the exercise of authority" (no. 15). To express this, a bishop normally ordains the priests and deacons of his diocese and must authorize all priests who enter the diocese to administer the sacraments. The bishop is the "chief priest" in each diocese—the chief representative of Jesus Christ in his royal priesthood. His main concern is to offer to the Father a people who are holy: "As those who lead others to perfection, bishops should be diligent in fostering holiness among their clerics, religious, and laity according to the special vocation of each...[and] to give an example of holiness through charity, humility, and simplicity of life" (no. 15).

Perhaps the most striking and important of all the roles of the bishop presented by Vatican II is his share in the kingly ministry of Christ. Far from "lording over" his flock, the bishop is presented as a "good shepherd" and a "true father" to his people:

> In exercising his office of father and pastor, a bishop should stand in the midst of his people as one who serves [cf. Lk. 22:26-27]. Let him be a good shepherd who knows his sheep and whose sheep know him. Let him be a true father who excels in the spirit of love and solicitude

for all.... Let him so gather and mold the whole family of his flock that everyone, conscious of his own duties, may live and work in the communion of love. (no. 16)

Many other aspects of the bishop's pastoral role are mentioned, such as his ecumenical concern (no. 16), his promotion of the lay apostolate (no. 17) and his care for other groups in need (no. 18). But what stands out is the fatherly and fraternal care that the bishop is to have for all people whom he is called to serve and his responsibility to preach and teach the Catholic faith in its fullness.

How do priests collaborate with their bishops?

The Extraordinary Synod of 1985 speaks of priests' having a participation in the bishop's ministry and thus a co-responsibility with him for the life and leadership of the church. As the Synod states:

> Between a Bishop and his presbyterate there exists a relationship founded on the Sacrament of Orders. Thus priests in a certain way make the Bishop present in the individual local assemblies of the faithful, and assume and exercise in part, in their daily work, his tasks and his solicitude (cf. *LG,* no. 28). Consequently, friendly relations and full trust must exist between Bishops and their priests. Bishops feel themselves linked in gratitude to their priests, who in the post-conciliar period have played a great part in implementing the Council (cf. *OT,* no. 1), and they wish to be close with all their strength to their priests and to give them help and support in their often difficult work, especially in parishes. (Synod, 57-58)

The priest shares in the fullness of the ministerial priesthood of the bishop. He participates in a way similar to the bishop in Jesus' roles of priest, prophet and king. The Second Vatican Council's *Decree on the Ministry and Life of Priests (Presbyterorum Ordinis)* states that priests "have as their primary duty the proclamation of the gospel of

God to all...not to teach their own wisdom but God's Word, and to summon all men urgently to conversion and holiness" (no. 4).

"The source and the apex of the whole work of preaching the gospel" is the Eucharist, over which the priest presides and where he strives to lead the faithful "to an ever-improved spirit of prayer" (no. 5). Priests extend the praise and thanksgiving of the Eucharist to the different hours of the day by reciting the Divine Office or Liturgy of the Hours.

As pastor or shepherd, the priest reflects the same fatherly care for the faithful as the bishop. Indeed, a priest is called "Father" in the Catholic tradition because he is a "father in Christ Jesus" to his people (see 1 Corinthians 4:15) and mirrors the love of God the Father to all. The decree notes that "priests must treat all with outstanding humanity, in imitation of the Lord. They should act toward men, not as seeking to win their favor but in accord with the demands of Christian doctrine and life" (no. 6).

There is no room for priests who are after popularity or who promote the values of the world: "Priests are never to put themselves at the service of any ideology or human faction. Rather, as heralds of the gospel and shepherds of the Church, they must devote themselves to the spiritual growth of the Body of Christ" (no. 6). The goal of their ministry is to lead people to Christian maturity (no. 6).

As if this were not enough of a challenge, one short section of this decree catalogues those for whom priests are to have a *special* care: the poor and the lowly, youth, married people and parents, all religious men and women and, above all, the sick and the dying (no. 6). The same section proceeds to explain that "the office of pastor is not confined to the care of the faithful as *individuals,* but is also properly extended to the *formation of a genuinely Christian community*...[which] should not only promote the care of its own faithful, but filled with a missionary zeal, it should also prepare the way to Christ for all men" (no. 6, emphasis added).

How are priests to fulfill these "superhuman" responsibilities?

It would be tragic and irresponsible to give priests this tremendous list of duties and responsibilities without a corresponding list of resources and means of support for their lives and ministries. The *Decree on the Ministry and Life of Priests* includes the following sources of strength for priests.

1. A good relationship with the bishop is key. The bishop "should regard priests as his brothers and friends... [and] should have at heart the material and especially spiritual welfare of his priests. For above all, upon the bishop rests the heavy responsibility for the sanctity of his priests" (no. 7).

2. Holiness or sanctity is the key to a priest's ability to carry out his ministry successfully, because his relationship with God is the priest's primary support. Chapter three discusses the priestly call to perfection, which is fostered especially by daily Eucharist and the daily reading of God's Word in Scripture (no. 13), as well as by the other sacraments and spiritual reading, especially "a study of the Holy Fathers and Doctors and other annals of tradition" (no. 19), mortification (no. 12), the Divine Office and personal prayer.

3. Priests must support and help each other in various ways. Older priests should help younger priests and vice versa. There should be hospitality and recreation among priests, some form of community life and associations for mutual support and growth in holiness (no. 8).

4. Laypersons may be a significant personal support and source of practical assistance in ministry for priests (no. 9). They must especially pray for their priests (no. 11). Some laypeople may even form deep personal friendships with priests.

5. Finally, priests should receive a just recompense for their service and have a "vacation each year" (no. 20).

It is encouraging to see that the support for priests includes both the spiritual and the human dimensions!

Is it true that a priest does not need to be particularly holy?

All of us, including priests, are sinners who are redeemed and being redeemed by Jesus Christ. The Council reaffirms its long-held teaching that "the grace of God can complete the work of salvation even through unworthy ministers." This is the sacramental doctrine of *ex opere operate;* the efficacy of the sacrament does not depend on the worthiness of the minister. "Yet ordinarily God desires to manifest His wonders through those who have been made particularly docile to the impulse and guidance of the Holy Spirit. Because of their intimate union with Christ and their holiness of life, these men can say with the Apostle: 'It is now no longer I that live, but Christ lives in me' (Gal. 2:20)" (*Presbyterorum Ordinis,* 12). Priests should be holy to reflect the holiness of God.

Isn't celibacy a stumbling block for many priests?

Vatican II responds that even though celibacy is "not, indeed, demanded by the very nature of the priesthood," it "accords with the priesthood" in many ways. Jesus himself recommended it (Matthew 19:12), and priests consecrated to him in this way "more easily hold fast to Him with undivided heart" (*Presbyterorum Ordinis,* 16).

The "marriage" of the priest to Christ evokes the marriage of the church to Christ that will be fully manifested when Christ returns. At that time marriage between man and woman will cease (see Luke 20:35-36), and only marriage to Christ will remain. Priests become "a vivid sign of that future world which is already present through faith and charity" (no. 16). Hence, priestly celibacy is recommended by the Lord, fosters undivided devotion and service to him and is a sign of that total union with Christ in the world to come.

The document observes that "many men today call perfect continence impossible" (no. 16). The solution proposed is for priests and the whole church to pray perseveringly for the grace of fidelity, which "is never denied to those who ask" (no. 16). Also, priests must "make use of all the supernatural and natural helps" to live this calling, especially by observing the ascetical norms that have been tested by the church's experience.

With regard to a decline in vocations, the *Decree on the Ministry and Life of Priests* emphasizes that God is committed to providing priests for his church. It is the duty of the whole Christian people to cooperate with God's will for priestly vocations "by constant prayer and other means at their disposal, so that the Church may always have the necessary number of priests to carry out her divine mission" (no. 11). Recently I heard that vocations to the priesthood in a particular diocese have increased rapidly since parishes in the diocese started devoting periods of eucharistic adoration specifically to pray for vocations to the priesthood. Prayer is a key to priestly vocations.

Other means to foster vocations are discussed at length in chapter two of the *Decree on Priestly Formation*. In this task the whole Christian community—families, parishes, teachers, priests and bishops—has a role to play.

The approach of Vatican II to priestly vocations does *not* include loosening the requirements for priesthood. In fact, it insists that "necessary standards must always be firmly maintained, even when there exists a regrettable shortage of priests. For God will not allow His Church to lack ministers if worthy candidates are admitted" (*Optatum Totius, 6*). Neither does the Council consider changing the law of celibacy for the Latin Rite Catholic Church. Pope Paul VI instructed the Council fathers to focus on explaining the beauty of priestly celibacy, not to explore alternatives to it. The Council calls the church to faith, prayer and the living of a vibrant, dedicated Christian life that will attract candidates to the priesthood.

Have we been too ready in the past forty years to consider *other solutions* to the exodus of priests from active ministry and the decline in priestly vocations? Have we really pursued the solutions recommended by the Council? Do we have enough faith to see the priesthood flourish and triumph even as a small band, like Gideon's army? Just as the small group of apostles and Christians of the primitive church "conquered the world" through their witness, a small but dedicated and holy band of celibate priests can, with God's help, accomplish his will beyond our imagining. It is upon this faith that the Council's teaching rests.

What other special counsels does the Council call priests to embrace?

Besides chastity, the Catholic Church has always honored in a special way the two other "evangelical (gospel) counsels": poverty and obedience. Priests in religious orders vow to live faithfully the evangelical counsels. Diocesan priests in Roman Catholicism promise to live in obedience to the pope, to their bishop and to any others in legitimate authority over them in the church. For example, a priest serving as an assistant pastor in a parish is obedient to the pastor. Even though diocesan priests do not take a vow of poverty, "they are invited to embrace voluntary poverty. By it they will be more clearly likened to Christ and will become more devoted to the sacred ministry. For Christ became poor for our sakes" (*Presbyterorum Ordinis*, 17).

Commitments to voluntary poverty, obedience in imitation of Christ and chaste celibacy are not easy in a world that often flaunts and praises materialism, rebellion against authority and unrestricted sex. Yet this is what makes the living of these gospel counsels central to fulfilling the promise of Vatican II. Far from being outmoded, the traditional Catholic practices of poverty, chastity and obedience (by priests, religious *and* laypeople) is a powerful witness to the presence of Jesus Christ and to the eternal values of his kingdom.

What about the ordination of women to the priesthood?

There is no direct discussion of this issue in the *Decree on the Ministry and Life of Priests* or any other document of the Second Vatican Council. However, the Council defends the rights of women (see *Gaudium et Spes*, 29) and calls for an increased participation of women in the life and mission of the church (see *Apostolicam Actuositatem*, 9).

Concerning the ordination of women, the declaration of the Sacred Congregation of the Doctrine of the Faith, *On the Question of the Admission of Women to the Ministerial Priesthood* (October 15, 1976), and the teaching of recent popes, including Pope John Paul II, affirm and explain the reasons for the unbroken tradition of the Catholic Church, now nearly two thousand years old, on this issue. On May 22, 1994, Pope John Paul II issued an apostolic letter on ordination and women *(Ordinatio Sacerdotalis)*. There he explained that the Catholic Church has no authority to ordain women to the priesthood, as there is no precedent for women's ordination in sacred Scripture or Tradition:

> Although the teaching that priestly ordination is to be reserved to men alone has been preserved by the constant and universal tradition of the church and firmly taught by the magisterium in its more recent documents, at the present time in some places it is nonetheless considered still open to debate, or the church's judgment that women are not to be admitted to ordination is considered to have a merely disciplinary force.
>
> Wherefore, in order that all doubt may be removed regarding a matter of great importance, a matter which pertains to the church's divine constitution itself, in virtue of my ministry of confirming the brethren (cf. Lk. 22:32) I declare that the church has no authority

whatsoever to confer priestly ordination on women and that this judgment is to be definitively held by all the church's faithful. (no. 4)

The question was raised whether this papal statement was definitive and whether the ordination of men only to the priesthood should be considered part of the "deposit of faith." On October 28, 1995, the Congregation for the Doctrine of the Faith responded in the affirmative: this is a "formal declaration, explicitly stating what is to be held always, everywhere, and by all as belonging to the deposit of the faith."

As we see from the example of countless women saints, both lay and religious, there has never been a lack of women leading the church to sanctity through their example and teaching. The Extraordinary Synod of 1985 urged the church to "'do its utmost so that [women] might be able to express, in the service of the Church, their own gifts, and to play a greater part in the various fields of the Church's apostolate' (cf. *Apostolicam Actuositatem*, 9). May pastors gratefully accept and promote the collaboration of women in ecclesial activity" (Synod, 58).

Did Vatican II introduce any significant changes in priestly formation?

Vatican II's *Decree on Priestly Formation* presents some general rules that episcopal conferences throughout the world need to apply and sometimes adapt. The document emphasizes the importance of sound theological, spiritual, pastoral and liturgical formation. It places equal weight on seminarians' intellectual formation, balanced human development and emotional maturity (no. 3).

There is no indication that seminarians should be artificially isolated from the world or their families. Their "course of studies ought to be so arranged that students can continue them elsewhere without disadvantage if they choose another state of life" (no. 3). They should be "duly aware of the duties and dignity of Christian marriage…as well [as] the superiority of virginity consecrated to Christ" (no. 10).

What might be most surprising to some is chapter five on ecclesiastical studies. Seminarians are still instructed to "acquire a command of Latin." Philosophy remains at the heart of priestly training, working harmoniously with the study of theology.

The Extraordinary Synod of 1985 calls attention to article 16 of this decree concerning the manner of teaching theology.

1. Theological studies for seminarians should be based on divine revelation and authentic Catholic doctrine. They should be trained to "understand that doctrine, profoundly nourish their own spiritual lives with it, and be able to proclaim it, unfold it, and defend it in their priestly ministry." Seminarians should be trained with special diligence in sacred Scripture, "which ought to be the soul of all theology."

2. Biblical themes are to be presented *first* in dogmatic theology, followed by a historical study of the transmission and development of doctrine through the Catholic tradition.

3. A strictly Thomistic education is not required, but the meaning of doctrine should be penetrated "more deeply with the help of speculative reason exercised under the tutelage of St. Thomas."

4. Finally, all other theological studies should flow from the mystery of Christ and the history of salvation, and moral theology's "scientific exposition should be more thoroughly nourished by scriptural teaching." The education of seminarians should aim "at a genuine and deep formation of students" (no. 17). Practice in developing the call to the priesthood in pastoral areas is also

an indispensable part of this formation. Continuing education of priests is strongly encouraged (no. 22).

The Extraordinary Synod of 1985 particularly highlights the need for formation in holiness. Seminarians "must be seriously introduced to a daily spiritual life: prayer, meditation, the reading of the Bible, the sacraments of Penance and the Eucharist." In their pastoral ministry and activity they need to find spiritual nourishment so that they might truly build up God's people by their example of holiness and offer correct spiritual counsel and guidance.

Is this a "rosy" picture of the priesthood?

No. The last paragraph of the *Decree on the Ministry and Life of Priests* looks at some of the difficulties that confront priestly life today, including loneliness, social pressures, loss of faith and "the seeming sterility of their past labors" (no. 22). The *Decree on Priestly Formation* states that in training seminarians, "no hardship of priestly life should go unmentioned," including the challenge of celibacy (no. 9).

However, amid the challenges and trials of priestly life, there is an unshakeable source of strength and hope:

> Priests should remember that in performing their tasks they are never alone. Relying on the power of Almighty God and believing in Christ Who called them to share in His priesthood, they should devote themselves to their ministry with complete trust, knowing that God can intensify in them the ability to love.
>
> Let them be mindful too that they have as partners their brothers in the priesthood and indeed the faithful of the entire world. For all priests cooperate in carrying out the saving plan of God. (*Presbyterorum Ordinis*, 22)

With God, their brother priests and the faithful people of God to support them, priests will find strength and hope even in their most difficult struggles.

What about the renewal of religious life?

The *Decree on the Appropriate Renewal of Religious Life (Perfectae caritatis)* called for two things to be undertaken simultaneously: First "a continuous *return* to the sources of all Christian life and to the original inspiration behind a given community, and [second] an *adjustment* [or adaptation] of the community to the changed conditions of the times" (no. 2, emphasis added).

The decree specified that this renewal "should go forward under the influence of the Holy Spirit and the guidance of the Church" according to certain principles.

1. The "following of Christ as proposed by the gospel...is to be regarded by all communities as their supreme law," since this is the fundamental norm of religious life.

2. Each religious community has its own special character and purpose, which is enshrined in "the spirit of founders" and in other traditions at the heart of each community's heritage.

3. "All communities should participate in the life of the Church," taking as their own and fostering in every possible way the church's objectives in every field. The mission and goals of the whole church are also to be those of each religious community.

4. Members of religious communities must be aware of contemporary human conditions and of the needs of the church, so that they can combine "the burning zeal of an apostle with wise

judgments" about the circumstances of the modern world and hence come to the aid of others more effectively.

5.   Finally, "the religious life is intended above all else to lead those who embrace it to an imitation of Christ and to union with God through the profession of the evangelical counsels.... Even the most desirable changes made on behalf of contemporary needs will fail unless a renewal of spirit gives life to them. Indeed such an interior renewal must always be accorded the leading role even in the promotion of exterior works" (*Perfectae Caritatis,* 2).

These principles are to guide the renewal of religious life. Special attention must be given to the last point about the importance of a "renewal of spirit" or interior renewal. The source of this renewal is the gospel of Christ and a discovery or rediscovery of the religious community's foundation and its purpose in the modern world.

This conciliar teaching led some Third Order Franciscans to begin studying the origins of their particular branch of the Franciscan family. Although hundreds of small Third Order Franciscan groups exist around the world, they had a very diverse understanding of their particular mission and gift for the church. This historical research and meetings of Third Order Franciscan groups from around the world yielded an agreement on the common identity and mission of this branch of the Franciscans. This has led to updated constitutions and, more significantly, a reunification of Franciscan life and spirituality among the Third Order Regular Franciscans and the lay secular Franciscan Order that is associated with it.

It should be noted that there are no directives in the Vatican II decree that justify a compromise of basic gospel values; rather it identifies the divine call of "dying to sin" and "renouncing the world" (no. 5). The decree highlights the living of the evangelical counsels with zeal (nos. 12, 13, 14). Community life should follow the example of the primitive church (no. 15).

There is to be a certain streamlining or simplification of religious life to remove unnecessary rules and distinctions between persons (no. 15) and to "avoid every appearance of luxury, of excessive wealth, and accumulation of possessions" (no. 13). Religious habits may be adopted that are more suited to modern circumstances, but they should remain "simple and modest, at once poor and becoming" (no. 17) as a sign of consecrated life.

All of these changes are designed to focus attention upon the heart of religious life and commitment. Even when adaptations or adjustments to the needs of the present time are made, the decree states that "the missionary spirit" of the religious community should by all means be maintained (no. 20).

Whether applied to contemplative communities (no. 7), clerical or lay institutes devoted to the apostolate (no. 8), monasteries (no. 9), lay religious communities of women or men (no. 10) or secular institutes (no. 11), the focus of the *Decree on the Appropriate Renewal of Religious Life* is a more fervent and dedicated following of Jesus Christ and his teaching in the modern world.

If this is so, why have so many left the religious life?

Confusion was not *caused* primarily by the Council document. The principles stated there are sound and readily understandable. What happened?

Religious communities were challenged to a monumental task: to reexamine every aspect of their identity and lives and to conform these to the standards of the gospel, their founding vision, their heritage and the new circumstances and needs of the time. This is a tall order!

Obviously, some difficulty would result when members of religious communities met to discuss and decide how to remain loyal to the spirit of their founder and how to adapt to modern circumstances without compromising essentials. It was a matter of balancing many important values and demands, especially when what was right and wrong was not clear but a matter of discernment. In the process many religious whose vocation was not firm, or who had depended unduly on certain external or secondary expressions of religious life, naturally had a difficult time.

Second, there are many forces in the world vying for the allegiance and support of religious communities. In the process of renewal, some communities lost a clear sense of the basic identity and purpose of religious life. Some may have lost the sense of their own unique calling and mission, instead becoming caught up in other agendas and causes. Without a firm grasp of the reason for and importance of one's identity and mission in Christ and his church, it is understandable how a religious community could struggle, decline and even disappear.

What is the solution to this crisis in religious life?

Forty years after the Council, we see certain religious communities flourishing and joyfully carrying on the mission of Christ in full loyalty to the teaching of the church. We have witnessed the phenomenal growth of Blessed Teresa of Calcutta's Missionaries of Charity and other religious orders rooted in prayer and loyalty to the church's magisterium. It would seem reasonable to look for guidance and direction from these flourishing communities who have responded faithfully to the authentic norms of renewal as presented in this Vatican II decree.

Catholics also should look to the example and intercession of Mary, the Mother of God. The decree on religious life closes: "With the prayerful aid of that most loving Virgin Mary, God's Mother, 'whose life is a rule of life for all,' religious communities will experience a daily growth in numbers, and will yield a richer harvest of fruits that bring salvation" (no. 25).

Conclusion

In the last two chapters we have explored what the Second Vatican Council teaches about the unique gifts and call of the laity, bishops, priests, deacons and religious. They are called together as members of one people, working together to advance the cause of Jesus Christ and the mission for which he founded the church. Above all, that mission is to bring the good news of salvation in Jesus Christ to all people. The next chapter will explore that great "missionary challenge" to the people of God: to make disciples of all nations (see Matthew 28:19).

Christus Dominus, Presbyterorum Ordinis, Optatem Totius and *Perfectae Caritatis* in the *Catechism of the Catholic Church*

In the *Catechism* there are fourteen references to the *Decree on the Pastoral Office of Bishops,* mainly in the explanation of the hierarchy of the church in Part I (nos. 882-886) and in Part II regarding episcopal ordination (nos. 1548-1586). References to the documents on priests and priestly formation are cited twenty-four times and twice, respectively, mainly in the discussion of the celebration of the sacraments (nos. 1136-1175) and particularly the sacrament of holy orders (nos. 1548-1582) in Part II of the *Catechism.* The decree on religious life is cited seven times in the *Catechism,* with regards to the consecrated life in Part I (nos. 914-918), virginity for the sake of the kingdom (no. 1620) in Part II and prayer (nos. 2684-2691) in Part IV. There are also many references from *Lumen Gentium* chapter three (on bishops and priests) and chapter six (on religious).

Recent Magisterial Documents on Bishops

Pope John Paul II. *Apostolos Suos (On the Theological and Juridical Nature of Episcopal Conferences).* May 21, 1998.

Pope John Paul II. *Pastores Gregis (Post-Synodal Apostolic Exhortation on the Office of Bishops),* October 16, 2003. *Origins* 33, no. 22 (November 6, 2003).

Recent Magisterial Documents on Priests and Priestly Formation

Congregation for the Clergy. "Directory on the Ministry and Life of Priests," 1994.

Congregation for the Clergy. "The Priest, Pastor and Leader of the Parish Community," August 4, 2002.

Pope John Paul II. *Pastores dabo Vobis (I Will Give you Shepherds: On the Formation of Priests in the Circumstances of the Present Day),* 1992.

Recent Magisterial Documents on Religious

Congregation for Institutes of Consecrated Life and Societies of Apostolic Life. "Starting Afresh from Christ: A Renewal Commitment to Consecrated Life in the Third Millennium," May 2002. *Origins* 32, no. 8 (July 4, 2002).

Pope John Paul II. *Vita Consecrata (The Consecrated Life).* March 25, 1996. *Origins* 25, no. 41 (April 4, 1996).

Favorite Quotes from *Christus Dominus*

In exercising their duty of teaching, they should announce the gospel of Christ to men, a task which is eminent among the chief duties of bishops. (no. 12)

In exercising his office of father and pastor, a bishop should stand in the midst of his people as one who serves. Let him be a good shepherd who knows his sheep and whose sheep know him. Let him be a true father who excels in the spirit of love and solicitude for all and to whose divinely conferred authority all gratefully submit themselves. Let him so gather and mold the whole family of his flock that everyone, conscious of his own duties, may live and work in the communion of love. (no. 16)

Favorite Quote from *Optatam Totius*

The task of fostering vocations devolves on the whole Christian community, which should do so in the first place by living in a fully Christian way. Outstanding contributions are made to this work by families which are alive with the spirit of faith, love, and reverence and which serve as a kind of introductory seminary; and by parishes in whose pulsing vitality people themselves have a part. (no. 2)

Favorite Quote from *Perfectae Caritatis*

The appropriate renewal of religious life involves two simultaneous processes: (1) a continuous return to the sources of all Christian life and to the original inspiration behind a given community and (2) an adjustment of the community to the changed conditions of the times. It is according to the following principles that such renewal should go forward under the influence of the Holy Spirit and the guidance of the Church. a) Since the fundamental norm of the religious life is a following of Christ as proposed by the gospel, such is to be regarded by all communities as the supreme rule. (no. 2)

Favorite Quotes from *Presbyterorum Ordinis*

By their vocation and ordination, priests of the New Testament are indeed set apart in a certain sense within the midst of God's people. But this is so, not that they may be separated from this people or from any man, but that they may be totally dedicated to the work for which the Lord has raised them up. (no. 3)

Toward all men...priests have the duty of sharing the gospel truth in which they themselves rejoice in the Lord.... The task of priests is not to teach their own wisdom but God's Word, and to summon all men urgently to conversion and to holiness. (no. 4)

CHAPTER TWELVE

Proclaiming the Gospel

This chapter will discuss three documents of the Second Vatican Council that are closely related: the *Declaration on Religious Freedom (Dignitatis Humanae)*, the *Declaration on the Relationship of the Church to Non-Christian Religions (Nostra Aetate)* and the *Decree on the Missionary Activity of the Church (Ad Gentes Divinitus)*. What these documents have in common is that they all describe basic attitudes that Catholics must have as they approach non-Christians. We must defend the freedom of others to believe what they want and to practice their religion freely. We must respect whatever is true and good in other religions. And we must tirelessly witness in word and deed to the fullness of truth revealed in Jesus Christ to those who do not yet know or believe in him.

There are many misconceptions about the teaching of Vatican II on these topics. Some Catholics, even missionaries, are not aware that the Council clearly teaches that the gospel of Christ must be proclaimed. This is an urgent command from the Lord that is central to the church's mission. Although missionaries should also seek to alleviate hunger and promote the human development of the people to whom they are sent, their primary mission is to lead others to faith and life in Christ and to his church, through which people will find spiritual nourishment and eternal life.

A second common misconception is that the Second Vatican Council encouraged Catholics to seek wisdom and truth from non-Christian religions, even to incorporate certain non-Christian practices into their lives as Christians. This is not the case. It is true that in missionary countries some non-Christian beliefs and practices that are compatible with Christianity may be incorporated into the church's faith and life in some way. However, this is far different, for example, from Western Christians' seeking to incorporate non-Christian elements from other cultures into their own religious practice and belief—as if the rich spiritual tradition of Western Christianity were inadequate or incomplete.

Why would a person who owned the world's richest gold mine go to the ends of the earth to obtain a few gold pieces from other mines? The owner might examine the pieces out of curiosity or for comparison, but certainly it would not be necessary to possess them. Catholics should thoroughly mine the rich storehouse of saints and mystics of their own tradition before seeking nuggets of truth elsewhere.

Finally, lest Catholics fall into arrogance or pride, the Second Vatican Council stresses that all Catholics—even bishops and priests—need to be converted ever more deeply to the Lord so that we can be more effective witnesses to Jesus Christ in word and deed. The missionary activity of the church is never completed. It requires our constant transformation by the grace of Christ.

Hence, the challenge presented here by the Second Vatican Council can be simply stated: How do we fulfill Jesus' great commission to his followers, "Go therefore and make disciples of all nations" (Matthew 28:19)?

In the modern context we recognize that this is part of a broader question that is often asked today: How do Christians view and relate to those who are not Christian? Many specific questions flow from this one: Are they saved? Should Christians work with non-Christians on common projects? Should we dialogue with them or simply try to convert them? Do non-Christians have anything to teach Christians? Could we adopt or adapt some of their religious practices? How should Christianity be adapted to other cultures? If non-Christian religions are *not* true, should they have a right to exist, or do they have any rights?

Let us turn to the Council documents themselves for responses to these questions.

What is the approach of the *Declaration on Religious Freedom?*

The *Declaration on Religious Freedom* is formally addressed to all people. Sometimes called the American contribution to the Council, it embodies the ideal of religious freedom very similar to that enunciated in the United States Constitution, including the very phrase concerning the "free exercise of religion" that is found in the First Amendment (no. 1).

However, the concern for religious rights and freedom has been constant in the church for centuries. This declaration openly proclaims its intention "to develop the doctrine of recent Popes on the inviolable rights of the human person and on the constitutional order of society" (no. 1).

This document may be seen as the crown of a long history of the church's deepening insight into this subject, guided by the Holy Spirit. Religious freedom was a hallmark of the teaching of Pope John Paul II in his speeches and pastoral visits.

Although this chapter focuses on the implications of this declaration for the relationship of Catholics to non-Christians, *Dignitatis Humanae* has monumental significance for the causes of all people who are struggling to secure their religious freedom. Until recently this struggle was often seen primarily in countries that were openly atheistic or anti-religious. In an ironic twist, many of those countries are now opening up to religious freedom, while in democratic countries like the United States, the free exercise of religion is being threatened and challenged in courts and legislative bodies.

What is the basis of the Council's teaching on religious freedom?

The *Declaration on Religious Freedom* is addressed to all people because it wishes to propound principles that deserve universal recognition. The two basic principles that underlie this concept are (1) the dignity of the human person, which dictates that each person be able to exercise responsible freedom and to act on his or her own judgment, especially in matters of conscience such as religion; and (2) the duty of government and society to protect and foster individual rights and freedoms.

The document's argument develops in this way:

1. All people are bound to seek the truth and to embrace the truth they come to know.

2. The nature of truth is such that a person accepts something as true because he or she is convinced of it.

3. Therefore, the acceptance of the truths of religion must be made freely, without any coercion, whether physical or psychological. "Nor is anyone to be restrained from acting in accordance with his own beliefs, whether privately or publicly, whether alone or in association with others, within due limits" (no. 2).

4. Because the right to religious freedom is known both through reason and God's revelation, this freedom is to be recognized by governments and societies as an inalienable civil right (no. 2).

How does religious freedom affect our approach to non-Christians?

Lest the Council be accused of teaching religious indifferentism (that is, that one religion is as good as another), the first paragraph of the

Declaration on Religious Freedom announces: "We believe that this one true religion subsists in the Catholic and apostolic Church, to which the Lord Jesus committed the duty of spreading it abroad among all men" (no. 1). Catholics firmly believe that the Christian faith, as taught in fullness by the Catholic Church, is the one religion containing the fullness of truth, which God desires all people to embrace.

Nonetheless, this true religion must be embraced in authentic *freedom.* Non-Christians have a right to act according to their beliefs and consciences, especially in religious matters. Even in countries where Catholicism is established by law as the "official" religion, it is essential that the rights of all citizens and religious bodies be recognized and practically respected (no. 6).

Likewise, in non-Christian nations the Catholic Church claims freedom for herself and for all others. Individuals and groups should be able to practice and profess their faith freely and openly, in private and in public, without restraint or coercion, as long as the rights of others and the just requirements of the public order are respected and upheld (no. 13).

Catholics reject all forms of coercion or undue pressure in bringing non-Christians to the Catholic faith. This would include promises of political or economic advantage, food or other gifts that would be offered to a person for becoming a Catholic. "In spreading religious faith and in introducing religious practices, everyone ought at all times to refrain from any manner of action which might seem to carry a hint of coercion or of a kind of persuasion that would be dishonorable or unworthy, especially when dealing with poor or uneducated people" (*Dignitatis Humanae,* 4; see also *Ad Gentes Divinitus,* 13).

The *Declaration on Religious Freedom* openly admits that Catholics have sometimes violated this teaching, although the church has always firmly taught the error of such measures. They are unworthy of the gospel and opposed to human freedom and dignity (no. 12).

How does Jesus exemplify this teaching?

Both Jesus and the early church acknowledged the rights of civil government. Yet the early church "did not hesitate to speak out against governing powers which set themselves in opposition to the holy will of God: 'We must obey God rather than man' (Acts 5:29)" (*Dignitatis Humanae*, 11).

Both Jesus and the early church boldly proclaimed the truth without imposing it by force on anyone. "They preached the Word of God in the full confidence that there was resident in this Word itself a divine power able to destroy all the forces arrayed against God and to bring man to faith in Christ and to His service" (*Dignitatis Humanae*, 11).

What about the relationship of the church to non-Christian religions?

The *Declaration on the Relationship of the Church to Non-Christian Religions* states that the church "gives primary consideration in this document to what human beings have in common and to what promotes fellowship among them" (no. 1). Realizing that in this age people of different faiths are being drawn closer together, the Catholic Church wishes to present here the basis for respect, cooperation and fellowship among them.

Catholics are instructed to recognize and respect what is true and holy in non-Christian religions (no. 2) and to root out all discrimination based on beliefs. This latter point is based on Scripture's teaching that we cannot claim to love God, whom we do not see, if we fail to love our brother or sister whom we do see (see 1 John 4:20). God created all people in his own image, and Christians must therefore act respectfully toward all.

How do we regard what is "true and holy" in non-Christian religions?

The declaration notes some particular points of agreement between the Catholic faith and Hinduism, Buddhism (no. 2) and Islam (no. 3). These religions "often reflect a ray of that Truth which enlightens all men" (no. 2). The church exhorts Catholics to "prudently and lovingly…acknowledge, preserve, and promote the spiritual and moral goods" found among these people (no. 2).

Fully one third of the declaration is devoted to the relationship of Catholics to the Jewish people, who share with Christians a close spiritual bond. The Catholic Church recognizes that "the Jews still remain most dear to God because of their fathers" and wishes to foster "that mutual understanding and respect which is the fruit above all of biblical and theological studies, and of brotherly dialogue" (no. 4).

It is clear from this that neither the Jewish people nor other non-Christians possess the fullness of truth in Christ that resides in the Catholic Church. Nor is there any indication in this document that Catholics should adopt or integrate into their own beliefs or practices any of those found in non-Christian religions. We are to acknowledge and affirm in them whatever "ray" or portion of the truth they possess.

It is disconcerting to observe that Catholics today often seek spiritual truth and religious practices in non-Christian religions, while failing to explore and integrate all the rich treasures found in the two-thousand-year spiritual tradition of Catholic Christianity. There is a big difference between respecting truths and goodness found in non-Christian religions (which the Council approves) and adopting these beliefs as part of Catholic life, worship or theology, which the Council does not call for.

What about religious persecution and discrimination?

The declaration calls for an end to all quarrels and "any discrimination against men or harassment of them because of their race, color, condition of life, or religion" (no. 5). It calls for Christians and Muslims "to forget the past and to strive sincerely for mutual understanding" (no. 3).

A serious statement of reconciliation is made regarding the Jewish people. Article 4 states first that the death of Jesus "cannot be blamed upon all the Jews then living, without distinction, nor upon the Jews of today." Second, the Catholic Church "repudiates all persecutions" and "deplores the hatred, persecutions, and displays of anti-Semitism directed against the Jews at any time or from any source."[1]

Third, the Catholic Church proclaims that Christ "freely underwent His passion and death because of the sins of all men, so that all might attain salvation. It is, therefore, the duty of the Church's preaching to proclaim the cross of Christ as the sign of God's all-embracing love and as the fountain from which every grace flows" (no. 4).

Rather than discrimination or persecution, the Second Vatican Council points to the sacrificial death of Christ as the sign of God's unconditional love for all people. Christians are to reflect this love and compassion in their attitudes and dealings with all.

Can non-Christians be saved?

Yes, non-Christians *can* be saved, but not all *will* be saved. "His saving designs extend to all men (cf. Wis. 8:1; Acts 14:17; Rom. 2:6-7; 1 Tim. 2:4)" (*Nostra Aetate,* 1). The *Dogmatic Constitution on the Church* explains:

> Those also can attain to everlasting salvation who through no fault of their own do not know the gospel of Christ or His Church, yet sin-

cerely seek God and, moved by grace, strive by their deeds to do His will as it is known to them through the dictates of conscience. Nor does divine Providence deny the help necessary for salvation to those who, without blame on their part, have not yet arrived at an explicit knowledge of God, but who strive to live a good life, thanks to His grace. (no. 16)

We conclude that non-Christians *can* be saved if they meet a number of important conditions:

1. through no fault of their own they do not *know* the gospel of Christ (and thus have not rejected the truth);

2. they sincerely seek God;

3. they strive by God's grace to live a good life and do God's will as they know it through the dictates of conscience.

Do non-Christians then need to hear the gospel of Jesus Christ?

While it is *possible* for non-Christians to be saved, by the sheer mercy of God, the *Dogmatic Constitution on the Church* explains that the goodness and truth that may be found in non-Christian religions are only partial and dim reflections of the fullness of life, grace and truth that reside in the gospel of Jesus Christ. The constitution states: "Whatever goodness or truth is found among [non-Christians] is looked upon by the Church as a preparation for the gospel. She regards such qualities as given by Him who enlightens all men so that they may finally have life" (no. 16; see also *Ad Gentes Divinitus,* 2).

In sum, God intends the "rays" of the truth and goodness found in non-Christian religions to lead their members to the source and fullness of the truth found in the Son of God made man, Jesus Christ. Possessing partial truth and goodness does *not* always and necessarily lead to full truth and goodness, nor to eternal salvation. The constitution boldly states: "But rather often men, deceived by the Evil One, have become caught up in futile reasoning and have exchanged the truth of God for a lie, serving the creature rather than the Creator (cf. Rom. 1:21, 25). Or some there are who, living and dying in a world without God, are subject to utter hopelessness" (*Lumen Gentium,* 16).

The constitution acknowledges that the kingdom of God is engaged in a cosmic battle against the evil one and that there are many casualties. Satan is striving to lead people away from the truth and goodness. "Rather often" (not "rarely" or even "half the time") he succeeds. The problem with possessing only part of the truth of Christ and a portion of his grace is that it is easier to end up denying God, serving false gods (including money, power, sex and so on) or falling into despair.

What are Christians to do about this? The very next sentence gives us the answer: "Consequently, to promote the glory of God and procure the salvation of all such men, and mindful of the command of the Lord, 'Preach the gospel to every creature' (Mk. 16:16), the Church painstakingly fosters her missionary work" (*Lumen Gentium,* 16).

Thus we have the reason behind the missionary challenge to Catholics. Without the proclamation of the gospel of Jesus Christ, "rather often" those who do not know Christ will fail to attain salvation. Even more importantly, Jesus himself commanded his followers to preach the gospel to every creature and to make disciples of all nations (Matthew 28:19). God's will is that all come to salvation through believing the Good News of Jesus Christ. The Council declares: "This missionary activity finds its reason in the will of God, 'who wishes all men to be saved and to come to the knowledge of the truth. For there is one God, and one Mediator between God and men, himself man, Christ Jesus, who gave himself a ransom for all' (1 Tim. 2:4-5), 'neither is there salvation in any other' (Acts 4:12)" (*Ad Gentes Divinitus,* 7).

If this were not yet clear enough, the next section of the *Dogmatic Constitution on the Church* (no. 17) is dedicated entirely to the church's missionary outreach. The Holy Spirit compels the church to proclaim the gospel, since God has established Christ as "the source of salvation for the whole world." The same Spirit prepares those who hear the gospel to believe it and be baptized, so that they are snatched from "the slavery of error" and invited to grow up into full maturity in Christ.

In his encyclical letter *On the Permanent Validity of the Church's Missionary Mandate,* often referred to as *Mission of the Redeemer,* Pope John Paul II quotes Acts 4:12, in which Peter says there is salvation in no other name but that of Jesus. The pope writes: "This statement…has a universal value, since for all people—Jews and Gentiles alike—salvation can come only from Jesus Christ" (*Redemptoris Missio,* 5).

The Council boldly states that whatever good is found in non-Christian religions "is not only saved from destruction" by acceptance of the gospel of Christ "but is also healed, ennobled, and perfected unto the glory of God, the confusion of the devil, and the happiness of man." This missionary work is so essential to the life and mission of the church that every disciple of Christ is obligated to participate in it according to his or her ability (*Lumen Gentium,* 17; see also *Ad Gentes Divinitus,* 9).

Isn't there a conflict between the call to dialogue and the call to conversion?

No. Concerning dialogue with non-Christians, the Extraordinary Synod of 1985 stated:

> Dialogue must not be opposed to mission. Authentic dialogue tends to bring the human person to open up and communicate his interiority to the one with whom he is speaking. Moreover, all Christians have

received from Christ the mission to make all people disciples of Christ (Mt. 28:18). In this sense God can use the dialogue between Christians and non-Christians and between Christians and non-believers as a pathway for communicating the fullness of grace. (Synod, 65)

When Christians open themselves to communicate what is most important to them with non-Christians in authentic dialogue, they will witness to the gospel of Jesus Christ, as well as listening to the important values and beliefs of the partner in the dialogue. In this way the dialogue may become, as Pope Paul VI first called it, a "dialogue of salvation." The work of Catholic missionaries, then, may include or even begin with "dialogue," but this must always lead to a clear call to faith in God through Jesus Christ, through whom we receive life and salvation.

What is the missionary task of the church, and how does it differ from evangelization?

The *Decree on the Missionary Activity of the Church (Ad Gentes Divinitus)* explains that "the pilgrim Church is missionary by her very nature. For it is from the mission of the Son and the mission of the Holy Spirit that she takes her origin, in accordance with the decree of God the Father" (no. 2).

The church itself is the result of God's own missionary activity! The Father sent Jesus on mission to establish the kingdom on earth (no. 3). The Father and the Son sent the Holy Spirit on mission to give birth to the church at Pentecost (no. 4). The church continues the mission of spreading the message and the reality of the kingdom of God "in obedience to Christ's command and in response to the grace and love of the Holy Spirit" (no. 5).

The general term for spreading the gospel and converting others to Jesus Christ is *evangelization.* Pope Paul VI's great apostolic exhortation *On Evangelization in the Modern World* (December 8, 1975) explains that the church "exists in order to evangelize, that is to say in order to preach and teach, to be the channel of the gift of grace, to reconcile sinners with God" (no. 14).

The Extraordinary Synod notes that "evangelization takes place through witnesses. The witness gives his testimony not only with words, but also with his life." It is not coincidental that the Greek word for testimony is *martyrium*. The ultimate witness is the martyr, who testifies by losing his life for the faith.

What then distinguishes missionary activity from evangelization? The term *missions* usually refers to "preaching the gospel and planting the Church among peoples or groups who do not yet believe in Christ.... The specific *purpose* of this missionary activity is evangelization and the planting of the Church among those peoples and groups where she has not yet taken root.... The chief *means* of this implantation is the preaching of the gospel of Jesus Christ" (*Ad Gentes Divinitus,* 6, emphasis added).

Is missionary activity really all that urgent?

In 1965 the Second Vatican Council reported that "the gospel message has not yet been heard, or scarcely so, by two billion human beings. And their number is increasing daily" (*Ad Gentes Divinitus,* 10). Even if more people have heard of Jesus Christ, millions do not yet believe in him. Recent statistics estimate that the world population now comprises about 19 percent Catholics, 14 percent other Christians and 67 percent non-Christians. Two thirds of the world's people do not believe in Jesus Christ! The urgency of missionary activity is evident.

The *Decree on the Church's Missionary Activity,* article 7, sets forth a bold and impassioned challenge to the church to engage in missionary activity. The document concludes:

Therefore, *all* must be converted to Him as He is made known in the Church's preaching. *All* must be incorporated into Him by baptism, and into the Church which is His body.... Though God in ways known only to Himself can lead those inculpably ignorant of the gospel to that faith without which it is impossible to please Him (Heb. 11:6), yet a necessity lies upon the Church (cf. 1 Cor. 9:16), and at the same time a sacred duty, to preach the gospel. Hence missionary activity today as always retains its power and necessity. (no. 7, emphasis added)

Pope John Paul II's *Redemptoris Missio* reinforces and expands upon the teaching of Vatican II on the missionary activity of the church:

Above all, there is a new awareness that *missionary activity is a matter for all Christians*, for all dioceses and parishes, Church institutions and associations.

Nevertheless, in this "new springtime" of Christianity there is an undeniable negative tendency, and the present document is meant to help overcome it. Missionary activity specifically directed "to the nations" (*ad gentes*) appears to be waning, and this tendency is certainly not in line with the directives of the Council and of subsequent statements of the Magisterium. Difficulties both internal and external have weakened the Church's missionary thrust toward non-Christians, a fact which must arouse concern among all who believe in Christ. For in the Church's history, missionary drive has always been a sign of vitality, just as its lessening is a sign of a crisis of faith....

I wish to invite the Church to *renew her missionary commitment*. The present document has as its goal an interior renewal of faith and Christian life. For missionary activity renews the Church, revitalizes faith and Christian identity, and offers fresh enthusiasm and new incentive. *Faith is strengthened when it is given to others!* It is in commitment to the Church's universal mission that the new evangelization of Christian peoples will find inspiration and support.

But what moves me even more strongly to proclaim the urgency of missionary evangelization is the fact that it is the primary service which the Church can render to every individual and to all humanity in the modern world, a world which has experienced marvelous achievements but which seem to have lost its sense of ultimate realities and of existence itself. "Christ the Redeemer," I wrote in my first encyclical, "fully reveals man to himself.... The person who wishes to understand himself thoroughly...must...draw near to Christ.... [The] Redemption that took place through the cross has definitively restored to man his dignity and given back meaning to his life in the world."

...The number of those who do not know Christ and do not belong to the Church is constantly on the increase. Indeed, since the end of the Council it has almost doubled. When we consider this immense portion of humanity which is loved by the Father and for whom he sent his Son, the urgency of the Church's mission is obvious. (nos. 2, 3)

Why do many Catholics lack zeal to evangelize or to do missionary work?

"Why did twelve fishermen convert the world, and why are half a billion Christians unable to repeat the feat? The Spirit makes the difference."[2]

That the Holy Spirit is the source of zeal and power for evangelization and mission is evident from the Acts of the Apostles and Jesus' own teaching. This is why Pope John XXIII accompanied the convocation of Vatican II with prayer for a "new Pentecost," in which the Lord would "renew his wonders in our time." Pope John Paul II gave a telling title to the third chapter of his encyclical letter *Mission of the Redeemer:* "The Holy Spirit: The Principal Agent of Mission."

Many signs indicate that the Catholic Church has experienced some of the grace of Pentecost since the close of the Council. Nonetheless, in his December 1988 apostolic letter on the laity, Pope John Paul II called for a *re-evangelization* of Christian countries, whose "moral and spiritual patrimony...[is under attack from] secularization and a spread of sects. Only a re-evangelization can assure the growth of a clear and deep faith" (*Christifideles Laici,* 34).

Obviously, countries that are losing or weakening in the Catholic faith will not readily be in a position to evangelize or send missionaries to others. The same is true on a personal level. If we lack the zeal to evangelize others, either we are not fully converted or empowered to witness ourselves, or else we lack an understanding of the church's missionary nature. The Extraordinary Synod of 1985 states bluntly: "The evangelization of non-believers in fact presupposes the self-evangelization of the baptized and also, in a certain sense, of deacons, priests, and Bishops" (Synod, 50).

How remarkable that a group of bishops would openly acknowledge that even they need to evangelize themselves! And yet only this sort of humility will enable Catholics to turn to God in prayer and repentance. We need to ask him for the same boldness and power of the Holy Spirit that first filled the apostles and the early church at Pentecost. Only this will enable Catholics to evangelize others and to support the missionaries God calls to plant the gospel where it has never been heard.

I frequently hear from people about non-denominational or Pentecostal churches that are made up largely of ex-Catholics. Apparently many Catholics think that they have not heard the basic gospel message clearly proclaimed in the Catholic Church and have gone elsewhere. Our own church needs to be re-evangelized, so it is clear to all that the Catholic Church is rooted and constantly nourished in the *full gospel* of Christ.

The saying "You can't give what you ain't got" is also an important truth. Only after this re-evangelization can Catholics undertake what Pope John Paul II set forth as "a giant step forward" in his challenge to the laity: a renewed effort in the evangelization of the world.

> The Church today ought to take *a giant step forward* in her evangelization effort, and enter into *a new stage of history* in her missionary dynamism. In a day when speedy travel and communication make the world increasingly smaller, the Church community ought to strengthen the bonds among its members, exchange vital energies and

means, and commit itself as a group to a unique and common mission of proclaiming and living the Gospel. (*Christifideles Laici*, 35, emphasis added)

Does missionary activity include social justice and service to the poor?

Yes. Missionary activity includes care for persons in every aspect of their lives, including physical needs and human rights and freedoms. A complete view of missionary activity contains many elements. We see this in chapter two of the *Decree on Missionary Activity*, which divides mission work into three parts.

The first part discussed is "Christian witness" in both word and deed. This section recommends drawing people to Christ "through truly human conversations" and insists on the importance of knowing the people, their culture, social life and national and religious traditions (no. 11).

Christian charity extended toward all is at the heart of this witness. The examples offered demonstrate that there is no human struggle or concern outside the scope of the church's missionary endeavor. Rather than contribute mere material progress and prosperity, the ultimate goal of the missionary is "to render to others true witness of Christ, and to work for their salvation" (no. 12).

The second part focuses on the church's missionary task of *preaching the gospel*. Christians should take advantage of any open door and announce "to all men…with confidence and constancy…the living God, and He whom He has sent for the salvation of all, Jesus Christ" (no. 13). The section notes that an ever deeper conversion must complete the initial conversion to Christ (no. 13).

The third part deals with *forming the Christian community*. Missionaries are urged to "raise up congregations of the faithful" as signs of God's presence in the world and as means of forming those who have been converted to Christ (no. 15).

To sum up, "it is not enough for the Christian people to be present and organized in a given nation. Nor is it enough for them to carry out an apostolate of good example. They are organized and present for the purpose of announcing Christ to their non-Christian fellow citizens by word and deed, and of aiding them toward the full reception of Christ" (no. 15).

Who carries out the missionary work of the church?

Many are involved, and a variety of ministries are necessary. The bishops who oversee the work must have a missionary vision and zeal. Priests and deacons are needed, and new churches are encouraged to form their own indigenous clergy. Men and women catechists are of "maximum importance," especially due to the shortage of priests (no. 17). Religious orders are important, too. Finally, the laity "have the greatest importance," especially as they bring the gospel into the everyday life of secular society (no. 15).

What is the goal of missionary work?

The final goal of this work is not simply the conversion of individuals but the planting of new churches. The *Decree on Missionary Activity* explains that the missionary work of the church has been fulfilled when the local church that has been planted "enjoys a certain stability and firmness." This is achieved when the local church has its own supply of priests, religious and laypeople, sufficient to keep the church running strong (no. 19). Further, the Council urges that the young churches "participate as soon as possible in the universal missionary work of the Church," sending their own missionaries out to the world (no. 20). In fact, the Council fathers state that one sign of a church's maturity is its ability and desire to spread the gospel to others. Thus more people are brought to Christ, and the church grows.

How is Christian faith to be adapted to different cultures?

The question of how Christianity is expressed in different cultures, now commonly called "enculturation," is as old as the church and one that has not been finally resolved. The *Decree on the Church's Missionary Activity* calls for missionaries to be fully trained in the culture and language of the country to which they are sent (no. 26). Article 22 deals with the question most specifically. It states that the "young churches" can borrow from their cultures "all those things which can contribute to the glory of their Creator, the revelation of the Savior's grace, or the proper arrangement of Christian life."

But this can only be achieved through theological investigation of sacred Scripture and Tradition, which reveals what legitimate adaptations of beliefs and practices of different cultures may be made. Examples of legitimate adaptation would be the use in the liturgy of musical instruments and garb common to the culture or the use of new analogies from the system of thought to express or explain Christian doctrine. Inappropriate adaptations would be acceptance of thought or practices intrinsically opposed to or incompatible with Christian revelation, such as cannibalism or polygamy.

"Thanks to such a procedure [of discernment]," the decree states, "every appearance of syncretism and of false particularism can be excluded, and Christian life can be accommodated to the genius and the dispositions of each culture. Particular traditions…can be illumined by the light of the gospel, and then be taken up into Catholic unity" (no. 22). The key is that all customs, traditions and values of non-Christian origin must be tested and examined in light of the gospel of Jesus Christ.

The Extraordinary Synod of Bishops explains that the Catholic Church "takes from every culture all that it encounters of positive value." However, enculturation is not merely an external adaptation of different cultures to Christianity; "it means the intimate transformation of authentic cultural values" through their immersion in Christ and his gospel.

Sometimes it is thought that when Christianity or Catholicism confronts a new culture, the faith will lose something in the process of adaptation. To the contrary, the church is enriched and the culture is transformed through encounter with the gospel of Jesus Christ.

Conclusion

The Catholic Church has two patron saints of the missions, Saint Francis Xavier, the great Jesuit missionary, and Saint Thérèse of Lisieux, the contemplative Carmelite nun. They show us that everyone has a part to play in the church's missionary activity, whether it be working in the missions or praying for the missions and the conversion of all people to Christ.

For this to happen, the Second Vatican Council recognizes the need both for conviction about the church's evangelistic and missionary nature and for the interior conversion and spiritual power necessary to carry out the missionary task. This is the Lord's missionary challenge to the church, summarized by the *Decree on the Missionary Activity of the Church*, which reminds us that the whole church is missionary. Evangelization is a duty for *every* Christian.

The first thing a Catholic can do to fulfill this obligation to spread the faith is to lead a profoundly Christian life, "for their fervor in the service of God and their charity toward others will cause new spiritual inspiration to sweep over the whole Church." The decree adds that "this living testimony will more easily achieve its effect if it is given in unison with other Christian communities, according to the norms of the *Decree on Ecumenism*" (no. 36).

The last thought indicates another challenge to Catholics today. The modern ecumenical movement was born on the mission field, when Protestant missionaries at the turn of the twentieth century realized the scandal that their division caused to non-believers. This motivated them to seek greater unity with each other to promote the gospel of Jesus Christ.

The Second Vatican Council recognizes this same fact. It teaches that although missionary activity differs from ecumenical efforts, they are closely connected. Since the division among Christians obstructs the spread of the gospel, the work of restoring Christian unity also enhances the power of the church's witness of Christ to the world (*Ad Gentes Divinitus*, 6). The missionary challenge mandates the work of ecumenism, which will be the topic of the next chapter.

Dignitatis Humanae, Nostra Aetate and *Ad Gentes Divinitus* in the *Catechism of the Catholic Church*

The *Catechism* contains twenty-two references to the *Declaration on Religious Liberty,* in the sections on the freedom of faith in Part I (no. 160), on human freedom (no. 1738), moral conscience (no. 1785) and, most extensively, on "the social duty of religion and the right to religious freedom" (nos. 2104-2109; 2137) in Part II.

The *Decree on the Church's Missionary Activity* is cited fourteen times, mainly in the sections on the church (nos. 763-767) and on the church's missionary mandate and apostolate (nos. 849-870) in Part I and on baptism (nos. 1233-1271) and bishops, priests and deacons (nos. 1560-1571) in Part II.

Finally, the document on non-Christian religions has eight references in the *Catechism,* primarily in the discussion of the church and non-Christians (nos. 839-843) in Part I.

Recent Magisterial Documents

Commission for Religions Relations with the Jews. "We Remember: A Reflection on the Shoah," March 16, 1998.

Pope John Paul II. "Message to Cardinal Cassidy: Interreligious Dialogue," September 21, 2000.

Pope John Paul II. *Redemptoris Missio* (Encyclical Letter *Mission of the Redeemer*), December 7, 1990.

Pope John Paul II. *Slavorum Apostoli* (Encyclical Letter *In Commemoration of the Eleventh Centenary of the Evangelizing Work of Saints Cyril and Methodius*), June 2, 1985.

Favorite Quotes from *Dignitatis Humanae*

Truth cannot impose itself except by virtue of its own truth, as it makes its entrance into the mind at once quietly and with power. (no. 33)

In all his activity a man is bound to follow his conscience faithfully, in order that he may come to God, for whom he was created. It follows that he is not to be forced to act in a manner contrary to his conscience. Nor, on the other hand, is he to be restrained from acting in accordance with his conscience, especially in matters religious.

For, of its very nature, the exercise of religion consists before all else in those internal, voluntary, and free acts whereby man sets the course of his life directly toward God. No merely human power can either command or prohibit acts of this kind. (no. 3)

This truth appears at its height in Christ Jesus, in whom God perfectly manifested Himself and His ways with men. Christ is our Master and our Lord.... He wrought miracles to shed light on His teaching and to establish its truth. But His intention was to rouse faith in His hearers and to confirm them in faith, not to exert coercion upon them.... Taught by the word and example of Christ, the apostles followed the same way. From the very origins of the Church the disciples of Christ strove to convert men to faith in Christ as the Lord—not, however, by the use of coercion or by devices unworthy of the gospel, but by the power, above all, of the Word of God. (no. 11)

Favorite Quotes from *Ad Gentes Divinitus*

The pilgrim Church is missionary by her very nature. For it is from the mission of the Son and the mission of the Holy Spirit that she takes her origin, in accordance with the decree of God the Father. (no. 2)

"Missions" is the term usually given to those particular undertakings by which the heralds of the gospel are sent out by the Church and go forth into the whole world to carry out the task of preaching the gospel and planting the Church among peoples or groups who do not yet believe in Christ.... The chief means of this implantation is the preaching of the gospel of Jesus Christ. (no. 6)

This missionary activity finds its reason in the will of God, "who wishes all men to be saved and to come to the knowledge of the truth. For there is one God, and one Mediator between God and men, himself man, Christ Jesus, who gave himself a ransom for all" (1 Tim. 2:4-5), "neither is there salvation in any other" (Acts 4:12). (no. 7)

Favorite Quotes from *Nostra Aetate*

The Catholic Church rejects nothing which is true and holy in these religions. She looks with sincere respect upon those ways of conduct and of life, those rules and teachings which, though differing in many particulars from what she holds and sets forth, nevertheless often reflect a ray of that Truth which enlightens all men. (no. 2)

The Church repudiates all persecutions against any man. Moreover, mindful of her common patrimony with the Jews, and motivated by the gospel's spiritual love and by no political considerations, she deplores the hatred, persecutions, and displays of anti-Semitism directed against the Jews at any time and from any source.

Besides, as the Church has always held and continues to hold, Christ in His boundless love freely underwent His passion and death because of the sins of all men, so that all might attain salvation. It is, therefore, the duty of the Church's preaching to proclaim the cross of Christ as the sign of God's all-embracing love and as the fountain from which every grace flows. (no. 4)

CHAPTER THIRTEEN

The Call to Christian Unity

The phrase "To be Catholic is to be ecumenical" best sums up the teaching of the Second Vatican Council on the subject of Christian unity. Pope John XXIII made this a top priority for the Council, and his own efforts in this regard were strikingly successful. Witness, for example, the way he is affectionately remembered, by Catholic and Protestant alike, as "Good Pope John." Now all Catholics have been commissioned by Christ and the church to carry on and advance this mission of Christian unity, which is so close to the heart of God.

I personally did not become aware of the ecumenical dimension of my faith until I was exposed to the charismatic renewal. Through this movement God brought many Christians of different churches together to pray, to share Scripture and to love each other in Jesus Christ. The Holy Spirit, who is the source of all true unity, was evidently calling forth Catholics to this new advance in Christian unity that was spoken about theologically by the Second Vatican Council.

The Holy Spirit has continued to foster this work of Christian unity through the emergence of ecumenical groups of committed Christians. These groups have demonstrated that it *is* possible for Christians of different churches to commit themselves to love and serve each other, to pray together, to reach out to the world to bring others to Jesus Christ and to work together for the transformation of society.

While not always easy, there are great rewards in following the Lord's call to join together with other Christians in this ecumenical age. More and more we see Christians of different traditions working side by side in service to the poor, in pro-life activities and in other outreaches designed to foster the advance of the kingdom of God. Yet Catholics need accurate guidance on working with other Christians, which we find provided in Vatican II's *Decree on Ecumenism (Unitatis Redintegratio)* and more recently in Pope John Paul II's 1995 encyclical letter *Ut Unum Sint (That They May Be One)*.

Thus the Second Vatican Council inaugurated a new era in the relationship of Catholics to other Christians. The schism between the Catholic Church and the Orthodox churches of the East in 1054 and the Protestant Reformation of the sixteenth century not only divided the one church of Christ but led to a polarization among Christian bodies. The resulting division was marked by a breakdown in communication, misunderstanding, intolerance, even hostility and open warfare. As Vatican II's *Decree on Ecumenism* observes in its introduction, "Without doubt, this discord openly contradicts the will of Christ, provides a stumbling block to the world, and inflicts damage on the most holy cause of proclaiming the good news to every creature" (no. 1).

Until the twentieth century, Catholics normally felt that those who left the Catholic Church were responsible for these divisions. The Catholic approach was to pray and work for their return to the "one, true church of Christ." Often Catholics made little effort to understand what other Christians believed. They seldom appreciated the truly Christian aspects of their beliefs and heritage.

Although the love of Christians for each other had grown cold, "nevertheless, the Lord of Ages wisely and patiently follows out the plan of His grace on behalf of us sinners. In recent times He has begun to bestow more generously upon divided Christians remorse over their divisions and a longing for unity" (*Unitatis Redintegratio,* 1).

The concern about Christian division that surfaced among Protestant missionaries at the beginning of the twentieth century gave rise in the 1920s to the "Faith and Order" and the "Life and Work" movements, which sought to restore Christian unity. These movements coalesced in the 1940s to form the World Council of Churches.

The Catholic Church, in the meantime, was pleased to see Protestant and Orthodox groups working out their divisions but did not become involved in this effort. Catholic theology still insisted that the only authentic movement toward unity would be a return to the fullness of truth and Christian life found only in the Catholic Church.

However, the Holy Spirit began to work a remarkable change in the Catholic Church's attitude toward other Christians. In the mid-twentieth century the Catholic Church began to send observers to the organizations working toward unity. The popes began to consider the efforts of a few individuals and small Catholic groups promoting Christian unity.

This process culminated during the papacy of John XXIII, who took some remarkable steps in promoting Christian unity. He invited delegates from the Protestant and Orthodox churches to observe the Second Vatican Council, seating them in St. Peter's "front and center," directly across the aisle from the cardinals. He established a Secretariat for Promoting Christian Unity, giving it equal status with the other Council commissions. Thus he accentuated the fact that the restoration of unity among Christians was among the primary goals of the Second Vatican Council.

Where does this issue stand today in the Catholic Church? Is the pursuit of Christian unity still a top priority for Catholics? Has the ecumenical spirit become so much a part of the Catholic outlook and mentality that we can honestly say that "to be Catholic is to be ecumenical"?

Pope John Paul II answered these questions clearly in his 1995 encyclical letter on commitment to ecumenism, *Ut Unum Sint (That They May Be One)*. Here the pope reaffirmed the importance of every point of the teaching of the *Decree on Ecumenism* and made it absolutely clear that participation, in some form, in the effort for the restoration of Christian unity is essential for every Catholic. He wrote:

Jesus himself, at the hour of his Passion, prayed "that they may all be one" (Jn. 17:21). This unity, which the Lord has bestowed on his Church and in which he wishes to embrace all people, is not something added on, but stands at the very heart of Christ's mission. Nor is it some secondary attribute of the community of his disciples. Rather, it belongs to the very essence of this community. God wills the Church, because he wills unity, and unity is an expression of the whole depth of his *agape*....

To believe in Christ means to desire unity; to desire unity means to desire the Church; to desire the Church means to desire the communion of grace which corresponds to the Father's plan from all eternity. Such is the meaning of Christ's prayer: "*Ut unum sint.*"

In the present situation of the lack of unity among Christians and of the confident quest for full communion, the Catholic faithful are conscious of being deeply challenged by the Lord of the Church. The Second Vatican Council strengthened their commitment with a clear ecclesiological vision, open to all the ecclesial values present among other Christians. The Catholic faithful face the ecumenical question in a spirit of faith....

"Concern for restoring unity pertains to the whole Church, faithful and clergy alike. It extends to everyone, according to the ability of each, whether it be exercised in daily Christian living or in theological and historical studies" [*Unitatis Redintegratio,* 5].

All this is extremely important and of fundamental significance for ecumenical activity. Thus it is absolutely clear that ecumenism, the movement of promoting Christian unity, *is not just some sort of "appendix"* which is added to the Church's traditional activity. Rather, ecumenism is an organic part of her life and work, and consequently must pervade all that she is and does; it must be like the fruit borne by a healthy and flourishing tree which grows to its full stature.

This is what Pope John XXIII believed about the unity of the Church and how he saw full Christian unity. With regard to other Christians, to the great Christian family, he observed: "What unites us is much greater than what divides us." The Second Vatican Council for its part exhorts "all Christ's faithful to remember that the more purely they strive to live according to the Gospel, the more they are fostering and even practicing Christian unity" (*Unitatis Redintegratio,* 5). (*Ut Unum Sint,* 9, 10, 19, 20)[1]

There have been some great moments in ecumenism since the close of Vatican II: the lifting of the mutual excommunications of 1054 by Pope Paul VI and the Orthodox patriarch Athenagoras; historic meetings between the pope and the archbishop of Canterbury and other Christian leaders; the establishment of official dialogues between the Catholic Church and other Christian churches and so on. But these efforts have also revealed how difficult and deep-rooted some of the issues and emotions are that divide us.

To be honest, the efforts of the Catholic Church toward the restoration of Christian unity have barely begun. In many quarters Catholics are not sufficiently informed about or interested in this topic. Unity among Christians sometimes bears greater resemblance to a secular indifferentism about matters of Christian faith than to an honest seeking of unity based upon the truth. For many people, to be "Christian" means little more than being loving and accepting, being a good person or sharing common social concerns.

On the other hand, in some places we find old hostilities and antagonisms being revived in the name of preserving Christian truth or "defending the faith." It is easy for Catholics to respond in kind to anti-Catholic sentiments and attitudes by launching our own "truth crusade" against others in a defensive spirit.

What is the challenge of ecumenism today? As we return to studying Vatican II's *Decree on Ecumenism* and Pope John Paul II's *Ut Unum Sint*, let us pray that the same Holy Spirit who stirred up this vision of Christian unity would rekindle this vision and power today.

Catholics are now faced with the reality that Christian unity will not be attained and preserved by a short flurry of ecumenical enthusiasm but will take many years of persistent study, commitment, dialogue and prayer. We must be in it for the long haul if God's purpose is to be accomplished. Catholics also must remain faithful to their church's teaching and norms for ecumenism if true unity is to be achieved. Let us examine, then, what direction the Second Vatican Council has provided concerning Christian unity.

What is ecumenism?

According to Vatican II's *Decree on Ecumenism,* ecumenism is "a movement, fostered by the grace of the Holy Spirit, for the restoration of unity among all Christians. Taking part in this movement are those who believe in the Triune God and confess Jesus as Lord and Savior" (no. 1).

Efforts for unity with non-Christians, which would include the Jewish people, are not properly part of the ecumenical movement. Also excluded from consideration here are groups that claim to be Christian but do not believe in God as Trinity nor in the divinity or lordship of Jesus, such as the Mormons and the Jehovah's Witnesses. It is important to note that the restoration of Christian unity is not to be achieved by human efforts alone. From beginning to end it must be "fostered by the grace of the Holy Spirit."

Why seek unity with other Christians?

Catholics have always believed that the church is one—that unity is an essential mark or characteristic of the true church of Christ. Hence the Second Vatican Council proclaims that the restoration of unity among Christians is not optional; it is a gospel mandate. Jesus himself prayed fervently for the unity of his followers as the will of his Father and as a sign "that the world may believe that thou [the Father] hast sent me" (John 17:21).

The Holy Trinity is the model of the unity that Jesus' followers are to have with each other in the church (*Unitatis Redintegratio,* 2). Saint Paul taught that the church is "one body and one Spirit" (Ephesians 4:4). He spent much of his ministry healing or preventing divisions among Christians for the sake of the unity of the Body of Christ.

Christian unity is worth the effort because Jesus Christ wills it. He paid the price for unity, shedding his blood to form us into one people, one body—his people and his body on earth. As Saint Paul exclaimed when he heard about disunity in the church at Corinth, "Is Christ divided?" (1 Corinthians 1:13). Catholics must echo that same sentiment. "To be Catholic is to be ecumenical."

How should Catholics think about other Christians?

After the Protestant Reformation it was common for Catholics and Protestants to think of each other as "heretics" (those who believed false doctrine), "schismatics" (those who divided the church) or "apostates" (those who renounced the true faith). This was also true of the relationship between Catholics and Orthodox Christians. These groups have had difficulty recognizing each other as true Christians.

What a radical departure from such a posture is the teaching of the Second Vatican Council! The Council proclaims, "All those justified by faith through baptism are incorporated into Christ. They therefore have a right to be honored by the title of Christian, and are properly regarded as brothers in the Lord by the sons of the Catholic Church" (*Unitatis Redintegratio,* 3). Catholics look upon all those baptized into Christ as our brothers and sisters in Christ, although they are "separated brethren" since "they do not profess the faith in its entirety or do not preserve unity of communion with the successor of Peter" (*Lumen Gentium,* 15).

Not only do Catholics recognize these baptized believers as Christians, but at Vatican II the Catholic Church officially recognized for the first time the bodies to which these Christians belong as "churches and (ecclesial) communities." The Council recognized that the Spirit of Christ has used these churches as a means of salvation for their members.

Furthermore, the *Decree on Ecumenism* urges Catholics to "joyfully acknowledge and esteem" the Christian elements in other churches and even to learn from certain practices of other Christians, knowing that "whatever is wrought by the grace of the Holy Spirit in the hearts of our separated brethren can contribute to our own edification. Whatever is truly Christian never conflicts with the genuine interests of the faith; indeed, it can always result in a more ample realization of the very mystery of Christ and the Church" (*Unitatis Redintegratio,* 4).

How do Catholics now view the Orthodox churches?

Chapter three of the *Decree on Ecumenism* highlights the many common beliefs held by Catholics and Eastern (Orthodox) Christians. The Eastern churches are of apostolic origin and provide "a treasury from which the Church of the West has amply drawn for its liturgy, spiritual tradition, and jurisprudence" (no. 14). The first seven ecumenical councils, recognized by both Eastern and Western Christianity, were held in the East.

The Second Vatican Council praises the Eastern churches' love of the sacred liturgy, especially the Eucharist, their devotion to Mary and the saints, the rich spiritual traditions coming from the fathers of the church and monasticism and their possession of true sacraments through apostolic succession.

The Council often sees even the points of difference between the Catholic Church and the Eastern churches, such as differences of theological expression, as complementary rather than conflicting. For example, while Catholics speak of the life-giving presence of God in a person through the Holy Spirit as "sanctifying grace," the Orthodox speak of the "divine energies." The varying disciplines of the Eastern churches only add to the diverse beauty of the church.

In summary, the Second Vatican Council clearly indicates the great respect that the Catholic Church has toward the Eastern Christian churches and their traditions. Catholics cherish the hope of attaining full unity with these churches, possibly in the near future. In seeking this unity, the Catholic Church wishes to "'impose no burden beyond what is indispensable' (Acts 15:28)" (*Unitatis Redintegratio,* 18).

What about the differences between Catholics and Protestants?

The perspective of the *Decree on Ecumenism* on the Protestant churches is noticeably different than its approach to the Orthodox Christian churches. While the common elements of belief among Catholics and Protestants are indeed listed, the Council alludes to "weighty differences" in understanding these elements and in the interpretation of revealed truth (no. 19).

These differences include the varying Catholic and Protestant understandings of the redemptive work of Christ, the role of Mary and the church in God's work of salvation (no. 20); the meaning of sacred Scripture and the relationship of Scripture to the church (no. 21); and the number and power of the sacraments (no. 22). Concerning the latter, the Council notes that Protestant churches "lack that fullness of unity with us which should flow from baptism.... Especially because of the lack of the sacrament of orders they have not preserved the genuine and total reality of the Eucharistic mystery" (no. 22).

It is necessary to be realistic about the unresolved differences that still divide Catholic and Protestant Christians. Nonetheless, the Council recognizes that our Protestant brethren are spiritually nourished by faith in Christ, baptism, hearing and meditating on God's Word in the Bible, private prayer, Christian family life and community worship, which sometimes "displays notable features of an ancient, common liturgy" (no. 23).

What then is the goal of the ecumenical movement?

By definition, ecumenism seeks to bring Christians and their churches toward closer unity. Every step toward greater respect for other Christians and their traditions, working together in common mission and service while respecting doctrinal differences, and any progress toward agreement in doctrine advances the cause of Christian unity.

The 1985 Extraordinary Synod expressed succinctly the final goal of ecumenism: "We Bishops ardently desire that the incomplete communion already existing with the non-Catholic churches and communities might, with the grace of God, come to the point of full communion" (Synod, 60).

Full communion would mean recognizing the same apostolic authority, professing the same essential Christian beliefs and sharing fully in the same sacraments. For Catholics the climactic expression of full communion would be receiving the Eucharist together, after the necessary agreements about doctrine, worship and common life had been reached. At that point Christians could joyfully and sincerely join together as one to partake of the great sacrament of unity, the Body and Blood of the Lord in the Eucharist.

Until that day Catholics must refrain from receiving communion in other Christian churches, save in exceptional circumstances. (In very limited and clearly defined circumstances, Catholics can receive the Eucharist in Christian churches that have a valid sacrament of holy orders and believe as we do about the real presence of Christ in the Eucharist.)

Likewise, Christians of other churches are normally not permitted to receive Holy Communion in the Catholic Church. For Catholics, receiving the Eucharist requires a belief in Jesus' real presence. This sacrament expresses the full unity of faith and life that we share with each other as Catholics and with the ordained apostolic ministers of the Catholic Church. The Eucharist is a living sign of that deep unity and enriches that unity by the grace of Christ. We pray for the day when that depth of unity is established among all Christians, which is the goal of ecumenism.

Are renewal and repentance necessary for ecumenism?

They are imperative. The *Decree on Ecumenism* states that the "primary duty" of Catholics in ecumenical work is to honestly appraise what needs to be renewed and strengthened within the church. The Council calls all of us to repentance and reform. The decree states, "For although the Catholic Church has been endowed with all divinely revealed truth and with all means of grace, her members fail to live by them with all the fervor they should. As a result, the radiance of the Church's face shines less brightly in the eyes of our separated brethren and of the world at large, and the growth of God's kingdom is retarded. Every Catholic must therefore aim at Christian perfection (cf. Jas. 1:4; Rom. 12:1-2)" (no. 4).

It is significant that rather than pointing a finger at the errors or faults of our separated brethren, the Council calls us to first reform and renew ourselves.

I have heard many ex-Catholics say that they joined other churches because they were not being spiritually nourished in the Catholic Church. Others say that they did not experience in their parish the fullness of Christian life that Catholic doctrine claims the church possesses. When the Catholic Church lives out its doctrine fully and vibrantly, then Catholics will have no reason to leave. Then some of the greatest obstacles toward unity with other Christian churches and communities will be removed.

One of the mottos of the Catholic Church must continue to be *Ecclesia semper reformanda:* "The church is always reforming herself." This is a prerequisite for successful ecumenism. "There can be no ecumenism worthy of the name without a change of heart.... Let all Christ's faithful remember that the more purely they strive to live according to the gospel, the more they are fostering and even practicing Christian unity" (no. 7).

What is the soul of the ecumenical movement?

The *Decree on Ecumenism* declares that "this change of heart and holiness of life, along with public and private prayer for the unity of Christians, should be regarded as the soul of the whole ecumenical movement, and can rightly be called 'spiritual ecumenism'" (no. 8).

The decree notes that Catholics already pray for Christian unity, and it urges Catholics to "join in prayer with their separated brethren" (no. 8), petitioning the Lord for the grace of unity. This teaching reminds Christians that unity is a gift from the Lord; and therefore, prayer for unity must be at the heart of all our ecumenical efforts. The annual Week of Prayer for Christian Unity in January is an important response to this call for prayer.

Who is to initiate efforts for Christian unity?

After many years of peripheral involvement with the ecumenical movement, the Catholic Church now realizes that if unity is God's will, Catholics must take a role of leadership. The Council states that "Catholics must assuredly be concerned for their separated brethren, praying for them, keeping them informed about the Church, *making the first approaches towards them*" (no. 4, emphasis added). Catholics are not to wait until we are approached but are to take the initiative.

Is there a contradiction between ecumenism and leading other Christians to join the Catholic Church?

The decree teaches that "the work of preparing and reconciling those individuals who wish for full Catholic communion is of its nature distinct from ecumenical action. But there is no opposition between the two, since both proceed from the wondrous providence of God" (no. 4).

This is certainly a sensitive area, but both activities are legitimate. If an individual hears God's call to join the Catholic Church, the person must follow his or her leading of conscience, and the Catholic Church should readily prepare and receive the person.

However, the *Decree on Ecumenism* reminds us that Christian unity will not be accomplished primarily by individual decisions to join the Catholic Church. God's deepest desire is that Christian churches and ecclesial groups move together to restore the full unity of the one church of Jesus Christ. As all Christians focus on Jesus Christ and seek to conform their lives more fully to his teaching, Catholics believe that God will draw his people from all churches into one.

What are some practical steps that we can take in seeking Christian unity?

The *Decree on Ecumenism* outlines some practical steps for ecumenical endeavors.

1. Catholics are to "eliminate words, judgments, and actions which do not respond to the condition of separated brethren with truth and fairness" (no. 4).

2. Catholics are to study the beliefs of other Christians in order to understand them correctly (no. 9).

3. Competent experts are to engage in ecumenical dialogue in order to know and appreciate the teaching and religious life of each communion and possibly reach agreement in certain areas (nos. 4, 9).

4. Christians of different churches can cooperate in projects and service for the common good (no. 4).

5. Christians should come together for common prayer in ways that are permitted by their churches (no. 4).

6. After examining their own faithfulness to Christ's will for the church, all Christians should "undertake with vigor the task of renewal and reform" (no. 4).

7. Instruction in sacred theology, history and other branches of knowledge must be presented from an ecumenical point of view.

Any Catholic who has friends from other Christian churches, or who has simply struck up a conversation regarding Christianity with those of other traditions, knows how useful and important these guidelines can be in building unity. These steps lead to closer communion among individual Christians and among the churches and ecclesial bodies to which they belong.

What are some pitfalls to ecumenism?

There appear to be two opposite dangers to true ecumenism that particularly affect Catholics. The *first* is an attitude that other Christian churches have nothing to offer us, since the Catholic Church possesses the fullness of truth and the means of salvation. Catholics need to be reminded that there is no room for arrogance, pride or "triumphalism" in approaching other Christians. Why?

First because we Catholics often fail to live the gospel as we should, despite the truth we possess and all the means of grace at our disposal. Humility is a more honest and Christian attitude. In fact, the *Decree on Ecumenism* calls Catholics to repentance for our sins and failures. "St. John has testified: 'If we say that we have not sinned, we make him a liar, and his word is not in us' (1 Jn. 1:10). This holds good for sins against unity. Thus, in humble prayer, we beg pardon of God and of our separated brethren, just as we forgive those who trespass against us" (no. 7).

The *Decree on Ecumenism* reminds Catholics that the lives and witness of other Christians can instruct and edify us. We will surely miss this if we are caught up in our own "fullness." One leading ecumenist warns of "Catholic sectarianism"—that is, Catholic refusal to recognize the truly Christian elements in other Christian churches and ecclesial communities, pretending that we have no need of their witness of faith.

The *second danger* that threatens Catholic ecumenical efforts is a type of "religious indifferentism" or "non-denominationalism." This views different forms of Christianity as equally true and valid and seeks unity based on minimal doctrinal content. Perhaps you have heard people say things like "All churches are pretty much the same" and "It doesn't matter what church you belong to or what you believe, as long as you are sincerely trying to be a Christian." (Often the term *good person* becomes interchangeable with the word *Christian*.)

While it is true that ecumenism is more fruitful when Christians *begin* by seeking and recognizing areas of agreement in faith and practice, true ecumenism cannot deny or overlook the differences that divide Christians. The *Decree on Ecumenism* states: "It is…essential that doctrine be clearly presented in its entirety. Nothing is so foreign to the spirit of ecumenism as a *false conciliatory approach* which harms the purity of Catholic doctrine and obscures its assured genuine meaning. At the same time, Catholic belief needs to be explained more profoundly and precisely, in ways and in terminology which our separated brethren too can really understand" (*Unitatis Redintegratio,* 11, emphasis added).

The temptation to water down or compromise doctrine in ecumenical dialogue is actually a disservice to the cause of unity. We must face and resolve our disagreements honestly. Truth must be the basis of unity.

Christians are genuinely united, even now, through love, the work of the Holy Spirit and the beliefs and religious practices we hold in common. Yet we cannot settle for a "least-common-denominator" Christianity. We seek the fullness of Christian faith and life. We are not opposing ecumenism, therefore, when we speak in an open, honest way, that is neither defensive nor aggressive, about specifically Catholic doctrines—such as teaching about Mary, purgatory and intercommunion. We are sharing aspects of our understanding of the fullness of Christian belief and life.

On the other hand, the *Decree on Ecumenism* advises Catholics: "When comparing doctrines, they should remember that in Catholic teaching there exists an order or 'hierarchy' of truths, since they vary in their relationship to the foundation of the Christian faith" (no. 11). In other words, Catholics should distinguish between truths of the faith that are close to the "heart" or foundation of Christianity and those beliefs that are not central to the basic gospel message— such as purgatory, indulgences and devotions to particular saints. There is no official listing of these truths in order of importance or priority, but our ongoing study of the sacred Scriptures and Catholic doctrine can give us a sense of this.

Catholics usually find that we agree with other Christians on most (if not all) of the primary elements of our faith, such as the Incarnation, the Resurrection and the Second Coming. However, we will still find disagreements about what doctrines *are* most important and central to Christianity. Ecumenical dialogue seeks to reach agreement even concerning what is at the heart of Christian belief and practice, as well as discussing the specific beliefs that divide us.

Why shouldn't all Christians simply return to the Catholic Church?

The *Decree of Ecumenism* does claim that "it is through Christ's Catholic Church alone, which is the all-embracing means of salvation, that the fullness of the means of salvation can be obtained" (no. 3). In its doctrine the Catholic Church lacks nothing.

However, because of the division of Christianity, the Catholic Church does not possess *in actuality* all of the essential marks of the true church of Christ in their perfect form. For example, since the one church has been divided, it is therefore no longer fully "catholic" or universal (no. 4). Elements of true apostolic succession exist outside the Catholic Church as well.

The conclusion to be drawn may sound contradictory: by Christ's gift, the Catholic Church possesses the fullness of grace and the means of salvation, but because of the sin of division, the Catholic Church is lacking in the actual expression of that fullness. Catholics must therefore join with other Christians in seeking the restoration of unity, so that the "one, holy, catholic and apostolic church" may be visibly present in the world in all its splendor and fullness.

Nowhere does Vatican II speak of ecumenism explicitly as a return to the Catholic Church. Rather it speaks of Catholics joining with other Christians, focused on Jesus Christ, to seek the unity that God intends for his church. The result of this effort "will be that, little by little, as the obstacles to perfect ecclesiastical communion are overcome, all Christians will be gathered, in a common celebration of the Eucharist, into that unity of the one and only Church which Christ bestowed on His Church from the beginning" (no. 4).

How will this unity look? When and how will it come about?

We need to be open to God's action and the inspiration of the Holy Spirit. The closing words of the *Decree on Ecumenism* remind Christians not to prejudge or obstruct the ways that God will use in the future to bring his church together into one. It also reminds us that this task is utterly beyond all human energies, ingenuity and ability, and consequently the church "places its hope entirely in the prayer of Christ for the Church, in the love of the Father for us, and in the power of the Holy Spirit. 'And hope does not disappoint, because the charity of God is poured forth in our hearts by the Holy Spirit who has been given to us' (Rom. 5:5)" (no. 24).

The concern and work for ecumenism continues to be one of the greatest challenges yet to be accepted and undertaken by most Catholics. The final chapter of this book will discuss two other widely recognized areas of concern and challenge for Catholics: education and the communications media.

Unitatis Redintegratio in the *Catechism of the Catholic Church*

The *Decree on Ecumenism* is referred to forty-two times in the *Catechism*. (To put this in perspective, Saint Thomas Aquinas is only cited sixty-one times, and the entire Council of Trent 101 times!) Apparently the writers of the *Catechism* thought it very important to discuss the unity of Christians, which is done primarily in the section on "The Church is One" (nos. 813-829), with mention in the discussions of baptism (no. 1271) and the Eucharist (nos. 1399-1400) in Part II and in the treatment of the Our Father (no. 279) in Part III.

Recent Magisterial Documents

Pontifical Council for Promoting Christian Unity. "Directory for Ecumenism," March 25, 1993. In *Origins* 23, no. 9 (July 29, 1993).

Pope John Paul II. *Ut Unum Sint* (Encyclical Letter *On Commitment to Ecumenism*), May 25, 1995.

Favorite Quotes from *Unititas Redintegratio*

There can be no ecumenism worthy of the name without a change of heart. For it is from newness of attitudes (cf. Eph. 4:23), from self-denial and unstinted love, that yearnings for unity take their rise and grow toward maturity. We should therefore pray to the divine Spirit for the grace to be genuinely self-denying, humble, gentle in the service of others, and to have an attitude of brotherly generosity toward them. (no. 7)

Everywhere, large numbers have felt the impulse of this grace, and among our separated brethren also there increases from day to day a movement, fostered by the grace of the Holy Spirit, for the restoration of unity among all Christians. Taking part in this movement, which is called ecumenical, are those who invoke the Triune God and confess Jesus as Lord and Savior. (no. 1)

This change of heart and holiness of life, along with public and private prayer for the unity of Christians, should be regarded as the soul of the whole ecumenical movement, and can rightly be called "spiritual ecumenism." (no. 8)

CHAPTER FOURTEEN

The Critical Challenges of the Media and Education

Documentation is increasing every day about the tragic effects of pornography and violence in the media on the minds and lives of children and adults. Nearly every conceivable blasphemy and sin can be found graphically exhibited in movies and on television—not only in "adult" productions but even in "prime-time" programming and animated productions. Yet many parents still use the television as a "baby-sitter" without reviewing what their children watch. The same type of problem exists in the media of music, periodicals, comic books and newspapers.

These media have become some of the most powerful educational tools of our time. As with nearly every facet of modern life, they can be of great benefit when used to present good morality, sound education, helpful information, wholesome entertainment and even the truths of religion. But they can harm when they are disengaged from the moral order and from the things that contribute to the authentic human life God intended.

Adults, especially parents, are the key figures today in determining what sort of media exposure and education they will choose for themselves and allow for their children. *We* must decide what to read, watch and listen to in order to promote our own growth. *We* must decide how we will respond to media or educational institutions when they present things we judge to be good (Will we support them?) or evil (Will we speak out against them?).

Parents must take responsibility for what their children see and hear and for how they are educated. They need to help their children discern what is true and worthwhile and what is not. Parents must take seriously their own role as educators, especially with regard to faith. It is irresponsible to simply leave this to others, regardless of how qualified teachers may be.

Since there are few things that shape and form the human person and society today as decisively as educational institutions and the communications media, the fathers of the Second Vatican Council decided to devote separate documents to these topics. They wisely saw that each of these subjects merited its own document.

Some have criticized these documents because of their brevity and allegedly superficial analysis. To the contrary, if Catholics put into effect all that is in these two documents, the Catholic Church (and our society) would be in a much better position. The documents lay out general principles and suggestions, leaving the development of more specific and in-depth strategies to the labor of others.

It has been argued that the Catholic bishops do not speak as professional educators nor as experts in the mass media. Generally they are not, but in these documents they speak with competence as the church's shepherds, commenting on the pastoral implications of these forces upon the faith and life of God's people. The church itself is an educator and a communicator and has a deserved interest and concern for how all education and the mass media affect society. Let us look at each document to discover the principles and guidelines they present.

What is the purpose of education?

The *Declaration on Christian Education (Gravissimum educationis)* states, "A true education aims at the formation of the human person with respect to his ultimate goal" (no. 1) and with respect to the good of society. Therefore, not only does each person have "an inalienable right to an education corresponding to his proper destiny" (no. 1), but each Christian "is entitled to a Christian education" (no. 2).

Besides developing a person's physical, moral and intellectual endowments, a Christian education (1) introduces a person into a knowledge of the mystery of salvation, based on the gift of faith; (2) teaches a person to adore God in spirit and truth (see John 4:23), especially through liturgical worship; (3) trains the person to conduct his or her personal life in righteousness and truth, modeled after Christ himself (see Ephesians 4:13, 22-24); (4) helps the person grow accustomed to giving witness to the faith and hope that is in him or her (see 1 Peter 3:15) and to promoting the Christian transformation of the world (no. 2).

Whose obligation is education?

Parents are the "first and foremost educators of their children." The Christian education document stresses that their role as educators is so decisive that scarcely anything can compensate for their failure in it. It is the parents' responsibility to create a family atmosphere "animated with love and reverence for God and men." The goal is that the children will grow in virtue and become well-rounded in personal and social skills (no. 3). In the family, children first learn to know and worship God, to love their neighbor, to experience human companionship and to belong to the church and society.

Society as a whole must assist in the work of education by supporting "the rights of parents and of others to whom parents entrust a share in the work of education" (no. 3). This support is part of society's responsibility to promote the common good. Note that society is not given the task of being the primary educator, but the state is to assist the parents and those whom the parents authorize to teach their children.

In the United States it often appears that the government has established itself as the primary educator. It is the parents who must conform to the dictates, wishes and guidelines of the state. This is *not* the Catholic Church's perspective!

The church educates by announcing and teaching the way of salvation in Jesus Christ, especially through the liturgy and catechetical instruction (no. 4). The church also promotes and supports the full human development of each person for his or her own welfare and that of society. Let us discuss now the place of schools in this scheme.

What is the church's position concerning schools?

Schools are viewed as particularly valuable agencies of education. The vocation of a schoolteacher is praised as "beautiful" and "truly solemn" (no. 5). Parents should be free in their choice of schools, even from the standpoint of economics. The document calls for the allocation of public subsidies to enable parents to send their children to the schools of their choice (no. 6).

The declaration warns against any attempt of the state to monopolize the educational system. The faithful are urged to get involved with the teachers and the school system, such as through parents' associations.

Finally, the church must recognize her "very grave obligation to give zealous attention to the moral and religious education of all her children" and to offer special services and programs, such as CCD (Confraternity of Christian Doctrine) religious education classes, for those not in Catholic schools. The goal here is that children "pace their development as Christians with their growth as citizens of the world" (no. 7).

What about Catholic schools?

The Catholic school is recommended to all Catholic parents, since it can create "an atmosphere enlivened by the gospel spirit of freedom and charity" (no. 8). The Catholic school aims to match spiritual development with human and cultural development.

Despite changing times, this declaration asserts the "immense importance" of Catholic schools and asserts "the Church's right freely to establish and run schools of every kind and at every level" (no. 8). It is a sad irony that in some countries, such as the United States, thousands of Catholic schools have closed since the Second Vatican Council due to lack of financial support and decline in dedicated religious and priests available to teach, as well as other factors.

Even now the future of Catholic schools in many countries remains uncertain. Catholics face many challenges with regard to Catholic education, including how to provide suitable Catholic education for their children when the Catholic schools have closed; how to maintain a strong Christian orientation for existing Catholic schools; and how to keep tuition for Catholic schools low enough so that poor and even middle-class Catholics are not excluded.

The declaration emphasizes the importance of good teachers in the success of the Catholic school. It urges that they be certified, be trained with care in both secular and religious knowledge and have up-to-date educational skills. More importantly, "bound by charity to one another and to their students, and penetrated by an apostolic spirit, let them give witness to Christ, the unique Teacher, by their lives as well as by their teachings. Above all, let them perform their services as partners of the parents" (no. 8).

Catholic schools must deal with specific issues in a Christian way, such as recognition of the importance of sexual differences. The Council states, "They should pay due regard in every educational activity to sexual differences and to the special role which divine Providence allots to each sex in family life and in society" (no. 8).

In responding to the demands of modern conditions, the declaration recommends the founding of professional and technical schools, institutes for adult education, social services, schools for students with special needs, schools for preparing Catholic teachers and so on. Whatever the school or program attended, "the purpose in view is that by living an exemplary and apostolic life, the Catholic graduate can become, as it were, the saving leaven of the human family" (no. 8).

What about Catholic institutions of higher learning?

The *Declaration on Christian Education* affirms the church's support of schools of higher learning, especially colleges and universities. The declaration advocates the pursuit of truth "with the freedom of scientific investigation," while believing that "faith and reason give harmonious witness to the unity of all truth," as Saint Thomas Aquinas and all the church's most illustrious teachers have taught (no. 10).

No one could have foreseen the traumatic changes that have occurred in these Catholic institutions, at least in the West, since the close of the Second Vatican Council. Today many Catholic colleges and universities are declaring their independence from the magisterium of the Catholic Church, as if faith and reason were at odds. How un-Catholic!

Pope John Paul II clarified the proper relationship between faith and reason in his encyclical letter *Fides et Ratio* of September 14, 1998. This declaration assumes that the magisterium has the right to teach the Catholic faith authoritatively. Those who teach in a Catholic university should be expected to respect this role of the magisterium and not advocate views that contradict Catholic teaching. The Apostolic Constitution *Ex Corde Ecclesiae* (August 15, 1990) gives definitive guidelines for the identity and mission of Catholic colleges and universities today and their proper relationship to the pastors of the church.

In session with some United States bishops on October 15, 1988, Pope John Paul II explained that faith does not limit freedom in the pursuit of knowledge. Faith does not stifle the inquiries of reason or science, which are properly governed by their own principles and methodologies. Rather, faith assists reason in achieving the full good of the human person and society by recognizing the transcendent dimension of the human person. Faith preserves the full truth about humanity. "For this reason the university by its nature is called to be ever more open to the senses of the absolute and the transcendent, in order to facilitate the search for truth at the service of humanity."[1]

Besides advancing the quest for knowledge in consonance with the fundamental truths about humanity's nature and true good, the Catholic university also can assist in the "reevaluation" of society that Pope John Paul II called for. In order to engage in this, Catholics must know their faith. Pope John Paul II spoke of the *right* of Catholic university students to receive a Catholic formation, both doctrinal and moral, that corresponds to the level of their scholastic abilities. It is obvious that if Catholic students hope to have an impact on higher culture and witness to their faith before the world, they must be clear about their own Catholic identity, and so must the colleges and universities in which they are formed. The pope insisted, "This Catholic identity has to be present in the fundamental direction given to both teaching and studies."[2]

Returning to the Council's *Declaration on Catholic Education,* Catholic institutions should be located around the world and distinguished for their academic pursuits rather than the size of their enrollment. They should open their doors to students of special promise "even though of slender means, especially those who come from young [developing] nations." The church should also establish residences and outreaches to support the spiritual life of Catholics and other students at colleges and universities that are not Catholic (no. 10).

What are we to make of the freedom of Catholic theologians?

Since theology deals with the exposition of truth as seen through the light of faith, the bishops of the church, who have been given special authority by Christ to discern and teach matters of faith, must oversee it. (This authority is discussed regarding the interpretation of Scripture in the *Constitution on Divine Revelation,* article 12, and in the *Dogmatic Constitution on the Church,* articles 23, 25.)

All of the Vatican II documents encourage advanced scholarship, including scientific research, even in theology. In an age marked by competition between different fields of study and among schools, the call for cooperation among Catholic scholars and schools is refreshingly significant. A broad range of theological inquiry may be carried on within the wide boundaries of theological orthodoxy set by the church's teaching office over the centuries.

Yet considerable tension still exists between some theologians and the magisterium of the church, and the Extraordinary Synod of 1985 recommends a priority be set on resolving this (see Synod, 51, the section concerning "the relationship between the magisterium of the Bishops and theologians"). The Sacred Congregation for the Doctrine of the Faith has taken a major step in clarifying the proper relationship between theologians and the official teachers (magisterium) of the church by publishing *Instruction on the Ecclesial Vocation of the Theologian.*[3] Through study and discussion of this document, Catholics can gain a better understanding of the theologian's role in the church and in the formation of our faith.

What is the purpose of ecclesiastical universities and faculties of sacred science?

Section two of the *Declaration on Christian Education* underscores the importance of these faculties, which prepare students for the priesthood and advanced chairs of teaching and research. These faculties seek to develop a deep understanding of sacred revelation, unfold the treasures of Christian wisdom in the church and foster dialogue with our separated brethren and with non-Christians (no. 11).

In April of 1979 Pope John Paul II issued an important apostolic constitution, *On Christian Wisdom (Sapientia Christiana)*,[4] giving specific guidelines for ecclesiastical universities and faculties.

What are the prospects for Catholic education?

The conclusion of this document focuses on the debt of gratitude that Catholics owe to "those priests, religious men and women, and laypeople who in their evangelical self-dedication devote themselves to the surpassing work of education." Young people are "urgently" implored to consider teaching as a vocation (no. 12).

The future of Catholic education does hinge largely on Catholic *teachers*. Will there continue to be enough priests and religious men and women involved in education to support even a steadily declining number of Catholic schools? Will laypeople be paid enough to make teaching in a Catholic school a realistic option, especially those married and desiring to raise families according to the church's own teaching? At present we may *say* that Catholic teachers are important, but we don't *pay* them as if they were. Even more critically, where will Catholic teachers be instructed in the authentic and full teaching of the Catholic faith, without confusion or compromise, so they will be able to hand on a living faith to their students?

The future of Catholic education also hinges on Catholic *schools*. Will they preserve their authentic *Catholic identity* and thus be able to influence both their students and the broader society with the truths and values of the kingdom of God? Pope John Paul II has said, "The adjective 'Catholic' must always be the real expression of a profound reality."[5] Schools that are Catholic in name only are useless to God and to his people.

The promise of Vatican II in education is that the church is called to support and promote all forms of education that are academically sound and genuinely Catholic in every respect.

What forms of media are discussed in the *Decree on the Means of Social Communication?*

Inter Mirifica is one of the shortest documents of the Council and one of the first two to be passed, along with the *Constitution on the Sacred Liturgy*. Because of the ever-increasing influence of the contemporary media (as I described in opening this chapter), the church's teaching on the proper use of it is crucial. Although this decree spells out only the rudimentary principles to be considered, certainly if these basic principles had been taught and followed, the media and society today would be significantly improved, at least in the West. Let us test this hypothesis by outlining the teaching and asking whether it has been heard and followed.

Included in this discussion are means of communication that by their very nature can reach and influence the whole of society: the press, movie theaters, radio, television and similar media. The church, as a mother, naturally is concerned about the influence they have on her children:

> Mother Church, to be sure, recognizes that if these instruments are rightly used they bring solid nourishment to the human race. For they can contribute generously to the refreshment and refinement of the spirit, and to the spread and strengthening of God's own kingdom.
>
> But the Church is also aware that men can employ these gifts against the mind of the divine Benefactor, and abuse them to their own undoing. In fact, the Church grieves with a motherly sorrow at the damage far too often inflicted on society by the perverse use of these media. (no. 2)

What should the church's goals be with regard to the mass media?

This decree specifies two goals: first, to *use* the instruments of social communication to proclaim to the world the good news of redemption in Jesus Christ; second, to *instruct* humanity in the worthy use of these instruments and to animate their use "with a humane and Christian spirit" (no. 3).

How can we insure the media are used properly?

The first step is that all who use the media know the norms of morality and apply them faithfully. Catholics must be educated to recognize what is moral and what is immoral through the study of the sacred Scripture and the church's teaching and tradition. Catholics must examine the moral quality of the subject matter, as well as the "context" (such as intention, audience, place and time), which can modify the media's moral quality or even reverse it entirely (no. 4).

An evident example is that some TV productions, such as a graphic documentary portraying warfare, might be harmful for children yet be unobjectionable for adults. Therefore they should not be aired when or where children would be a large part of the audience.

The Council notes that some instruments of the media are so powerful and compelling "that people, especially if they are caught off guard, may scarcely be able to appreciate it, to moderate it, or, when necessary, to reject it" (no. 4). An extreme case of this would be subliminal or subaudial messages. A more frequent situation involves public transportation or other public facilities where constant music and a barrage of commercial messages are practically impossible for people to ignore.

What are some key areas for taking a stand morally?

This decree gives three specific examples in which an upright conscience will desire to follow moral norms:

First is the *"right to information."* People have the right to know about affairs that affect them individually and collectively. The moral standards involved here insist that information "always be true and complete as charity and justice allow." Further, "in the gathering and publication of news…the legitimate rights and dignity of a man must be held sacred" (no. 5). In other words, the right to information does not entail the right of anyone to know about another person's private affairs, unless those affairs pose some threat to the common good. Also, information cannot be obtained by morally illicit means.

Second, *concerning art.* Sometimes people justify as "art" the presentation of questionable material in the media—even something as abominable and degrading to persons as pornography. The Council warns against "ethical and artistic theories which are false." It "asserts that the primacy of the objective moral order demands absolute allegiance" (no. 6). Only the moral order established by God proposes and judges the true value of all human endeavors, including art.

Third, *portrayal of moral evil.* There is some justification for the portrayal of moral evil by the media. Nonetheless, "moral norms must prevail if harm rather than spiritual profit is not to ensue. This requirement is especially needed when subjects treated are entitled to reverence, or may all too easily trigger base desires in man, wounded as he is by original sin" (no. 7). Unfortunately, a Hollywood tendency since the late 1970s has been to produce movies that glorify anti-heroes—men and women who lack any authentic morality and have no recognizable redeeming virtues.

Who has moral responsibility for the proper use of the media?

This is the heart of the *Decree on the Instruments of Social Communication.* Moral responsibility for the proper use of the media falls primarily on three groups: (1) the "consumers" or users of the media, (2) the "makers" and transmitters of the media and (3) the civil authorities. The document discusses each of these in detail.

What is the moral responsibility of consumers?

The first and primary responsibility for the correct use of the media falls on "those readers, viewers, or listeners who personally and freely choose to receive what these media have to communicate" (no. 9). It may appear obvious, but the easiest way to avoid moral evil in the media, or even presentations of questionable value, is to turn off the TV or radio or put down the offending book or magazine. The Council instructs us, in our selection of media, to amply favor "whatever fosters virtue, knowledge, or art. People should reject whatever could become a cause or an occasion of spiritual harm to themselves, whatever could endanger others through bad example, and whatever would impede good selections and promote bad ones" (no. 9).

Consumers of the media must *learn* to make good judgments and to form their consciences according to the moral law by listening to competent authorities. This process must begin in youth. Just think of how much the following advice has been *needed* over the past forty years, especially with the use of TV and radio, and how little it has been *heeded:* "People, especially the young, should take care to develop moderation and self-control in the use of these instruments. Their goal should be an ever more discerning grasp of what they see, hear, and read. Discussions with educators and appropriate experts will school them to make mature judgments" (no. 10).

Even more critical is the following instruction: "Parents should be mindful of their duty to guard against shows, publications, and the like which would jeopardize faith or good morals. *Let them see that such things never cross the thresholds of their homes and that their children do not encounter them elsewhere*" (no. 10, emphasis added).

Would a parent readily invite a drug pusher, someone sexually perverted or a user of foul language to sit down with the children and instruct them? And yet we allow media figures of questionable morals into our homes to entertain our youth. Catholics must assume *primary moral responsibility* for what comes into their homes and into their own minds and the minds of those whom they raise or pastor.

What is the moral responsibility of the makers of the media?

The church says that the "chief moral duties" for the proper use of the media fall on "newsmen, writers, actors, designers, producers, exhibitors, distributors, operators, and sellers, critics, and whoever else may have a part of any kind in making and transmitting products of communication." Through their activity they can lead the human race "upward or to ruin" (no. 11).

Is this an exaggeration? When you consider the influence of the media—no. The Council demands that the producers of the media regulate their own activity according to moral standards and the pursuit of the common good, not merely according to the profit they can make. "These responsible persons should never forget that much of their audience consists of young people who have need of literature and shows that can give them decent amusement and inspiration" (no. 11). Jesus said something about millstones around the necks of those who led the "little ones" astray (see Matthew 18:6; Mark 9:42; Luke 17:2).

What moral responsibility do civil authorities have?

The mass media are subordinate to the common good, which civil authority is pledged to uphold. Civil authority must insure the availability of true information and should "foster religion, culture, and fine arts" (no. 12).

Public authority also has a *protective* role, which is to ensure "that serious danger to public moral and social progress do not result from a perverted use of these instruments" (no. 12). Civil authorities have a right and a duty to pass laws that protect public morality and the dignity of persons and to energetically enforce these laws. This watchfulness on behalf of the common good is not an infringement on individual rights any more than are laws against robbery, assault or murder. The decree again stresses that "particular effort should be expended to protect youngsters from literature and shows which would be injurious to them at their age" (no. 12).

In summary, when the consumers of the media are not discriminating nor willing to speak out and the makers and transmitters of the media are irresponsible in what they produce and transmit, then the civil authority is the last line of protection against the misuse of media. Realistically, such pervasive misuse could destroy a nation from within—by destroying its moral fiber and commitment to promoting the good of all.

What should the church do?

The church should be the most effective and influential moral force behind the proper and constructive use of mass media. The decree encourages pastors to use the media to spread the gospel and urges Christian laypersons involved with their use to "be busy giving witness to Christ, especially by performing their duties skillfully and with apostolic ardor" (no. 13).

Catholics are to provide leadership in the media: by establishing "a Catholic press worthy of the name"; by "the production and showing of films which serve honest relaxation as well as culture and art"; by patronage of "theatres managed by upright Catholics and others"; by supporting decent radio and television productions, "particularly those which are proper family fare"; and even by making efforts "to establish Catholic stations" that "excel in professional quality and forcefulness" (no. 14).

The question is whether Catholics will heed the Council's challenge to support and assist Catholic newspapers, magazines, movie enterprises and radio and television stations and programs "whose main purpose is to spread and defend the truth and to strengthen the Christian texture of human society" (no. 17). The decree comments that "it would be dishonorable indeed if sons of the Church sluggishly allowed the word of salvation to be silenced or impeded by the technical difficulties or the admittedly enormous expenses which are characteristic of these instruments" (no. 17). The emergence of Catholic radio and TV stations and even cable networks such as EWTN prove that nothing is impossible, technically or financially, to those who have faith and seek only to do God's will.

In order for Catholic media leadership to grow, priests, religious and laity must be trained to carry out this task through schools and institutes where they can obtain up-to-date, well-rounded formation animated by a Christian spirit (no. 15).

The decree recommends that the bishops of the church plan a media apostolate (no. 21) and oversee and promote proper use of the media in their dioceses (no. 20). Bishops are further advised to "devote a day of each year to instructing the faithful in their duties on this subject," so that the faithful might pray for the media and support Catholic institutes and enterprises meeting the needs of the world in this field (no. 18). In fact, the United States bishops have worked together toward this end. Pope Paul VI inaugurated a day for the church to speak on the use of media: the annual "World Communications Day."

The decree rightly observes in its concluding statement, "The fate of humanity grows daily more dependent on the right use of these media" (no. 24). Catholics need further instruction and reflection on this vast and important area.[6]

Can Catholics win, or win back, the educational establishment and the media fully to Christ and his church? Prayerfully and soberly, each of us needs to begin doing our own part in meeting these immense challenges.

Conclusion

The documents of Vatican II call each of us to embrace and to live to the fullest our Catholic Christian identity in every aspect of our lives.

We are the people gifted with God's Word, who are challenged to know and live that Word as it comes to us in sacred Scripture and sacred Tradition and through the teaching office of the pope and the bishops.

We are the people whose worship of God as a community in the liturgy is the fullest expression of who we are and the summit of our life. Thus we are challenged to worship our Lord reverently and faithfully, in spirit and truth.

We are the people of God whose fullness resides in the Catholic Church. Yet we recognize the gifts and grace of God at work in other baptized believers.

We are the people of God who have different gifts, callings and positions of service in the body of Christ. Yet all are equally called to holiness and Christian perfection. All of us must accept Christ's challenging call to be saints.

We are the missionary people of God, called by Christ to spread the good news throughout the world and to make disciples of all nations—including those closest to us, those with whom we live, work and recreate. At the same time we must respect each individual's right to believe as his or her conscience dictates. We must also respect what is good and true in other religions, as we present to them the truth found in Jesus Christ and his teaching.

We are the people of God, called to work with charity and understanding toward the unity of all Christians, even as we remain firmly committed to the fullness of our own Catholic faith.

We are the people of God, challenged to take up the mission of Christ in every sphere of human life: the family, politics, economics, social and cultural life, education and the mass media. Our aim is that Christ may truly be the Lord of all, in every aspect of life.

Relying on God's grace and guidance, we trust that our response to these challenges is only the beginning of a new endeavor among Catholic Christians to live and proclaim the gospel of Jesus Christ with new boldness and understanding at the dawn of the third millennium.

Gravissimum Educationis and *Inter Mirifica* in the *Catechism of the Catholic Church*

The *Declaration on Christian Education* is cited three times in the *Catechism,* both with regard to the duties of parents, in number 1653 of Part II (related to the sacrament of marriage) and in numbers 2221 and 2229 of Part III (in the section on the fourth commandment).

The *Decree on the Means of Social Communication* is referred to five times in the *Catechism*'s section on "The Use of the Means of Social Communications Media" (nos. 2493-2499) in the discussion of the eighth commandment in Part III. It is notable that this topic falls under the commandment "You shall not bear false witness against your neighbor"!

Recent Magisterial Documents

On Christian Education:

Pope John Paul II. *Catechesi Tradendae (On Catechesis in our Time)*. October 16, 1979.

Pope John Paul II. *Ex Corde Ecclesiae (Apostolic Constitution on Catholic Universities)*. August 15, 1990.

Pope John Paul II. *Fides et Ratio* (Encyclical Letter *On the Relationship Between Faith and Reason*). September 14, 1998.

Pope John Paul II. *Sapientia Christiana (On Ecclesiastical Universities and Faculties)*. April 29, 1979.

On Social Communications:

Pontifical Council for Social Communications. *Aetatis Novae (A New Era: On the Twentieth Anniversary of* Communio Et Progressio). 1992.

Pontifical Council for Social Communications. "The Church and the Internet" and "Ethics in Internet." February 2002.

Pontifical Council for Social Communications. "Ethics in Advertising." 1997.

Pontifical Council for Social Communications. "Ethics in Communication." 2000.

Favorite Quotes from *Gravissimum Educationis*

Since every Christian has become a new creature by rebirth from water and the Holy Spirit, so that he may be called what he truly is, a child of God, he is entitled to a Christian education. (no. 2)

Since parents have conferred life on their children, they have a most solemn obligation to educate their offspring. Hence, parents must be acknowledged as the first and foremost educators of their children. Their role as educators is so decisive that scarcely anything can compensate for their failure in it. For it devolves on parents to create a family atmosphere so animated with love and reverence for God and men that a well-rounded personal and social development will be fostered among the children. Hence, the family is the first school of those social virtues which every society needs. (no. 3)

Among all the agencies of education the school has a special importance.... Beautiful...and truly solemn is the vocation of all those who assist parents in fulfilling their task, and who represent human society as well, by undertaking the role of school teacher. (no. 5)

This sacred Synod urgently implores young people themselves to be aware of the excellence of the teaching vocation, and to be ready to undertake it with a generous spirit, especially in those parts of the globe where a shortage of teachers is causing a crisis in the training of the young. (no. 12)

Favorite Quotes from *Inter Mirifica*

Special duties bind those readers, viewers, or listeners who personally and freely choose to receive what these media have to communicate. For good choosing dictates that ample favor be shown to whatever fosters virtue, knowledge, or art. People should reject whatever could become a cause or an occasion of spiritual harm to themselves. (no. 9)

People, especially the young, should take care to develop moderation and self-control in the use of these instruments. Their goal should be an ever more discerning grasp of what they see, hear, and read.... Parents should be mindful of their duty to guard against shows, publications, and the like which would jeopardize faith or good morals. Let them see that such things never cross the thresholds of their homes and that their children do not encounter them elsewhere. (no. 10)

It would be dishonorable indeed if sons of the Church sluggishly allowed the word of salvation to be silenced or impeded by the technical difficulties or the admittedly enormous expenses which are characteristic of these instruments. Hence the sacred Synod admonishes these sons that they are duty bound to uphold and assist Catholic newspapers, magazines, movie enterprises, and radio and television stations and programs whose main purpose is to spread and defend the truth and to strengthen the Christian texture of human society. (no. 17)

Notes

Part One: The Crisis of Vatican II

Chapter One: Vatican II: The Crisis and the Critics

1. To borrow the title of Ralph McInerny's book *What Went Wrong with Vatican II?* (Manchester, N.H.: Sophia Institute Press, 1998). McInerny primarily focuses on the rejection of *Humanae Vitae* after the Council as a sign of growing dissent in the church.

2. Michael Davies, *Pope John's Council* (Kansas City, Mo.: Angelus, 1977), p. 10.

3. Davies, p. 9.

4. Davies, p. 4.

5. Davies, p. 52.

6. Davies, p. 11.

7. Davies, p. 4 (referring to *L'Osservatore Romano,* December 8, 1968).

8. Davies, p. 4.

9.   Davies, pp. 4, 10, 17, 27, 36, 38, 39, 53, 59, 60, 66, 73, 78, 94-95, 115, 118, 124, 148-149, 152, 213, 216, 254.

10.   Davies, p. 504.

11.   Davies, p. 507. Davies also presents what he considers convincing evidence that Bugnini was a Freemason who was banished by Pope Paul VI when this came to light (also see Davies, pp. 165-166, 172).

12.   Davies, p. 137.

13.   Michael Davies, *The Second Vatican Council and Religious Liberty* (Long Prairie, Minn.: Neumann, 1992), p. 121. This contradicts, according to Davies, the "tradition" that in a Catholic country the state has often repressed the religious practices of non-Christians or other Christian bodies and not allowed them to hold public services, since from a Catholic point of view their beliefs are erroneous (at least to some degree).

14.   Davies, *The Second Vatican Council,* p. 68.

15.   Davies, *The Second Vatican Council,* pp. 119, 120.

16.   Davies, *The Second Vatican Council,* p. 105.

17.   Davies, *The Second Vatican Council,* p. 155.

18.   Atila Sinke Guimarães, *In the Murky Waters of Vatican II,* 2nd ed. (Rockford, Ill.: TAN, 1999), p. lvi.

19.   Guimarães, pp. lviii, lix.

20. Guimarães, pp. lx, lxi.

21. Guimarães, p. 234.

22. Davies, *Pope John's Council,* p. 9.

23. Guimarães, pp. 295, 296.

24. Robert Sungenis, M.A., "Was God Behind the Ambiguities of Vatican II? A Biblical Answer to an Intriguing Question," *Catholic Family News,* February 2003.

25. Christopher A. Ferrara and Thomas E. Woods, Jr., *The Great Façade: Vatican II and the Regime of the Novelty in the Roman Catholic Church* (Wyoming, Minn.: Remnant, 2002), p. 16.

26. Ferrara and Woods, p. 17.

27. Ferrara and Woods, pp. 20-21.

28. Ferrara and Woods, pp. 21, 22.

29. Ferrara and Woods, p. 23.

30. Ferrara and Woods, p. 26.

31. Davies, *The Second Vatican Council,* p. 257.

32. Davies, *The Second Vatican Council,* p. 257.

33. James Hitchcock, *Catholicism and Modernity Confrontation or Capitulation?* (New York: Seabury, 1979), p. 223.

34. James Hitchcock, "The End of *Gaudium et Spes*?" *The Catholic World Report,* May 2003, pp. 54-58.

35. Michael Davies, *The Second Vatican Council,* pp. 280-281.

36. Gregory Baum in Michael R. Pendergast and M.D. Ridge, *Voices from the Council* (Portland, Ore.: Pastoral, 2004), pp. 132-134.

37. Hitchcock, "The End of *Gaudium et Spes*?" p. 56.

38. Hitchcock, "The End of *Gaudium et Spes*?" p. 56.

39. Hitchcock, "The End of *Gaudium et Spes*?" p. 58.

Chapter Two: The Deeper Crisis in the Church Since the Council

1. Daniele Menozzi, "Opposition of the Council (1966-84)" in Giuseppe Alberigo, Jossua, Jean-Pierre Jossua, and Joseph A. Komonchak, eds., *The Reception of Vatican II* (Washington: Catholic University of America Press, 1987), pp. 328-329.

2. Quoted in Ralph Martin, *A Crisis of Truth* (Ann Arbor, Mich.: Servant, 1982), p. 17.

3. Hitchcock, "The End of *Gaudium et Spes*?" p. 55.

4. See *L'Osservatore Romano,* November 16, 1972; also in *The Pope Speaks,* XVII, p. 316.

5. Thesen zum Thema "Zehn Jahre Vaticanum II," in Joseph Ratzinger with Vittorio Messori, *The Ratzinger Report* (San Francisco: Ignatius, 1985), p. 29.

6.   Ratzinger, pp. 29, 30.

7.   Ratzinger, p. 44.

8.   Martin, pp. 171-172.

9.   Hitchcock, *Catholicism and Modernity,* p. 28.

10.   "Critics: Kerry, Abortion Stances 'trying to have it both ways,'" *Lowell Sun* (Lowell, Massachusettes), August 24, 2004: "The Roman Catholic Church teaches that life begins at conception and opposes abortion. In his comments, Kerry said that Vatican II was clear in its teaching that Catholics have 'freedom of conscience.'"

    See also "Kerry Abortion Comment Stokes Fire on Both Sides, View on Stem Cell Widens Argument," *The Boston Globe,* July 18, 2004, Sunday *Third Edition,* National/Foreign section, p. 22: "Kerry has been a firm supporter of abortion rights in the U.S. Senate. Planned Parenthood of America gives him a 100% rating."

    Also see "Kerry's Latest Attacks on Bush Borrow a Page from Scripture," *New York Times,* October 25, 2004, Late-Edition-Final, Section A, Column 1, National Desk, 17: "Mr. Kerry also answered those Roman Catholics who have said that it is a sin to vote for politicians who, like him, support abortion rights and embryonic stem-cell research. 'I know there are some bishops who have suggested that as a public official I must cast votes or take public positions, on issues like a woman's right to choose or stem-cell research, that carry out the tenets of the Catholic Church,' he said, as audience members shouted 'No!' 'I love my church; I respect the bishops; but I respectfully disagree,' he said to a standing ovation."

11.   Menozzi, pp. 328, 329.

12. Hitchcock, *Catholicism and Modernity,* p. 228.

13. The Extraordinary Synod of 1985, "Final Report," pp. 41-42.

14. Ratzinger, pp. 30-31.

15. Ratzinger, pp. 30, 34.

16. Cardinal Karol Wojtyla (Pope John Paul II), *Sources of Renewal: The Implementation of Vatican II* (New York: Harper and Row, 1980; originally published in Polish in Cracow, 1972), pp. 9-11.

17. Pope John Paul II, Apostolic Constitution *Fidei Depositum,* quoting from his own discourse of January 25, 1985: *L'Osservatore Romano,* January 27, 1985.

18. *Catechism of the Catholic Church,* no. 2. In fact, in the index to the 1992 *Catechism* there are 809 specific references to the sixteen documents of Vatican II, compared with 101 references to the Council of Trent, 27 references to the First Vatican Council (which only had two documents), 138 references to teachings of Pope John Paul II (the most oft-cited pope), 87 references to Saint Augustine and 61 to Saint Thomas Aquinas (the most frequently cited theologians). Next to the sacred Scriptures (which are cited thousands of times in the *Catechism*), the Vatican II documents are by far the most oft-cited source.

19. Pope John Paul II, *Novo Millennio Ineunte,* p. 57.

Chapter Three: Setting the Record Straight

1. Letter dated August 7, 1870, written to O'Neill Dauvit; see *Lettre au duc de Norfolk (1874) et Correspondeance realtive à l'infallibilité (1865-1875)*, B.D. Dupuy, trans. (*DDB*, 1970), 457, in Dom Alberic Stacpoole, ed., *Vatican II Revisited by Those Who Were There* (Minneapolis: Winston, 1986), p. 349.

2. Wojtyla, *Sources of Renewal*, pp. 10, 11.

3. Ratzinger, p. 28.

4. Yves Congar commented on this in his article "A Last Look at the Council" in Stacpoole, p. 341: "The new aspects of Vatican II…had already been sketched out in the plans of Vatican I."

5. Walter M. Abbott, ed., *The Documents of Vatican II* (New York: Guild Press, 1966), p. 715.

6. Ratzinger, p. 35.

7. Available at www.praiseofglory.com/jp2vat2.htm.

8. For example, Peter Huizing states: "Vatican II neglected to translate its teachings into Church institutions…. This is the main reason for the failure of Vatican II. Vatican III should fill this gap. It should make a constitution on Church order." In David Tracy, ed., *Toward Vatican III: The Work That Needs to Be Done* (New York: Seabury, 1978), p. 214.

9. Ratzinger, p. 40.

10. John Paul II, *Novo Millennio Ineunte*, p. 57.

11. Available at www.praiseofglory.com//jp2vat2/htm.

12. Available at www.praiseofglory.com//jp2vat2/htm.

13. Cardinal Avery Dulles, "Vatican II: The Myth and the Reality," *America,* February 24, 2003, p. 9.

14. Cardinal Avery Dulles, "The Reception of Vatican II at the Extraordinary Synod of 1985" in *The Reception of Vatican II,* p. 350.

15. Congar, pp. 343-344.

16. Pope John Paul II, *Crossing the Threshold of Hope* (New York: Knopf, 1994), p. 159.

17. Cardinal John Krol, "Our Brotherhood and Unity," in Synod, 72.

18. In doing this "they make the definition in conformity with revelation itself.... They do not...admit any new public revelation" (*Lumen Gentium,* 25), since, as *Dei Verbum* indicates, there can be "no new public revelation" (*Dei Verbum,* 4), and the teaching office (magisterium) of the church "is not superior to the Word of God, it is its servant. It teaches only what has been handed on to it" (*Dei Verbum,* 10).

19. A phrase coined by Saint Irenaeus of Lyons in the second century A.D., who compared God's revelation to a rich man making a deposit of something valuable. The most valuable "deposit" is God's revelation of himself and his truth.

20. Pope John Paul II, *Novo Millennio Ineunte,* no. 57.

21. Abbott, p. 713.

22. Abbott, p. 715.

23. Yves Congar, "A Last Look at the Council," in Stacpoole, p. 347.

24. Pope John Paul II, *Crossing the Threshold of Hope,* p. 162.

25. Pope John Paul II, *Crossing the Threshold of Hope,* p. 160.

26. Cardinal Avery Dulles, "Vatican II: The Myth and the Reality," p. 11.

27. See, for example, the writings of Saint Ignatius, bishop of Antioch, martyred around A.D. 107-110, who wrote seven letters to the local churches on his way to martyrdom, encouraging all of them to avoid error by staying in union with their bishop and his directives. Cyril Richardson, ed., *Early Christian Fathers* (New York: Macmillan, 1970), pp. 88, 89, 95, 96, 99, 108, 110, 115.

28. One mistake in a generally excellent article, "Open Windows: Why Vatican II Was Necessary" by George Sims Johnston (*Crisis,* March 2004), is his statement: "The Word 'active' in the original text could better be translated as 'authentic,' and by 'participation,' they meant mainly internal participation. In other words, silence." While Johnston is right about the translation of 'active,' from the quote from the text of Vatican II's *Sacrosanctum Concilium* cited here it is clear that the participation the Council fathers had in mind (acclamations, responses, psalmody, antiphons and songs as well as actions, gestures and bodily attitudes) is much more than the "internal participation" of silence, though that is mentioned as necessary as well "at the proper times."

29.   See *Code of Canon Law,* nos. 337, 338.

30.   See *Code of Canon Law,* no. 341, par. 1.

31.   Johnston.

Part Two: Understanding Vatican II

Chapter Four: Background to Vatican II

1.   Pope John Paul II, quoted in "The teachings of Vatican II are sure compass," *L'Osservatore Romano* (English edition), October 16, 2002, p. 2, col. 2.

Chapter Five: Knowing and Living God's Word

1.   Ratzinger, p. 76.

Chapter Six: The Church: A Mystery and the People of God

1.   See Francis Sullivan, "The Significance of the Vatican II Declaration that the Church of Christ 'Subsists in' the Roman Catholic Church," in *Vatican II: Assessment and Perspectives,* vol. II, Rene Latourelle, ed. (New York: Paulist, 1989), pp. 272-287.

2. See Michael Schmaus, *Dogma 4: The Church* (London: Sheed and Ward, 1972), p. 209.

3. Johnston.

4. Pope John Paul II, *Vicesimus Quintus*, "On the 25th Anniversary of the *Constitution on the Sacred Liturgy*," December 4, 1988, in *The Pope Speaks*, September/October 1989, p. 225.

Chapter Seven: Touching Eternity: The Call to Worship

1. Ratzinger, p. 134.

2. On the Mystery and Worship of the Eucharist *(Dominicae Cenae)*, p. 13, February 24, 1980.

3. Ratzinger, p. 126.

4. Ratzinger, p. 126.

Chapter Eight: How Should a Catholic Act in the World?

1. Blaise Pascal, *Pascal's Pensées*, Martin Turnell, trans. (New York: Harper and Row, 1962), pp. 76, 94. "The greatness of man is great insofar as he realizes that he is wretched."

2. Saint Augustine, *Confessions*, 1:1, Henry Chadwick, trans. (Oxford: Oxford University Press, 1991), p. 3.

Chapter Ten: The Laity: A Call to Full Membership in the Church

1.   Johnston.

Chapter Twelve: Proclaiming the Gospel

1.   It is instructive to compare the official Catholic liturgical
        prayers for the Jewish people in the Good Friday liturgy as
        they have been revised according to this teaching of Vatican
        II. In the Roman Missal of Pope Pius V, used until 1966,
        Catholics prayed, "Let us pray for the perfidious [faithless]
        Jews; that Our God and Lord would withdraw the veil from
        their hearts; that they also may acknowledge Our Lord Jesus
        Christ."

            In the re-issued Roman Missal of 1966, Catholics prayed,
        "Let us also pray that Our God and Lord will look kindly on
        the Jews; so that they too may acknowledge the Redeemer of
        all, Jesus Christ, Our Lord."

            Finally, in the Roman Missal of 1975, in current use, we
        pray, "Let us pray for the Jewish people, the first to hear the
        word of God, that they may continue to grow in the love of
        His name and in faithfulness to His covenant."

2.   Peter Kreeft, *Fundamentals of Christian Faith* (San Francisco:
        Ignatius, 1988), p. 142.

Chapter Thirteen: The Call to Christian Unity

1.   Pope John Paul II reaffirmed the importance of the *Decree on Ecumenism* in an address given on the fortieth anniversary of the document's promulgation. On November 13, 2004, he stated:

> The implementation of this conciliar decree, desired by my predecessor Blessed Pope John XXIII and promulgated by Pope Paul VI, has been one of the pastoral priorities of my pontificate from the outset (cf. *Ut Unum Sint*, 99). Since ecumenical unity is not a secondary attribute of the community of Christ's disciples (cf. Ibid., 9) and ecumenical activity is not just some sort of appendix added to the Church's traditional activity (cf. Ibid., 20) but is based on God's saving plan to gather all [Christians] into unity (cf. Ibid., 5), it corresponds to the desire of our Lord Jesus Christ, who wanted only one church and on the eve of death prayed to the Father that they might all be one (cf. Jn. 17:21). Basically, to seek unity is to comply with Jesus' prayer. The Second Vatican Council, in making its own this desire of Our Lord, made no innovation. Guided and enlightened by the Spirit of God, it cast new light on the true, deep meaning of the church's unity and universality. The way of ecumenism is the way of the church (cf. *Ut Unum Sint*, 7); she is not a reality closed in on herself but permanently open to the missionary and ecumenical dynamic (cf. Ibid., 5).

Chapter Fourteen: The Critical Challenges of the Media and Education

1.   "The universal ordinary magisterium can be considered to be the usual expression of the Church's infallibility," Pope John Paul II, *L'Osservatore Romano*, English edition, October 24, 1988, p. 22.

2. Pope John Paul II, *L'Osservatore Romano*, English edition, October 24, 1988, p. 22.

3. *L'Osservatore Romano*, English edition, July 2, 1990, 1-4; *Origins*, Vol. 20, No. 8 (July 5, 1990), pp. 117, 119-126.

4. Pope John Paul II. "Apostolic Constitution on Ecclesiastical Universities and Faculties" *(Sapientia Christiana)*, April 29, 1979.

5. "Address to Bishops of U.S.A. on *Ad Limina* visit," *L'Osservatore Romano*, October 24, 1988, p. 22.

6. One post-conciliar document that complements and completes this decree of the Second Vatican Council is the Pastoral Instruction on the Means of Social Communication *(Communio et Progressio)*, January 27, 1971, which is published in the 1981 Austin Flannery edition of *Vatican II: The Conciliar and Post Conciliar Documents* (Grand Rapids, Mich.: Eerdmans, 1981).

Bibliography of Non-Magisterial Sources

Abbott, Walter M., ed. *The Documents of Vatican II.* New York: Guild Press, 1966.

Alberigo, Giuseppe, and Joseph A. Komonchak, eds. *History of Vatican II.* Maryknoll, N.Y.: Orbis, 1995 (vol. I), 1997 (vol. II), 2000 (vol. III).

Alberigo, Giuseppe, Jean-Pierre Jossua and Joseph A. Komonchak, eds. *The Reception of Vatican II.* Washington: Catholic University of America Press, 1987.

Cernera, Anthony J., ed. *Vatican II: the Continuing Agenda.* Fairfield, Conn.: Sacred Heart University Press, 1997.

Davies, Michael. *Pope John's Council.* Kansas City, Mo.: Angelus, 1977.

———. *Pope Paul's New Mass.* Kansas City, Mo.: Angelus, 1980.

———. *The Second Vatican Council and Religious Liberty.* Long Prairie, Minn.: Neumann, 1992.

Dulles, Cardinal Avery. "Vatican II: The Myth and the Reality." *America* 188, no. 6 (February 24, 2003).

Ferrara, Christopher A. and Thomas E. Woods, Jr., *The Great Façade: Vatican II and the Regime of Novelty in the Roman Catholic Church.* Wyoming, Minn.: Remnant, 2002.

Fesquet, Henri. *The Drama of Vatican II.* New York: Random House, 1967.

Flannery, Austin. *Vatican Council II: The Conciliar and Post Conciliar Documents. Vol. I.* Grand Rapids, Mich.: Eerdmans, 1975 (New Revised Edition, 1992).

Guimarães, Atila Sinke. *In the Murky Waters of Vatican II* (2nd ed.). Rockford, Ill.: TAN, 1999.

Hitchcock, James. *Catholicism and Modernity: Confrontation or Capitulation?* New York: Seabury, 1979.

———. "The End of *Gaudium et Spes?*" *The Catholic World Report.* May 2003.

John Paul II. *Crossing the Threshold of Hope.* New York: Alfred A. Knopf, 1994.

———. (then Cardinal Karol Wojtyla). *Sources of Renewal: The Implementation of Vatican II.* New York: Harper and Row, 1980. (Originally published in Polish—Cracow, 1972.)

Johnston, George Sim. "Open Windows: Why Vatican II Was Necessary?" *Crisis,* March 2004. (http://www.crisismagazine.com/march2004/johnston.htm.)

Kaiser, Robert Blair. *Pope, Council and World: The Story of Vatican II.* New York: Macmillan, 1963.

Kreeft, Peter. *Fundamentals of the Faith: Essays in Catholic Apologetics.* San Francisco: Ignatius, 1988.

Küng, Hans, Yves Congar and Daniel O'Hanlon. *Council Speeches of Vatican II.* Glen Rock, N.J.: Paulist, 1964.

Latourelle, Rene, ed. *Vatican II: Assessments and Perspectives.* New York: Paulist, 1998.

Martin, Ralph. *A Crisis of Truth.* Ann Arbor, Mich.: Servant Books, 1982.

McInerny, Ralph. *What Went Wrong with Vatican II?* Manchester, N.H.: Sophia Institute Press, 1998.

Miller, John H. *Vatican II: An Interfaith Approval.* Notre Dame, Ind.: University of Notre Dame Press, 1966.

Prendergast, Michael R. and M.D. Ridge. *Voices from the Council.* Portland, Ore.: Pastoral, 2004.

Ratzinger, Cardinal Joseph. *The Ratzinger Report.* San Francisco: Ignatius, 1985.

Richardson, Cyril, ed. *Early Christian Fathers.* New York: Macmillan, 1970.

Rynne, Xavier. *Vatican Council II.* New York: Farrar, Strauss and Giroux, 1962-1968.

Schindler, David L., ed. "Vatican Council II." *Communio,* vol. XVII, no. 4 (Winter 1990).

Schmaus, Michael. *Dogma 4: The Church.* London: Sheed and Ward, 1972.

Stacpoole, Dom Alberic., ed. *Vatican II Revisited By Those Who Were There.* Minneapolis, Minn.: Winston, 1986.

Sungenis, Robert. "Was God Behind the Ambiguities of Vatican II? A Biblical Answer to an Intriguing Question." *Catholic Family News* (February 2003).

Tracy, David, ed. with Hans Küng and Johannes B. Metz. *Toward Vatican III: The Work That Needs to Be Done.* New York: Seabury, 1978.

Vorgrimler, Herbert, ed. *Commentary on the Documents of Vatican II* (5 vols.). New York: Herder and Herder, 1967.

Wiltgen, Ralph M. *The Rhine Flows into the Tiber.* New York: Hawthorne, 1967.

Index

A

Ad Gentes Divinitus (Decree on the Missionary Activity of the Church), 57, 219, 223, 227–229, 231, 232, 239, 241

ambiguity
    in Scripture, 38
    in teachings of Vatican II, 9, 10–12

America magazine, 40

apostolate of the laity. *See* laity.

apostolate, 174–175

Apostolic Letter on Ordination and Women. See Ordinatio Sacerdotalis.

Apostolicam Actuositatem (Decree on the Apostolate of the Laity), 57, 171, 172, 174, 178–179, 181–186, 189, 190–191, 207–208

Apostolos Suos (On the Theological and Juridical Nature of Episcopal Conferences), 46, 59, 198–199, 216

B

background of Vatican II, 55–67

Battista Montini, Giovanni (Pope Paul VI). *See* Paul VI.

Baum, Gregory, 18

Benedict XVI (Pope). *See* Ratzinger, Cardinal Joseph.

Bible. *See* Scripture.

bishops
    teaching about, 194–195
    relationship with pope, 195–196
    collegiality of, 196–197
    episcopal conferences, 197–198
    concern for whole church, 199
    pastoral office, 200–201
    collaboration with priests, 201–202

Buddhism, 225

Bugnini, Archbishop Annibal, 6, 8, 66

C